The Complete Guide to

URBAN SELF PROTECTION VOL. 2

INTERMEDIATE – ADVANCED

BY JOHN BOWMAN

Copyright © 2017 by John Bowman
All rights reserved. This book or any portion thereof
may not be reproduced or used in any manner whatsoever
without the express written permission of the author
except for the use of brief quotations in a book review.

Printed in the United States of America

ISBN 9780244928308 90000

First Printing, 2017

www.kdp.amazon.com

Dedication

Both volumes in this series are dedicated to my beautiful wife Esther.

She always has my six.

"John Bowman is an Instructor who knows how to teach realistic self-defence because of his training and background. He's not theory, he's real world".

Jim Wagner

A former Soldier, Corrections Officer, Police Officer, S.W.A.T. Officer, Close Protection Officer, U.S. Federal Air Marshal, Military Police Soldier Reservist, Security Forces Soldier, Team Leader of a military Special Response Team specialising in Active Shooter/Terrorism response and founder of the **Jim Wagner Reality-Based Personal Protection system.**

"John Bowman has both significant experience and learning in the field of effective self-protection. This combination is what makes him a world-class Instructor.

His no nonsense approach, which strips away anything superfluous, and combines both physical and non-physical tools, puts what he teaches at the very centre of what anyone genuinely concerned to protect themselves should know."

David Stevens

A member of the **International Krav Maga Federation Global Instructors Team** (Expert Level 2), Urban Combatives Instructor, F.A.S.T Instructor and decades of training, competing and teaching amateur boxing, Muay Thai, Judo, Filipino Martial Arts, Brazilian Jiu-jitsu and MMA, alongside several years experience as a nightclub Door Supervisor and now an academic working in the field of religious radicalisation and counter-terrorism.

"The only defense against evil, violent people is good people who are more skilled at violence."

Rory Miller

Contents

Thanks	8
Martial Arts	9
What is Urban Self Protection?	12
Who is USP for?	20
Finding Your Own Way	21
The Founder	22
How to use the books	24
Training tips	28
Overall guiding principles	30
Related technique principles	31
Level 4: Combatives	36
Combinations	61
Ground	77
Self defence	94
Weapons	111
First aid	154
Conflict knowledge	158
Level 5: Combatives	174
Combinations	199
Ground	200
Self defence	222
Weapons	232

First aid	279
Conflict knowledge	281
Level 6: Combatives	287
Combinations	324
Ground	342
Self defence	354
Weapons	373
Conflict knowledge	440

Thanks

Dan Stevens	USP Instructor
Pete Miller	USP Instructor
Ed Broom	USP Instructor
Julian Whitehead	USP Instructor
David Stroud	USP Instructor
Kevin Brooks	USP Instructor
Daniel Hildrew	USP Black Belt
Stuart Winter	USP Black Belt
Alex Madge	USP Black Belt
Lawrence Tydd	USP Black Belt
James Stewart	USP Student
Dave Stevens	Continental Instructor Team member IKMF
Paul Grey	Founder of the British Krav Maga Association
Valerie Gyselman-Blane	IKMF Krav Maga Instructor
Jim Wagner	Founder of the Jim Wagner Reality Based Personal Protection System
Eyal Yanilov	Founder of Krav Maga Global
Amnon Darsa	Founder of SMART Krav Maga
Darren Levine	Founder of Krav Maga Worldwide
Phil Cawood	Founder of Kempo Ryu Karate Kickboxing
Marc Williams	Kempo Ryu Karate Kickboxing Instructor
James Johnson & Troy	Handler and his Dog

All of whom the author has been lucky enough to train with and all of whom have had a great influence on the system's foundation and/or development.

Martial Arts

A little look at different types of martial arts, may give some context to the next section – 'What is Urban Self Protection?'

Generally speaking, most martial arts can be described as being part of one of three groups:

Traditional, Sport Based or Reality Based.

That said, they can certainly cross over and each system will owe at least a little to another system in a different group.

Traditional martial arts

Traditional Martial Arts or TMA, are typically those which have been around for many, many years. They usually require a uniform to be worn in training, often require students to bow alongside other rituals and usually involve a great deal of set patterns, movements and even foreign language to learn.

These include, Karate, Kung Fu, Ninjitsu etc.

TMA's were originally designed to be no frills and effective in battle. However, as they have been passed down through the generations, Instructors have put their own spin on things, sometimes misunderstood ancient texts, failed to 'move with the times' and concentrated on other areas of the system such as spirituality giving a 'Chinese whisper' effect.

However, there are many TMA's that are very effective to varying degrees in a real life confrontation.

This is normally for one of two reasons:

The art emphasises contact in training and/or the Instructor has certain experience:

When an art emphasises contact in training, be it pad work or sparring, then anything that doesn't work is spotted fairly quickly and as such adjusted accordingly.

Other TMA's that display a degree of realism may also be as a result of the individual Instructor – if the Instructor is one of the very few who have practiced for years and years and is a true master of their art, then they will usually be able to make even a fancy move work in reality.

There may also be an Instructor teaching a TMA who has a background working in a violent environment – such as a soldier or law enforcement officer and uses this experience to teach what is needed and in a way that they know will transfer to the street.

TMA's promote discipline, respect and most will give you a good foundation in terms of body mechanics and proper forming of body weapons as well as improving your overall physical fitness and flexibility.

Sport based martial arts

Sport based martial arts are generally ring sports, which have developed from TMA's and form the basis for practicing various arts.

These include Muay Thai, Mixed Martial Arts (cage fighting), Boxing, Judo etc.

The general purpose of training in these disciplines is to prepare for a prize type fight – i.e. a one on one match in a set arena with rules and some form of scoring system.

These disciplines do not however, fully prepare a student for the realities of the street. For example, no weapons are involved, no shoes are worn, the fighting area is normally safely matted or sprung, both parties have agreed to fight and know when and where it will take place. There are a set of rules to limit injury to both parties and as already mentioned, fighters only have to fight one person.

This clearly bears little resemblance to a realistic self defence situation, where a surprise attack from multiple and/or armed aggressors with no rules or time limits is likely to take place in a dangerous environment such as a street or bar.

However, because of the heavy emphasis on contact training, both using pad work and sparring, sport based martial artists can definitely be effective in a myriad of realistic confrontations in the street – being able to knock someone out with a punch, or throw them to the floor have obvious benefits.

Reality based martial arts

Any Reality Based systems' prime goal, is to prepare the student to be able to defend themselves effectively in a real life confrontation. Anything that doesn't serve that purpose is ignored in training. This is not the case in TMA where often techniques are practiced to maintain the 'purity' of it's tradition.

Reality Based systems include Krav Maga, Jim Wagner's Reality Based Personal Protection System, Urban Combatives, Senshido, S.P.E.A.R and Urban Self Protection as well as many others. Terms such as Combatives or Defensive Tactics are often used to describe Reality Based systems. This is often because the system has roots in military or law enforcement training.

These systems generally look at what type of attack a student may encounter and create solutions in the form of techniques, principles or tactics.

Training environments tend to be as realistic as possible – usually training in normal clothes and shoes, in normal environments such as a car park, a confined space or darkness and involve subjects attacking WITHOUT the use of pre-set movements. Verbal aggression is usually included within training as is consideration of the adrenaline response to danger.

Sadly, many TMA's seem to be jumping on the Reality Based movement and marketing themselves as self-defence classes. Yet often this is no more than training Karate in jeans and removing some of the flashier moves. This is dangerous for the student as they are led into a false sense of security and is disrespectful to the origins of the specific TMA.

However, Reality Based systems often take a great deal from TMA or Sport Based martial arts. They may tweak it and only cherry pick what's useful to them, but there is no denying a great deal is owed to these other sections of the martial arts.

You will find very often that credible Reality Based systems have been developed by those who have experienced real life violence, do not pretend they have all the answers and have cross trained in other systems. You will also find that most Reality Based systems will have similar solutions to problems as each other.

The biggest difference between Reality Based Systems and TMA/ Sport Based Martial Arts however, is that Reality Based Systems almost always train for the pre-conflict, conflict and post conflict stages of a confrontation, described in the next section.

Every martial art, system and discipline, whether TMA, Sport or Reality Based have something to offer.

The goals of each are different and it is very much a matter of 'horses for courses', but each art, system and discipline should celebrate what it is good at, market itself for what it truly is and respect all others for what they can offer.

What is Urban Self Protection?

Urban Self Protection (USP) is a simple, effective and aggressive Reality Based system of self-protection, which covers not only the conflict itself, but the pre-conflict and post-conflict phases mentioned above.

Pre-conflict, is the phase *before* a physical attack and includes such subjects as awareness, avoidance, personal security, verbal diffusion, spotting signs of aggression and weapon concealment, knowing your enemy, knowledge of the law, criminal attack psychology, target hardening etc.

Conflict, is the *physical phase* and includes defensive (and sometimes pre-emptive) responses to conflict. I.e. striking, breaking free of a grab or hold, the body's reaction to danger, ground fighting, throwing, multiple subjects, control and restraint, third party protection, counter terrorist tactics, weapons defence/use and so on.

Post conflict, is the phase starting immediately *after* the physical incident and can potentially last a life time. Subjects in this area include, first aid, escape methods, Police contact, secondary dangers and coping with post-traumatic stress disorder etc.

Principle based

USP is principle based as no two attacks are ever the same; you need to be able to adapt and apply your skill to solve a variety of problems, not learn a different technique for every conceivable incident. Doing so is inefficient and does not lend itself to skill retention or use, especially when under the stress of a real life incident.

Well thought out and easily learned principles are what allow a self-protection system to be effective.

Simple

USP is simple, so it can be learned quickly and utilised easily under pressure – it is well known that stress reduces complex functions.

Effective

Any self-protection system must be effective. This is USP's primary goal – our methods may not look flashy or graceful, but they ARE effective. If self-protection is your aim, then you're reading the right book.

Aggressive

USP must be aggressive. Skill and strength help, but mindset is THE single most important characteristic of a self-protection practitioner. Aggression is nurtured in USP, but is also tempered into controlled aggression. We want people to be able to take swift and decisive action, but know when to stop.

As such, a great deal of research into combat psychology has been used to make the system as effective as it possibly can be, both through the tactics trained, but also in the WAY that they are trained.

Origins

USP is a hybrid of some of the most credible and effective defensive tactics systems and fighting styles available, alongside relevant knowledge bases, frontline experience and modern learning and development practices.

These include:

- Krav Maga
- Jim Wagner's Reality Based Personal Protection System
- Mixed Martial Arts
- Kempo Ryu Karate Kickboxing
- FAST defence
- FIST suit simulations
- Close protection training
- Law Enforcement Unarmed Defensive Tactics
- Modern learning and development practices
- First Aid Training

As well as knowledge and training from many other sources.

USP is fused together with sound principles and always considered with the realities of conflict in mind.

Other Influences:

Those people from the Reality Based community who have provided excellent information and study materials which have also had a huge influence on USP include:

Loren W. Christensen	Author of On Combat and others
Lt. Col. Dave Grossman	Author of On Combat and others
Peter Consterdine	British Combat Association
Geoff Thompson	British Combat Association
Rory Miller	Author of Meditations on Violence and others

Peyton Quinn	Founder of Rocky Mountain Combat Applications Training
Lee Morrison	Founder of Urban Combatives
Richard Dimitri	Founder of Senshido
Kenneth R. Murray	Author of Training at the Speed of Life

Those of you who have trained with, or studied the works of any of the fantastic people mentioned above in the *Thanks* or *Other Influences* section, will no doubt spot similarities in their systems and training methodology to those of USP.

Sometimes this is deliberate but sometimes by accident.

'Original' Solutions
More often than not, the people who know what they are talking about, having experienced real life combat, often come up with the same, or very similar solutions to the same problem's quite separately from each other. Most times not even being aware of each other's work.

'Gleaned' Solutions
It seems the sensible individuals learn and develop what's useful to them from the very rich melting pot of knowledge and experience already out there (whilst giving full credit to who they learnt it from).

USP includes both 'original' solutions and those 'gleaned' from others.

Levels:

USP has six levels. Each level has techniques from the following areas of self-protection:

Combatives
Fighting skill standing up including basic strikes, applying locks, takedowns and high level use of force although many of these skills can also be used on the ground.

Combinations
Multiple strikes put together.

Ground
Fighting skill and defensive tactics whilst on the ground including striking, falling and escape methods.

Self-Defence
Escapes from various chokes, holds and criminal attacks.

Weapons

Defence against common weapon attacks and training in the use of improvised weapons.

First Aid
Rescue methods and basic responses to conflict related injuries.

Conflict Knowledge
Conflict psychology and other tactics.

The reason the system has been broken down in this way is to aid the student's learning. In terms of simple to complex learning, students must learn a little bit at a time and build on their experiences, not have everything given to them all at once.

This breakdown also aids their motivation to learn:

When a Level 1 student trains in a class one week in ground work for example, they will be practicing Level 1 techniques, but will also be able to see their Level 4 colleague learning something more advanced within the ground work section, giving them something to strive for. This also allows advanced students to maintain their competency in the basics.

A grading system has been put in place, to assist students who need motivation and to offer feedback to students who would like it. However, it is completely optional.

Those grading to Level 1 will need to demonstrate all techniques from Level 1, carry out two pressure tests and one scenario.

They will be marked on – Technique, Effectiveness and Aggression. They will need to achieve the desired pass rate on each on these characteristics.

Each of these three are marked individually (although each of course overlap) to make sure we do not just have technically proficient students who can do the correct movement, but would be completely ineffective in reality. To do so is irresponsible and offers a false sense of security, putting students in more danger, not less.

Conflict based theory is also tested via a written exam to ensure a well balanced approach.

A student who is assessed as having a high level of competency in all three characteristics will be awarded a coloured wrist band signifying their rank. This is very similar to traditional martial arts awarding a coloured belt to signify rank, but is simply a modern version. Level 1 = Yellow, Level 2 = Orange, Level 3 = Red, Level 4 = Green, Level 5 = Blue and Level 6 = Black. USP still refers to these ranks as 'belts'. I.e. Level 6 = Black Belt. This is to give some measure of comparability to other systems and is a nod to the traditional arts.

To grade in higher levels, three random techniques from all previous grades passed must also be marked to ensure that the student is maintaining the basics and not simply replacing them with newer and more advanced techniques

Those who achieve Level 6 or Black, are entitled to have the USP Warrior Symbol tattooed on their skin should they wish to do so as a symbol of their achievement and a reminder of the importance of their training. This is a nod to traditional systems who sometimes 'branded' students as part of their final testing. It is also akin to the war paint of traditional warrior tribes and cultures.

Progression of the system:
USP is a system that adapts to new threats, improves current methods and discards that which is no longer useful.

As such, in the few years it has been around, it has been developed, dissected and improved upon and continues to do so. USP encourages students to experiment with techniques, try other systems and fighting styles and invites ideas from everyone.

This has seen simplified learning processes of various techniques, up to date conflict knowledge and new training methodology, making techniques more reflexive and easier to utilise under stress.

Some methods have been altered to combat the threat of so many people training in MMA for example – whilst not all MMA fighters are our enemy, many of our enemies have now trained in MMA.

The techniques have all been thoroughly tested. That is, they have either been used successfully in real life, or vigorously pressure tested with smaller, weaker people and scrutinized by highly experienced experts, some of whom are mentioned in our 'Thanks' section.

Most importantly though, superfluous methods and techniques have been stripped of the system, to stick to the important principle of learning a few techniques well, rather than trying to learn many, but which can only be done to a low standard as a result.

Being very good at that one general response means that you are more likely to be able to adapt it to suit unusual circumstances – allowing you to force a square peg into a round hole when the occasion requires it.

As Bruce Lee once said "I fear not the man who has practiced 10,000 kicks once, but I fear the man who has practiced one kick 10,000 times."

To add to this very profound statement, USP is honest with it's students, stating that techniques often require you to fight to get them to work – forcing the square peg into the round hole. So with the right aggressive mindset, often even the WRONG technique can potentially work effectively against a specific attack. As Peyton Quinn once said "Perfect intent is more important than perfect technique."

The following diagram gives an idea as to the process of deciding whether a technique/tactic/piece of information will be incorporated into the USP syllabus.

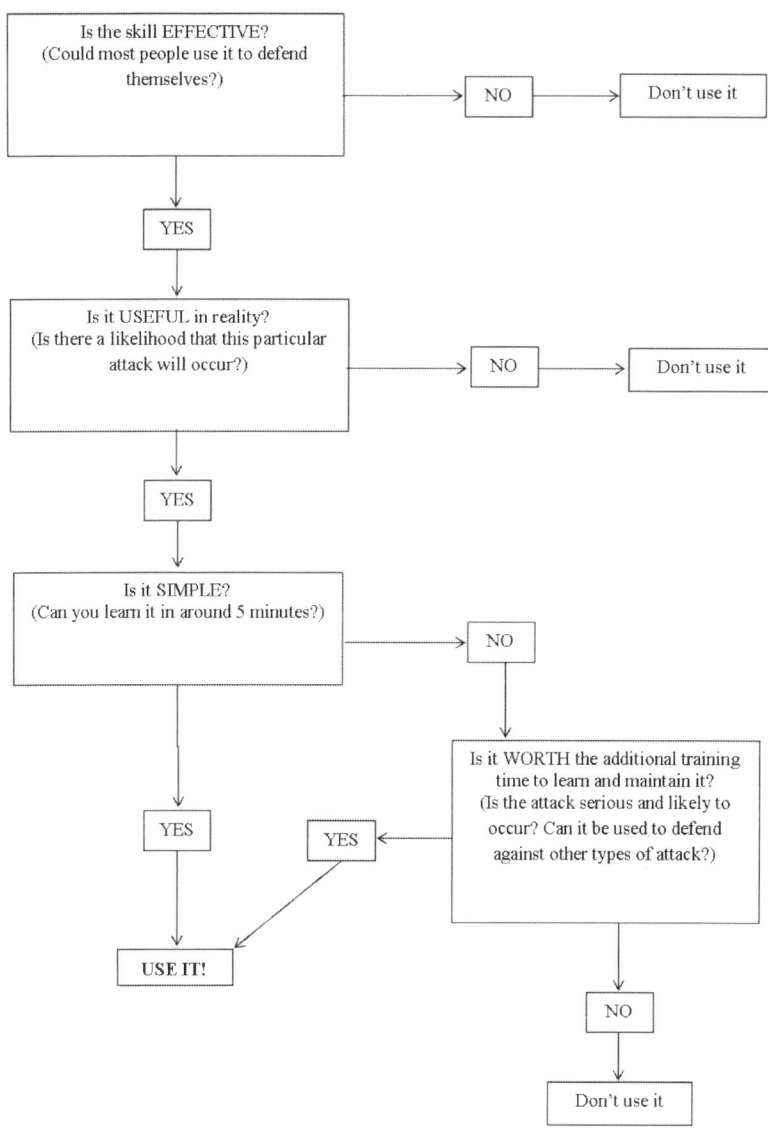

Specialisms:

USP also has specialist training programmes for those who wish to expand their knowledge and skill and become 'experts' in a certain area. These include:

USP High Risk Tactical
USP Women's Self Protection

USP Children's Self Protection

What's in the name?
Urban Self Protection was considered the most suitable name for the system.

There are subtle, but important differences between self-defence and self-protection.

Self-defence can be defined as 'to defend oneself when physically attacked' or 'the act of defending yourself'.

However, self-protection is more than just reacting as the above definitions imply. As already mentioned, self-protection involves pre-conflict, conflict and post conflict training.

'Urban', was chosen to connote the gritty and realistic nature of realistic self-protection that USP promotes.

Naming a system responsibly:
It is recognised that by failing to label a system in a responsible way, one can attract the wrong type of people into training.

We do not want to teach thugs or those with an ego, 'Walter Mitty' types or people who want to learn for the wrong reasons.

Calling your self-protection system something like 'Broken Bones Karate' or 'Military Fighting Systems' and wearing camouflage trousers in your training sends the wrong message.

We're not learning to be Commandos, action heroes or Special Forces soldiers. We are ordinary people who want to be able to protect ourselves and our loved ones effectively. Full stop.

Words can be powerful weapons to be used against you:
Imagine having used your self-protection skills, quite justifiably, in a real incident and having to explain your actions in a Court as, in protecting yourself, you injured the other party.

Now imagine a lawyer/solicitor cross examining you and presenting you as a thug or psychopath to the court by referring to your black belt in 'Lethal Arts Combat Training'……The Jury have already made their decision about the type of person you are, before they've even heard you speak, simply because of the aggressive sounding nature of your self-protection system.

A principle based system

USP was created using methods from the systems and knowledge bases by handpicking and tailoring techniques that would work together to make an easy and effective system of self-protection for the average person.

However, the focus for any self-protection system must be principles. This is because no two attacks are ever the same, no two people are ever the same and even the same person faced with a particular threat, may respond differently on different days.

When learning a technique, it might be to squat down when being bear hugged, but the *principle* is to make it difficult for the subject to lift you. A technique might be to poke a subject in the eye, but the *principle* may be to distract the subject.

However, we must start with techniques to hang the principles off of. Then in time, you will be able to create your own way of achieving good results, by tying these principles in with your own natural reactions and any individual circumstances you may encounter.

As such USP was created using the following principles:

- Techniques should be movements based on natural instincts – not just physical responses but psychological.
- Techniques must address the immediate danger first.
- Techniques must switch from defence to counter attack as soon as possible.
- One defence must work against a variety of attacks where possible.
- The system should be integrated so that movements learned in one area of the system complement, rather than contradict, movements in another area of the system.
- Techniques must be accessible to the average person.
- Techniques must work from a position of disadvantage.
- Training must include the stress experienced in real attacks.
- Techniques must work under, or even be improved by, stress. Stress should trigger the technique automatically.
- There must be a simple to complex learning pattern.
- Prevention techniques should also be practiced as well as the worst case scenario.
- Whilst you must not have too many techniques in your arsenal, there should always be a plan B, should the technique not work.
- Training drills should include determination – overcoming obstacles such as fatigue/pain.
- Techniques must be adaptable to the individual – if they are unable to utilise a technique due to physical limitations or their natural reaction, they must be able to be changed to suit that person but utilising the original principles.
- Techniques should try to exploit advantageous opportunities, but not use movement that is superfluous or useless.

Who is USP for?

The system was designed for the average person to be able to protect themselves and their loved ones.

Techniques were picked specifically for the types of threat that people are most likely to come across. Therefore, for example, USP includes defences against such things as dog attacks, as a trend has emerged recently whereby criminals are using dogs as weapons.

There are lots of other techniques that we could have included, but the overall aim was to allow someone to learn a handful of techniques that would be of actual use to them, not something that has a one in a billion chance of actually being required in real life.

Training for that one in a billion eventuality is effectively, a waste of time. It's far better to be proficient at defending against the few most likely attacks, than have a slight knowledge of hundreds of different ones covering every single conceivable possibility.

Having said that, in the most advanced levels of the system, there are some less likely attacks covered for those who may be travelling in higher risk environments – perhaps cities or abroad, where a few simple principles can save lives.

USP is designed to be a foundation system which covers a wide spectrum of common threats. However, once you have this foundation, USP can (and should) be adapted to suit your reality.

For example, if you work in Law Enforcement, then you might focus your training in the control and restraint aspects of the system. If you have a young family, then you can give additional training time to the third party protection techniques. Or perhaps you live somewhere where knife crime is particularly high and as such concentrate the majority of your training on knife threats and attacks.

USP is a Jack of all trades, master of none. You need to become a Jack of all trades to cover most possibilities, but then you need to master the areas relevant to your reality.

A Level 6 USP practitioner has really only begun their training, in so much as they now need to tailor it to their own requirements. This means adapting and/or focussing on techniques relevant to their specific reality. Make USP your own, but obtain an overall foundation before you do so and continue to maintain it.

Finding Your Own Way

If five different people go to the cinema and each fill a paper bag with pick n mix sweets, they will likely all have different sweets according to their different tastes. The five cinema goers have all achieved their goal by all having a bag of sweets to enjoy with the film. What's inside the bag isn't important as long as it suits their individual tastes.

Just as five different self-protection students can learn defensive principles against a headlock, yet execute a defence in different ways according to their different physiologies / psychologies / experiences and objectives. They have achieved their goal of defending against a head lock. How they carry out the defensive technique isn't important as long as it works.

By adhering to well thought out principles, mechanical variations on their execution should not reduce their effectiveness. In fact, provided the mechanical variations suit the individual, they will improve the effectiveness of the technique.

Principles shouldn't be changed, but techniques may be altered if necessary. However, alterations should only be made when the base technique is learnt and the techniques principle(s) understood.

The Founder

John Bowman, USP Founder and Chief Instructor runs a regular USP club in the UK, alongside Instructor Training, Syllabus Development and is a full time Law Enforcement Officer (LEO) in a Counter Terrorism role.

He initially started his training in Kempo Ryu Karate Kickboxing in 1996 in Exeter under Phil Cawood and Marc Williams. This system, whilst fairly traditional, is aggressive and carries out a lot of impact training rather than patterns and choreographed movements.

Whilst on his path to Black Belt within this system, John joined a Law Enforcement agency in 1997. (Unfortunately the Law Enforcement agency he works for cannot be divulged due to organisational policy. Neither can much of his training within the agency for the same reasons).

He eventually attained his Black Belt and began running a small club. However, at the same time, he was involved in various confrontations through his role as an LEO and realised much of what he had learnt was superfluous, although the aggressive and high impact training had set him in good stead.

Of course, he was also trained in the agency Unarmed Defensive Tactics programme and learnt a lot from this.

He began to look for other realistic systems and came across Krav Maga. He attended a few classes in 2004 under Valerie Gyselman-Blane in Plymouth and loved how no-nonsense it was. Practitioners of Krav Maga train in shoes, in darkness, in uneven areas and against realistic attacks with realistic responses.

John enrolled on the next International Krav Maga Federation (IKMF) Instructors course in 2005 and trained long hours in London under some of the worlds best including Eyal Yanilov and Amnon Darsa. He succeeded and became a Graduate Level 2 Instructor and set up a Krav Maga class as soon as he could. He ran this class for several years.

Despite Krav Maga being excellent and no doubt effective, John wanted to cross train to make sure he wasn't missing out on anything. He discovered Jim Wagner's Reality Based Personal Protection System.

Jim is an ex-Federal Air Marshal post 9/11 and has a great deal of Law Enforcement experience as well as Military, Counter Terrorism, Close Protection and Martial Arts training. John attended an Instructor Course in Ireland in 2005 and really enjoyed it. Jim's system is based more on principle than technique. It also emphasises more realistic training conditions. John loved both The Wagner System and Krav Maga, so taught both for a period of time.

He continued training under Jim for some time in various countries including

Ireland, Paris and Madrid and eventually became his UK Director. There were only 3 Levels in Jim's system, but due to John's Law Enforcement background and his continued study, he was given the honourary title of Level 4. There were only 5 Instructors in the world to have this honour and it meant he was entitled to train up Instructors for Jim.

Within John's Law Enforcement Agency, he became an Unarmed Defensive Tactics Instructor, First Aid Instructor and Law Trainer and over this 4 year period gained further qualifications in scenario creation and realistic training. He also created two realistic training programmes adopted by the agency – Edged Weapon Survival and Adrenaline Stress Training. John also gained qualifications and experience in teaching and coaching.

In 2009 John realised he could not continue to teach both Krav Maga and Jim Wagner's Reality Based Personal Protection system and was also coming up with ideas of his own as a result of operational experience and various other courses and seminars he attended. He also carried out experimental training with peers and absorbed information from various other sources.

John then spent some time formalising his own syllabus which incorporated what he felt were the most realistic techniques, the most useful tactics the best training methodologies and most importantly - sound principles.

This system was named Urban Self Protection or USP and was born September 20th 2009.

Since then, it has gone through various developments and will continue to do so where improvements can be made. This book represents version 5 of the system.

John continues to cross train and study other systems. Most recently he has qualified as an *Apprentice Rapid Assault Tactics Instructor*, the R.A.T system created by Paul Vunak for Navy Seal Team Six and has also studied and gained a diploma in: *'Understanding Terrorism and the Terrorist Threat'* from the University of Maryland's National Consortium for the Study of Terrorism and Responses to Terrorism, as well as a diploma from the Grossman Academy in *'On Combat'* studies, covering the psychology and physiology of combat.

John has continued to work on the frontline of Law Enforcement and has utilised USP during violent confrontations and has never been let down. Others in the same field who attend USP training have experienced the same.

As Lee Morrison says: *"Thirty seconds on the street is worth three years in the dojo any day of the week."*

In John's personal life, he enjoys spending time with family, teaching, training, syllabus development, kayaking, archery and going to the cinema. His guilty/geeky pleasure is an interest in disaster preparedness - probably as a result of watching too many zombie films!

How to use the books

'The Complete Guide to Urban Self Protection' is divided into two volumes – Vol. 1 Beginner – Intermediate and Vol.2 Intermediate – Advanced. The books describe the foundations of USP. They show you the techniques and describe the principles fundamental to them. This will improve your knowledge and make you safer – but when all is said and done – they are only books.

In order to improve your knowledge and make you safer, you must apply what you learn by training with a partner. Slowly to start with and safely build up resistance, speed and aggression until you are able to perform it at a realistic pace.

However, training like this is just the beginning and where many Martial Arts stop (in fact many don't even use resistant partners). We need to take this skill and develop it into a natural response to the stimulus (the physical/verbal assault itself).

In order to do so, you must repeat the technique with a training partner until you don't need to think about what you are doing. The skill then needs to be maintained and practiced regularly. This is called *'Operant Conditioning'* and is described in further detail later.

A conditioned response is still only half way there. There are sadly too many stories of highly trained Black Belts, incredibly proficient in their art, crumbling under the pressure of a real life incident.

So, once you have the conditioned response, you need to train so it can be operationalised under stress. To do so, you need to train the same technique with different partners, on different surfaces, in different conditions, different positions and under stress – be that physical or mental. This includes pressure drills, scenario training and sparring type drills.

This allows you to see if you can successfully ADAPT a technique using its principles when required and/or utilise it in challenging circumstances. This type of training is called *'Stress Inoculation'* and will be described in more detail In Level 2.

These methods of training will allow you to analyse your limitations and work to overcome them, as well as giving you confidence that you can succeed. Most importantly though, it will allow you the greatest chance of operationalising what you have learned when the occasion calls for it.

So, practice the moves slowly. When you're happy with the mechanics of the movement, increase your speed, aggression and the resistance level from your partner and repeat the technique until it becomes automatic. When you have a conditioned response, practice in different conditions and use various pressure drills to test yourself.

You will, of course, get the greatest benefit from training with a certified instructor. A list of which can be found on the official USP website – www.u-s-p.co.uk

The techniques in here are suggestions. You may need to adapt them to suit YOU. So, for example, if we suggest a counter attack using an elbow strike, but you prefer using a knee – DO IT! This system must adapt to suit you not the other way around. Stick with the principles of the technique, pressure test your variation and if it works for you – fantastic.

The Organisation of the Books:
The organisation is based on the USP syllabus for a reason. The USP syllabus is designed to teach a little bit at a time and build on it in the next level. As such, if you work through the books in order, you will learn effectively. Once you have a good base knowledge of USP, then use the books as a reference and dip in wherever you like. We will work through level's 1-3 in volume 1 (or Yellow – Red) and levels 4–5 in volume 2 (or Green - Black).

For each technique, you will be given the name of the technique and an explanation as to what the technique is under the heading: **'What is it?'**

You will then be given the reason the technique is used under the heading: **'Why do it?'**

You will then be presented with a detailed breakdown of the technique / tactic / method / principle and reasons behind this method under the heading: **'How to execute the technique'**.

You will also be given a reminder of the salient points to refer to when training under the heading: **'Essentials'.**

Lastly, *where applicable,* there will be a section referring to suitable specific training drills for the technique being discussed under the heading: **'Technique specific exercises'**

Where there are no 'Technique specific exercises' pad/bag work will be suitable for training most strikes. Drilling defences with a training partner starting with no resistance and safely increasing non-compliance will be suitable for most other techniques/tactics/principles described in the books.

Of course, there are many other drills used by USP that are beyond the scope of these books, but will be focus of a future publication.

(Note that some of the 'Conflict Knowledge' sections may be formatted differently to suit the specific subject.)

Photographs:
The people used in the photographs of the books are all USP Black Belts. For each technique, the Black Belt playing the role of the subject (the 'bad guy') will be

wearing a light coloured sleeveless hooded top to clearly identify their role as the subject for that specific technique.

Safety in Training:
It is important to know your limitations – consider any injuries or conditions you may suffer from. If you think that training may cause you to aggravate or worsen these, then you really should discuss these thoughts with your Doctor and take their advice.

We want you to train in the techniques presented within this book – to simply read it will be of only limited benefit, BUT, the techniques and knowledge are supposed to guard you from harm – if you get hurt during training, you have defeated the whole objective of self-protection!

So – take personal responsibility for your own safety and that of your training partners'. You must use the correct balance of realism and safety and remember, there will always be an element of danger in practicing these techniques – you must reduce that risk to an acceptable level.

To help do this, start slowly. Attacks must be realistic in their execution, but can still be slow and with minimal power. The defensive technique must also be realistic, but it too can start slowly and with minimal power. Speed, aggression and resistance can be built up as you progress.

Use the 'Tap out' rule in training. This is when, during training, you or your training partner need to quickly stop the action to prevent injury or stop pain. For example, your training partner puts on a rear headlock and it causes you pain and/or prevents you breathing. You need a method to let them know quickly that they need to release you immediately. The widely used method is the tap out rule, meaning that when someone repeatedly taps you with their hand, you must immediately release them and stop the action. They may also tap the floor or themselves depending upon what position they're in, so watch out for this and never continue training when the tap out is used. You will see this as a method of 'giving up' or 'submitting' in Mixed Martial Arts and at this point, the fight is immediately stopped.

Use appropriate safety equipment when required, such as matting, pads, gum shields, groin guards, eye protection, shin pads, gloves etc. NEVER use live weapons in training, use only safe versions – e.g. rubber knives instead of anything with a sharp edge.

When using airsoft or 'BB' guns in training, ALWAYS adhere to the following safety advice:
1. Everyone must wear wrap around eye protection as a MINIMUM safety precaution when the airsoft/BB gun is being handled. This includes the subject (i.e. the attacker), defender other students and anyone watching. Other advisable safety accessories include gloves, full face mask, hooded sweater (with the hood up to protect the head and neck), thick trousers and shoes.

2. Assume that the airsoft/BB gun is loaded, even when the magazine has been ejected.
3. Use appropriate signage if there is a chance that anyone who isn't involved with training could see, or walk in on, your training. This is to ensure they don't mistake your training for a real life event and to prevent them from being injured. Signs stating something like: "WARNING! AIRGUNS IN USE FOR TRAINING. PLEASE KNOCK AND WAIT" are useful.
4. If you are unsure as to whether the airsoft/BB gun is loaded once the magazine has been removed after training, point the gun in a safe direction AND fold a towel over its muzzle before pulling the trigger to test it. If it is still loaded, the towel will catch the BB projectile.
5. Lock up airsoft/BB guns when not in use.
6. Close shots can break the skin, so generally speaking; do not shoot at anyone within 6 feet during training. Closer shots could be used, for example when testing the deflection phase of a gun disarm. However, be sensible – do not shoot at bare skin and make sure you have tested the airsoft/BB gun (see below) prior to close range use.
7. 'Test' the airsoft/BB gun prior to its use in training by progressively decreasing shooting distances with a trusted training partner. For example, your training partner stands 20 metres from you whilst wearing thick clothing and full face protection. Shoot one shot at their chest. If your training partner doesn't feel anything upon contact, then carry out the same drill a metre closer and repeat until the training partner feels the shot but without it marking. (Do not wait until the projectile 'stings' your training partner, as they are wearing thick clothing as part of the test; other training partners may have only thin clothing or bare patches of skin). Once they do, this will give you an idea as to how close you can safely shoot at your training partner(s).
8. DO NOT use CO2 powered BB guns and ONLY use lightweight 6mm plastic ball bearings as ammunition. Do not use lead or metal BBs.
9. Spring powered airsoft/BB guns tend to be the least powerful and often are perfect for training. However, if you want to spend more money and have a more realistic rate of fire (i.e. semi-automatic/automatic) then battery or gas powered airsoft/BB guns may be suitable. Remember, do not use CO2 powered BB guns as they are too powerful to be used safely for force on force training.

If you are able, it is advised that you have at least a few lessons with a certified Instructor as they can offer advice on safe training principles.

Training tips

When training, counter attacks must include loud verbal commands, such as "GET BACK" whenever possible (don't use the command "BACK OFF" as this can be misheard as "F*** OFF" which can cause more problems). Loud verbal commands will cause stress and dysfunction to the subject.

Similarly, conflict communications with 'friendlies' should be incorporated whenever appropriate – e.g. to obtain assistance, or to tell an untrained person you are with to run.

You must use an A-Z approach to your training – i.e. the build-up to the conflict (e.g. any form of argument), the physical conflict itself and then the post conflict (e.g. running towards an exit).

When practicing the techniques within this book, practice from whichever stance is most comfortable for you to start with and then vary the stance as you progress.

Remember that techniques will not work by themselves - you need to fight to make them work and sometimes they will not happen instantly, but you must continue fighting aggressively and consider using a plan B when appropriate.

Training partners must allow each other to learn the techniques in a simple to complex manner, by complying and offering no resistance to start with. Later, when offering resistance, this must be realistic – i.e. if an effective counter attack is made, the partner must employ a suitable reaction.

Knowing your enemy and training like them is important – training partners should attack realistically (including things like the use of distraction) and aggressively whilst keeping in mind the simple to complex learning method.

Cross training – DO cross train in other systems to enhance your core training. Do not overload yourself with lots more techniques, instead, use other systems to refine your core technique or find ALTERNATIVES that suit YOU better.

Use a positive mindset when training – utilise mantras to aid determination, aggression and operating reflexively:

Determination: "When you're going through hell, keep going"

Aggression: "Forwards and finish it"

Operating reflexively: "Danger, Attack, Move, Scan, Breathe"

Use these whilst you train, so you have a mantra which will be 'with you' when you are involved in a real life situation.

Do not telegraph – wherever possible; do not give away what your intentions are.

Train in normal clothing.
Train in realistic conditions – with loud music, confined spaces, darkness etc.

Critique yourself – i.e. make sure you can lawfully justify anything you use in training as if it were a real life event.

Use impact training to develop striking – hitting pads or a heavy bag is the only way to train to be an effective striker in a real life incident.

Consider using video footage of your training sessions to critique yourself.

USP overall guiding principles

Distract if possible – using a question, misdirection or pain.

Deal with the immediate danger - without placing yourself in a worse position

Counter attack – immediately and aggressively, moving towards the subject, switching the psychology of the attack. Counter attacks prevent a secondary attack from the subject as well as preventing them from chasing you when you make your escape.

Move out of the 'fighting arc' – move around to the side / back of the subject where possible (this also allows you to escape their focussed tunnel vision).

Scan – look around for other subjects, weapons of opportunity, escape routes and cover whilst gaining space (this also allows you to mitigate your own focussed tunnel vision).

Breathe – take a slow, deep 'belly' breath to relieve excessive adrenaline response for -optimum performance under stress.

The list above can be overlapped, for example, counter attack aggressively WHILST moving out of the fighting arc AND scanning.

To make things easy to remember, the following can be used as 'jump start commands' when training – when used often in training these 'commands' should be readily available and help your recall when under stress, much the same as first aid training uses the DRSABC acronym which stands for:

Danger
Reaction
Shout for help
Airway
Breathing
Compressions

The USP acronym is: DAMSB, which stands for:

Danger
Attack
Move
Scan
Breathe

Although not included in this acronym, the principle of distraction is always practiced whenever appropriate as an added tactical advantage.

Related technique principles

The following are a list of principles that can be attached to techniques that are related to one another to give you some idea of why individual techniques have been designed in the way that they have as you progress through this book:

Striking/combinations:
All strikes must go beyond the target – i.e. don't just touch a punch bag or pad, hit it as though you are aiming six inches through it.

As you strike, you must remember to breathe! To hold one's breath when striking makes you too tense. However, releasing breath too quickly and freely provides less power in the strike. So we use a kettle's whistle analogy to describe how to release your breath:

The kettle's whistle when water boils is releasing pressure, but through a small channel. This means there is still pressure inside the kettle allowing the whistle to work (just as there will be enough pressure and tension in your body to strike powerfully) but by releasing the pressure, it prevents a dangerous build up (just as too much pressure in your body will cause you to be too tense and rigid).

Some people use a short, sharp word such as 'ice' as they tense their stomach quickly to obtain the correct breathing method when striking, others imagine blowing a pea off the end of their nose as hard and as quickly as they can. Whatever suits you is fine but get the right balance: don't hold your breath and don't release all of the pressure at once.

Strike continuously until the threat is neutralized/avenue of escape has been presented.

Do not miss opportunities to strike – e.g. when turning to face a subject the combination of a back kick, side hammer fist, and straight punches may be employed so as to strike continuously.

Always strike aggressively and as hard as you can, but find a balance between speed and power.

Keep target areas simple – where possible attack the head/face this is where the 'computer' is and if attacked, it helps to prevent thinking time for the subject. A punch to the arm hurts. A punch to the head hurts AND distracts.

Other effective target areas are the groin, knees and shins.

Closest (effective) target, closest (effective) weapon. This means that in any given position, we must strike the nearest target with the nearest body weapon optimising our time used in a conflict – however, this must be EFFECTIVE. It's no use if the nearest target is the subject's thigh and your nearest weapon is your head as a head butt to the thigh will (in most cases) be ineffective.

Recoil all strikes as quickly as you can. This helps to prevent the subject from grabbing the striking weapon, aides with concussive force and improves aggression. It also allows you to return to a ready state quickly so you can change tact should this be required.

Fighting:
Do not create a pause in conflict – counter attack continuously until the threat is neutralized/avenue of escape has been presented.

Generally, a fight in the street is not like a match fight, where subjects can almost take it in turns to throw strikes at each other. Instead, a street fight is usually asymmetrical in nature; one of the two parties involved will be taking the initiative with continuous attacks, overwhelming the other until they stop or the other party manages to 'change the tide'. So in a fight, you are either the hammer or the anvil – striking, or being struck. Don't be the anvil!

Do not become 'weapon focussed' i.e. do not try to use the same technique or strike over and over again if it is not working. Change your tactic.

Rest your vision on the chest of the subject allowing peripheral vision to be used during a physical conflict, but be sure to monitor their hands during a pre-conflict build up.

Do not show pain when fighting (or training) – it is a cue for the subject to become even more aggressive.

Strike if you can, grapple if you have to – do not go to the ground if you can help it. Do not vertically grapple (grappling whilst standing up) with the subject if you can help it. It is likely that you will end up vertical grappling if neither you nor the subject are down after the first or second strike.

Mix things up - consider hitting a high target area to raise the subject's guard and then finishing them with a hard low strike or vice versa.

Self-defence:
In general self-protection should be carried out in the following order of preference to be the most effective:

- Awareness and avoidance of conflict
- Escape conflict (walk/run away)
- De-escalate the situation if you are unable to escape
- Take pre-emptive action
- Fight aggressively until you can escape or the threat is neutralised

(This doesn't mean you have to work through all stages on every occasion of course. It may be that you are caught off guard and are grabbed by a subject for example. In which case, you must go to the final stage immediately).

If you are by yourself and are unable to avoid conflict, then escape is always the best option. However, if you are trapped or you have others to protect, then you must neutralise the threat before you can escape, whether that is through de-escalation, pre-emptive action or fighting aggressively.

Once you have broken free from a grab, hold or other type of attack, counter attacks are vital to prevent a secondary attack from the subject, or to stop them from chasing after you when you make your escape.

Visually check the hands of your subject frequently when conflict is building.

Trust your gut feeling – if something doesn't feel right IT ISN'T. Leave as soon as possible.

When practicing self-defence techniques, you should also practice physical prevention. Generally speaking this will be: long distance = kicking, closer = block and move, hold applied = defensive technique.

Ground work:
Get up and gain space as soon as possible as the subject may have weapons, the floor may be a dangerous environment (concrete floor, broken glass etc) and/or there may be other subjects.

Keep moving.

Keep your head off the floor.

Keep your knees bent.

Maintain close contact with the subject when you are in a top position to restrict their movement.

If you are unable to escape immediately, your priority is to get to a dominant position and strike the subject until you can escape.

If your subject is standing, keep your legs and feet between them and you.

Weapons (general)
Disarm the subject if you are going to remain at the scene.

Invite specific attacks by appearing passive and acting in a certain manner to manipulate positioning of both the subject and yourself if appropriate.

When you are in possession of a weapon – either your own or having just disarmed the subject – NEVER allow them to take it from you.

Control weapons as soon as possible preventing further use if you are unable to escape safely.

Improvised weapons
Conceal your improvised weapon whenever possible prior to its use to maximise the element of surprise.

Familiarise yourself with weapons on often travelled routes or in places frequented.

Equip yourself in advance when possible – i.e. when you sense possible danger get the weapon ready in your hand – do not wait for the attack.

Use the 10 angles of attack for stick, staff, flexi, edged and stone like striking weapons. The 10 angles are explained in Level 1, but are essentially:

- Forward & Back = 2 angles
- Horizontal (both ways) = 2 angles
- Vertical (both ways) = 2 angles
- The 4 diagonal angles along an imaginary 'X' = 4 angles

Firearms
Get out of/deflect the line of fire, control weapon, counter, disarm.

If at all possible, never run from the subject whilst they still have the weapon.

Knives
Deflect and run whenever possible.

If escape is impossible, control the weapon and prevent further usage.

Impact weapons (stick like objects – baseball bats, piece of scaffolding pipe, pool cue etc)
If you are unable to position yourself outside of the swinging arc of the weapon, get as far inside it as possible.

Multiple subjects
Use one to hinder the other – by positioning or shoving one into the path of the other or use as a shield.

Draw a 'line in the sand' during the conflict build up. (I.e. set an imaginary boundary that you will not allow a subject to cross). Should they do so, this will be your cue to pre-emptively respond or run.

Strike first.

Do not move through the middle and if you have to, do so aggressively and quickly.

If possible use hit and run tactics – hit the nearest subject and run.

Neutralize the most dangerous subject first if you have to fight more than one person – e.g. the one with a weapon.

Disarm if they have a weapon and use it against the other(s) if possible.

Use the wall to protect your back.

If you are unable to escape, then the attacking group's overall confidence can be significantly reduced if you effectively incapacitate one or more of the group very quickly.

Bear hugs
Drop your weight to make it difficult for the subject to throw you.

Choke holds
Gain space to breathe first.

LEVEL 4: COMBATIVES

Face shield

What is it?
A method to protect your head when overwhelmed with punches from a subject.

Why do it?
Multiple strikes to the head can sometimes be so fast and overwhelming, that it isn't possible to block each individual strike. As such, this is a general defence which affords some protection against this barrage of strikes and allows you to regain your composure.

How to execute the technique:
When overwhelmed with punches to the head, cover it with your hands and arms so that they take the impact of the strikes instead of your head and face.

Keep your hands and arms in tight to your head and face. This will help prevent strikes from making their way through your face shield and it also eliminates the chances of you striking yourself in the face as a knock on effect of being punched in your arms when they are only inches from you're your face!

Try to leave a small gap between your arms so you can still see the subject.

Actively move your arms and hands to best protect your head – as strikes may be coming at you from different angles.

As soon as you have regained your composure, drive your hands forwards towards the subject's eyes. This should cause a momentary distraction giving you time to gain some space and be ready to fight again.

As you drive your hands forwards, step forwards too, to put the subject on their back foot, both physically and psychologically.

A common mistake is to drive your hands into the chest of the subject. This technique relies on the distraction and flinch response from attacking the subject's face/eyes and as such, aiming for the chest won't be effective.

Essentials:
- Cover your head and face with your arms and hands
- Keep them in tight to your head
- Leave a gap to see through
- Actively move your hands and arms to best protect your head
- Drive your hands towards the subject's face and move towards them

Technique specific exercises:
Have both you and your training partner wear boxing gloves and at first, have them carry out light punches towards your head and face. Cover up and carry out the face shield for a few seconds, then drive your hands forwards towards their face.

This can be built up to harder and faster attacks.

Uppercuts

What is it?
This is a hand strike used to strike upwards at relevant body targets.

Why do it?
An uppercut is a close range tool where straight punches are less effective. An uppercut can be difficult for the subject to spot and can often help get around their guard.

How to execute the technique:
Uppercuts can be executed with the lead or rear arm and can also be carried out from passive stance.

Drop your weight slightly and turn inwards on the ball of the foot. This should be done with the foot that is on the same side as the striking hand. I.e. if you are striking with your right hand, turn on the ball of the right foot.

Turn the hips and shoulders in the same direction that your foot is moving. I.e. if striking with your right hand, the foot, hips and shoulders should be turning anti clockwise and if striking with the left, they should be turning clockwise.

Drop your striking hand from guard position slightly.

Your elbow should be bent at around a 90 – 120 degree angle.

Drive your fist directly upwards towards the target (usually the subject's jaw, or if you are on the floor and they are standing; their groin) along the centre line.

You should now drive your bodyweight upwards as you strike. This is where the power is generated.

Remember to recoil quickly, as usual.

Essentials:
- Drop your weight slightly
- Drop your striking hand slightly
- Turn on the ball of your foot
- Turn your hip and shoulder inwards
- Drive your body weight up as you strike with your fist
- Keep your elbow bent at around 90 – 120 degrees
- Recoil quickly

Stomp

What is it?
This is a foot strike which as the name implies, uses a stomping downwards action to various targets.

Why do it?
A stomp is a very easy technique to master and can be very effective. It can be used just after you have escaped a grab or hold on the subject's ankle or instep to ensure they do not run after you for example.

How to execute the technique:
A stomp essentially involves raising the knee, driving your heel downwards onto the target and retracting it.

Your shin should be kept vertical – because the targets can be various shapes, it is easy for your foot to roll off at an angle unless your drive straight down and back up again just like a sewing machine needle.

The important consideration when executing this technique is the target you are striking.

Stomping on the instep of the subject, perhaps when they are bear hugging you could break bones in their foot. When they are on the floor, stomping on limbs can also break bones. If you stomp on their head, throat, torso or groin, you have the potential to cause very serious injuries or even death. That's not to say you should discount these targets. The circumstances must be serious enough to strike them and your actions must be reasonable.

A few examples to help consider what may or may not be reasonable:

A small female has just had a larger stronger male try to pull her into some bushes. During the struggle he falls to the floor. She stomps on his ankle once to prevent him chasing after her and runs off. Refer to the section on law to see if you think this is reasonable in the circumstances.

A male has just tried to rob a corner shop by brandishing a knife. He has been wrestled to the floor by two members of the public, but is still continuing to fight and looks as though he is about to get up. A third member of the public stomps on the subject's head before he gets up, killing him. Again, refer to the section on law to see if you feel this is reasonable in the circumstances.

Remember to ask yourself if there was anything else that could have been done that would have caused less injury, but achieved the same result. If the answer is yes, then there must be justification for not taking that course of action.

Essentials:
- Raise your foot
- Drive your heel downwards into the target
- Keep your shin vertical
- Recoil along the same path
- Consider target areas

Technique specific exercises:
Stomping on a kick shield laid on the floor is fine to get used to the mechanics of the technique.

Regarding target choice, a realistic training dummy with soft sticks representing limbs, can be placed lying on the floor. You walk around the dummy and your training partner shouts 'Lethal' or 'Less lethal'. If they shout 'Lethal' you should strike the head, throat, torso or groin. If they shout 'Less lethal' then you should strike a limb. The reason the term 'Less lethal' is used is that there is still a potential for death when breaking bones in the limbs, albeit far less likely than the 'Lethal' targets.

Backwards head butt

What is it?
A strike using the head with the subject being behind you.

Why do it?
The head is a very effective striking tool and this is a simple strike. The head butt is very useful when you are unable to strike with your limbs because they have been grabbed or simply because of the position you're in.

How to execute the technique:
As per the forwards head butt, imagine you are wearing a crown on your head. The striking points of your head are along the line where the crown would sit at the rear of your head.

The strike is quick and simply driving backwards with the body rather than a whipping motion with the head and neck.

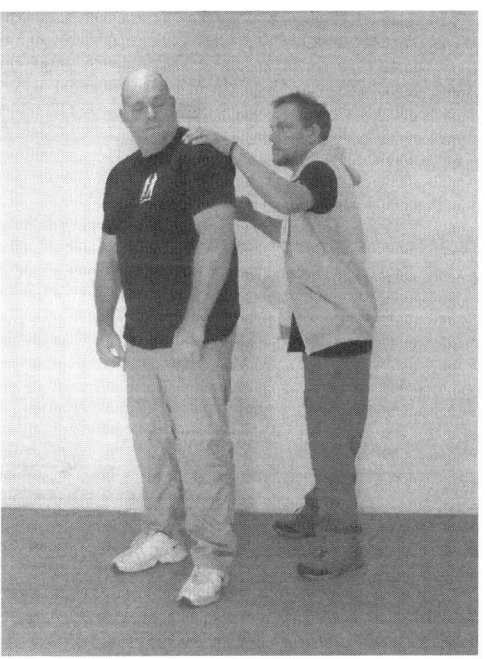 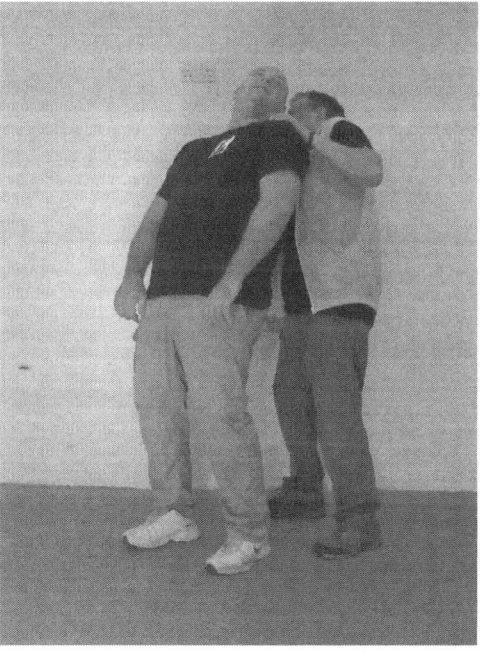

Make sure you clench your teeth as you strike so they don't smash together and break and/or bite the tip of your own tongue off.

Essentials:
- Strike with the rear part of your head where a crown would sit
- Drive the body backwards
- Clench your teeth

Technique specific exercises:
This technique can be practiced on a pad BUT do not do lots of repetitions or practice too regularly as you will give yourself a headache!

Two or three times once a month should be fine.

Use of a realistic training mannequin can also be helpful.

Barking

What is it?
Barking is a name given to a method of aggressive posturing to deter a subject. It is a higher level alternative to 'Command Presence' and a last ditch attempt to dissuade the subject before physical action and can also be used if verbal diffusion is not working.

Why do it?
This method employs no physical contact, so provided it works, you will be able to survive an encounter without having to risk injury by fighting. The common reaction to 'Barking' is the subject back-peddling and making some aggressive face-saving comment.

The only downside to this, is that it requires you to act very aggressively and should you end up having no choice but to fight, witnesses to the incident may claim you were overly aggressive during the incident showing you in a poor light.

However, should you be required to account for your actions, for example to the Courts, then provided you articulate that you acted in that manner to try and PREVENT a physical confrontation, then the behaviour is put into the correct context and your actions will seem more reasonable.

How to execute the technique:
Display the same 'Warning Signs' that you learned in Level 1. The following is a reminder of these:

- Direct prolonged eye contact
- Facial colour darkening
- Head back
- Standing tall to maximise height
- Standing square on to you
- Kicking the ground
- Exaggerated movements near to defender especially with hands
- Abrupt stopping and starting of nervous behaviour (e.g. tapping of fingers)
- Use of expletives
- Raised voice
- Heavier breathing
- Contorted face

Use expletives and act as if you are a feral animal making aggressive verbal threats such as "I'll rip your f***ing head off!"

Act as though you have lost control of yourself.

The intention is to scare the subject into leaving you alone without having to make contact with them.

46

This method can be used alongside weapon 'keep away swings' too.

Be prepared to fight if you have to.

Essentials:
- Display 'Warning Signs'
- Be verbally aggressive
- Act as though you have lost control

Technique specific exercises:
Have your training partner carry out some sort of verbal aggression towards you. Then carry out the technique.

Many people find it hard to act in this way in training. It is useful to consider what makes you angry and when you would be happy to use aggression. For example, if your children were being threatened. Just imagining this can put you in the right mind set to carry out the technique in just a training environment.

Groin grab

What is it?
This is a pain compliance method for obtaining a tactical advantage in close quarters.

Why do it?
This is a very simple and effective movement against a male subject for obvious reasons. It can cause a huge amount of pain and requires very little effort on the part of the defender. It's a useful tool for close quarter fighting standing up or on the ground and can be employed when you are in front or behind the subject.

How to execute the technique:
Get your open hand high into the groin to make sure you don't just grab clothing.

Crush whatever you grab in your hand and rip and twist at it.

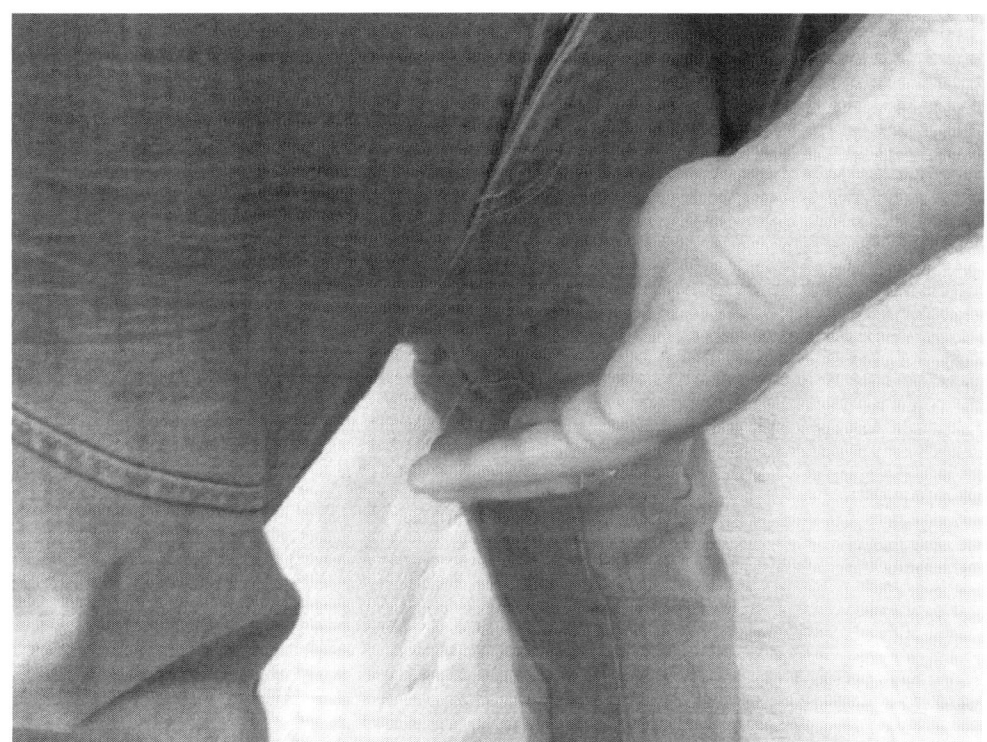

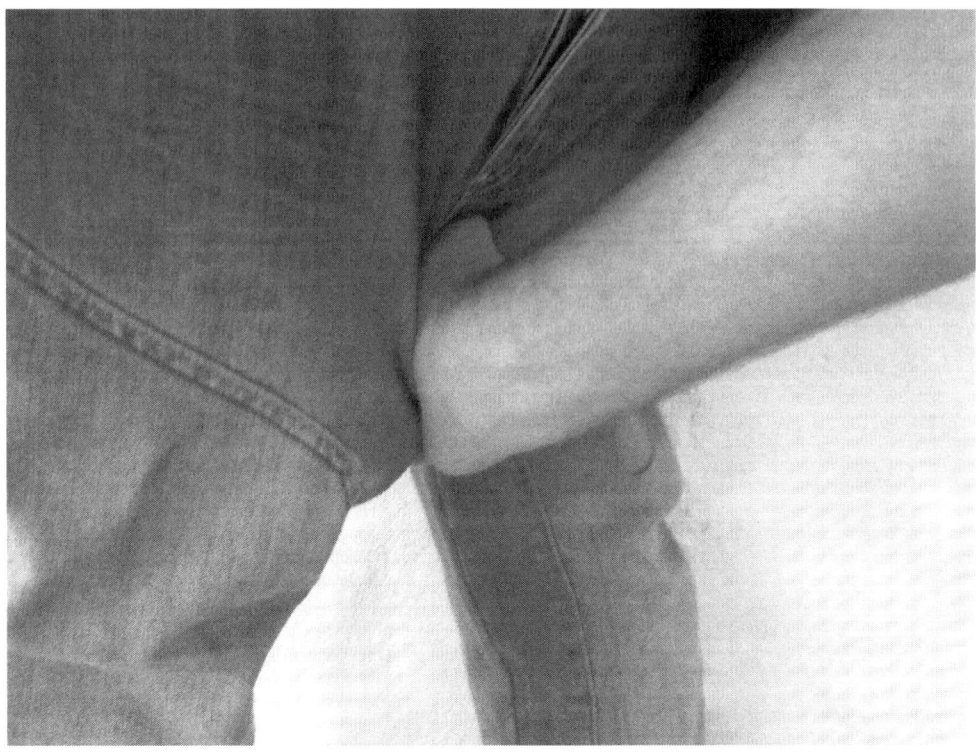

Essentials:
- Only really effective against male subjects
- Reach high up into the groin
- Crush, twist and tear at the genitals

Technique specific exercises:
Provided your training partner has baggy trousers on, the technique can be practiced by grabbing only their trousers in the groin area and twisting etc. as if you had hold of their genitals too.

This can be practiced carefully and with very little force when sparring if the opportunity arises and your training partner has given permission that this technique can be included the training exercise before you begin. This is obviously to make sure that no one makes inappropriate contact that could be deemed as a sexual assault during training.

Defence against a clinch

What is it?
This is a method of regaining control of a subject when they have you in a standing clinch position.

Why do it?
Many self-defence situations can end up with the parties vertically grappling. If the subject is able to put you into a 'clinch' then they have a degree of control over you in which they can use some devastating strikes on you and or throw you to the floor. As such, you need to regain the dominant position as soon as you can.

How to execute the technique:
The subject will have their forearms at either side of your neck and likely will be pulling your head forwards and downwards.

'Swim' your hands inside and under their arms, so that you can place your hands on the back of their head/neck in a 'Proper clinch' described in Level 1.

This is difficult and will likely require a lot of effort to achieve. It may be that you execute a distraction strike to give you an advantage

Essentials:
- 'Swim' your hands under and inside the subject's clinch
- Execute a proper clinch
- Be prepared to fight to achieve this

Technique specific exercises:
This can be practiced with a partner in a similar drill to 'pummelling' used to practice 50/50 and double under hooks positions.

One of you puts the other in a proper clinch. The other carries out the clinch defence. You simply take this in turns and gradually build up resistance and incorporate movement and striking.

Cavalier lock

What is it?
This is a wrist manipulation which is used as a takedown. It can also be an effective method of controlling a weapon in the subject's hand.

Why do it?
Wrist control techniques are only really effective on those who aren't resisting strongly (for example, drunk people) or when it is applied quickly and with surprise.

However, in these circumstances, the cavalier lock is very effective as it works against the wrist in two directions causing enough pain to easily control the subject and direct them to the ground. It is also safer for both you and the subject to take them to the ground this way as opposed to a throw because you are unlikely to be taken down with them and they are less likely to hit their head on the way down.

Once the subject is on the ground, it is easy to make your escape, counter attack or to transition into an effective restraint method.

How to execute the technique:
Grab the subject's hand. For the sake of explanation, we will assume you take hold of their right hand, obviously mirror the explanation if you take hold of the left.

The lock is carried out with both of your hands.

Grab their wrist with your left hand and have your left thumb on the back of their hand.

Your right hand should be placed on the back of their hand and wrap your fingers over theirs.

Bend the subject's wrist with their fingers moving towards the crook of their elbow.

Pivot to your left and drive the subject's hand in an anti-clockwise direction.

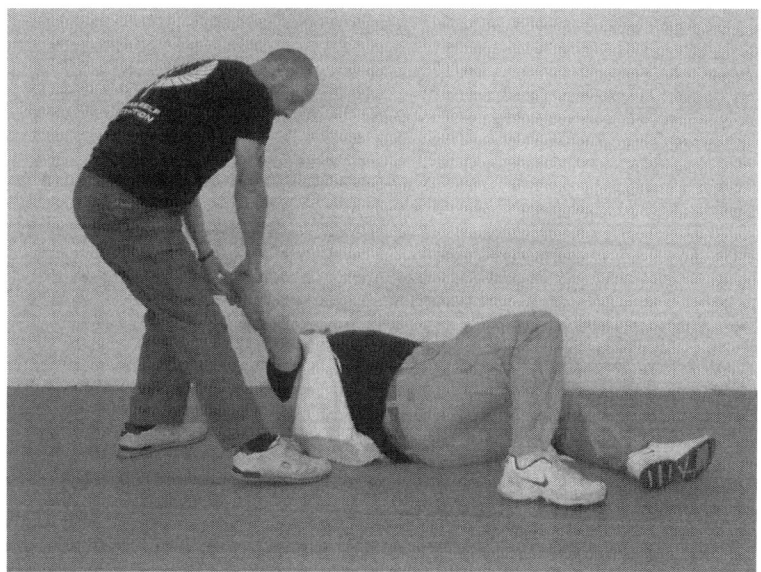

Their hand should be directed past the outside of their bicep and down towards the ground.

Essentials:
- Grab the subject's wrist
- Place your other hand over the back of their hand
- Bend their wrist
- Turn their hand to the outside
- Then direct the hand towards the ground past their bicep

Technique specific exercises:
This really can only be practiced on a training partner. To prevent injury, they need to be compliant and you need to be slow and cautious.

This can be tied into the 'Ground pin' technique described elsewhere in the book, by continuing the subject's movement into a prone position on the floor and turning the wrist back into a clockwise direction to assume the starting position for the ground pin.

Reverse head twist

What is it?
This is a pain compliance and control technique using a twisting motion of the subject's head.

Why do it?
Often, a physical confrontation can end up with the subject's head within reach. This could be during a ground fight, or perhaps they have pinned you against a wall with their shoulder. This is an easy and effective method for turning their whole body by using their head.

As the old Martial Arts adage goes, 'where the head goes, the body will follow'.

Applying this technique covers the face of the subject, distracting them and causing panic.

Contrary to how movies portray fighting, it is actually very difficult to kill someone with a head twist. To do so requires the spinal cord to be damaged. To do this requires the supporting cervical joints and ligaments to be broken. Whilst it is possible, it is difficult.

With any physical defence technique, there is potential for injury to varying degrees and these, of course, need to be considered. However, potential injuries from twisting the neck are worthy of special mention. There are, of course significant dangers to the subject when applying this technique. It is possible to damage their spine and / or spinal cord as well as other parts of their neck and throat, causing unconsciousness, brain damage, paralysis or death.

The more serious injuries tend to be caused when applied with speed, maximum force and for longer periods of time. That said, the body is quite robust and can take a certain amount of abuse without permanent injury. It must also be mentioned that the injuries described being caused, can be completely reasonable under the right circumstances.

How to execute the technique:
Using whichever hand is behind the subject's head, reach around the back of it and using your fingertips, hook the subject's nose and eye socket.

Pull their head on a horizontal path in the direction of the arm you are using which will cause them to face away from you. As you do so, drop your elbow down to keep their head in tight to you.

As soon as you are able, use the palm of your other hand to push against the subject's jaw which will aide the reverse head twist movement.

From here, you could continue the motion to push them to the floor, or push their head into a wall.

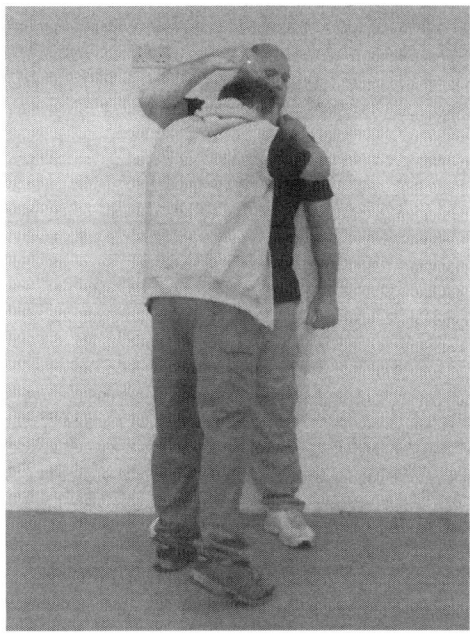
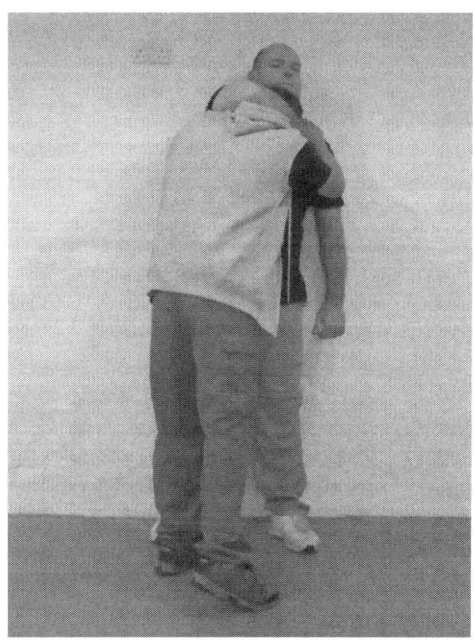

Essentials:
- Reach around the subject's head
- Hook their nose and eye socket with your finger tips
- Twist their head on a horizontal plane
- Use you other hand to push against their jaw

Head pull to ground

What is it?
The head to ground pull is a method of taking a subject to the floor from a proper clinch.

Why do it?
Taking someone to the floor can end an incident quickly. This method is a gross motor skill so is simple to remember. As per the 'Cavalier lock', it is also safer for both you and the subject to take them to the ground this way as opposed to a throw because you are unlikely to be taken down with them and they are less likely to hit their head on the way down as they have their arms in position to protect themselves as they make contact with the ground.

Once on the ground it is easy to make your escape or counter attack.

How to execute the technique:
Remember:

1. Only execute a takedown if you have 'softened up' the subject first. I.e. you have hurt them enough that they would be less likely to resist.
2. Only execute a takedown if a good opportunity arises. I.e. do not force a takedown to happen in difficult positions or circumstances – it should pretty much be a 'sure thing'.
3. Only execute a takedown if you are proficient in it's use.

When you have the subject in a proper clinch, keep their head tightly pulled in.

A knee strike to the groin will likely force them to bend in half making the take down easier.

Step backwards and drive their head towards the floor as you lean forwards.

 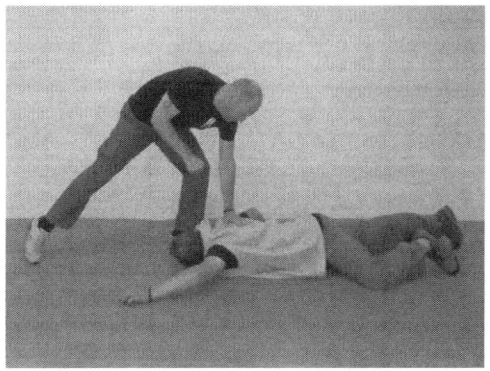

Consider grabbing the clothing around the subject's neck and using the same method of takedown as an alternative.
Beware of being bitten.

Essentials:
- From a clinch position execute a knee strike to the groin
- Step back
- Drive the subject's head towards the floor

Technique specific exercises:
This really can only be practiced on a training partner. Make sure you do so on mats and that your training partner is proficient at the forward break fall.

Increase their resistance but remember, in reality, you should only use this when the subject has been softened up anyway.

Wrestling throw

What is it?
This is a throw using the 'Gable grip' around the subject's body.

Why do it?
This is a simple method to use and is relatively safe for the defender to execute.

The throw can easily knock the wind out of the subject when they land.

Once on the ground it is easy to make your escape or counter attack.

How to execute the technique:
You need to be in a position where you can bear hug the subject with your arms low on their waist/underneath their buttocks.

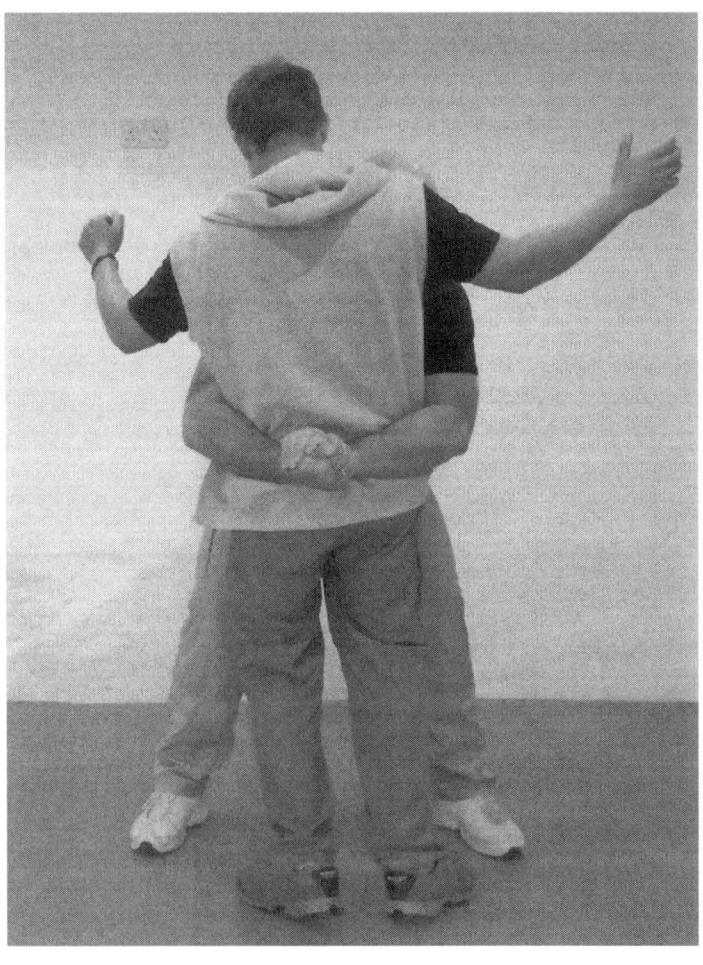

The technique works equally well from the front or the back of the subject and can be used with their arms free or pinned.

Use the 'Gable grip' (described earlier in this book) to secure your bear hug.

Move your feet either side of the subject, so your hips are as close as possible to them and drop your centre of gravity by bending your legs.

Straighten your legs and thrust your hips forwards. This should lift them off their feet. This movement is very similar to a kettlebell swing for those of you who are aware of it.

 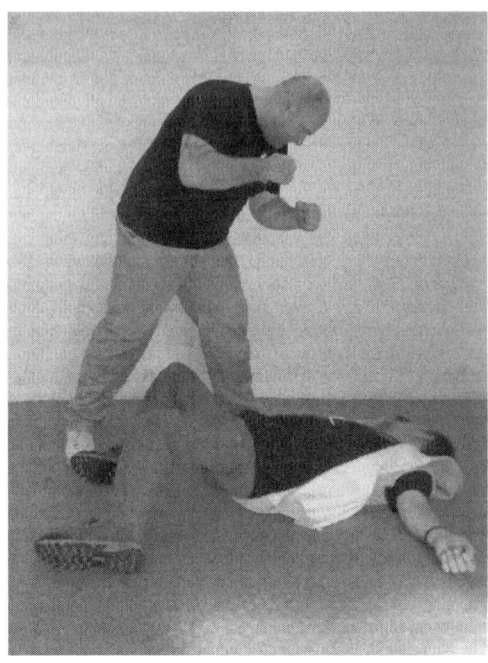

Use your head and arms to tip them sideways and drop them. Alternatively you can go with the throw and land on the subject, releasing your grip before they hit the floor.

Essentials:
- Bear hug and 'Gable grip' low on the waist or below the buttocks
- Place your feet either side of the subject and get hips close
- Straighten the legs and thrust the hips
- Turn them to one side

Technique specific exercises:
This can be practiced using a punch bag or a training partner provided you have crash mats to throw them onto.

Whilst using the 'pummelling' drill to gain 50/50 or double under hooks, you can compete to obtain a gable grip and lift your training partner off their feet without actually throwing them.

COMBINATIONS

Cross, lead hook

What is it?
A combination of punches.

Why do it?
This combination teaches moving in from mid, to close range striking as well as use of pivoting to produce power. It also teaches height changes for target acquisition. Lastly, whilst USP tends to stick to targeting the face for punching, this will also teach alternative appropriate targets.

How to execute the technique:
Execute a cross punch as usual.

Return to fighting stance and as you do so, step n drag pushing off your rear foot then execute a lead hook punch targeting the jaw of the subject.

The rhythm for this combination is simply 1-2.

Essentials:
- Execute a cross punch
- Step n drag forwards
- Lead hook punch to the jaw

Double elbow, double knee

What is it?
A combination of close range elbow and knee strikes.

Why do it?
This combination uses aggressive close range strikes with forward momentum designed to push the subject back and for you to learn how to follow them whilst continuing to strike, adjusting to distance and dynamic movement.

How to execute the technique:
Execute a rear forwards elbow on the horizontal plane.

The subject may step backwards. If they do, step n drag in order to close the distance and execute the second elbow as before.

Again, the subject may step backwards. If they do, take a drop step and reach to grab them in a proper clinch. Execute double rear forwards knee strikes.

Essentials:
- Execute two rear forward elbow strikes
- Step n drag to follow the subject if required
- Drop step if required and reach for a proper clinch
- Execute a double rear forwards knee strike

Back hammer fist (vertical plane), rear elbow (horizontal plane), side hammer fist, straight punches

What is it?
A combination of hand and elbow strikes.

Why do it?
This combination teaches how to carry out a seamless combination whilst turning to face a subject stood behind you, without wasting any time. It also teaches transition from passive stance to fighting stance whilst striking simultaneously.

How to execute the technique:
Execute a back hammer fist on the vertical plane to the subject's groin.

With the same hand, execute a rear elbow on the horizontal plane to the face of the subject. As you do so, take a step backwards towards the subject with the leg on the same side as your striking arm. Your strike should land at the same time as your step backwards to employ the 'Marriage of gravity' principle, described elsewhere in these books.

With the same hand, execute a side hammer fist on the vertical plane. As you make contact, the cross punch should begin to be executed. Then execute the jab and carry out alternate jab cross punches as necessary.

The rhythm for this combination is:

1-2…1-2-1-2

Essentials:
- Execute a rear hammer fist to the groin.
- Follow with a rear horizontal elbow as you step backwards and begin to turn using the marriage of gravity principle.
- Carry out a side hammer fist and continue turning into a forward stance pivoting on your rear foot as you carry out a cross punch.
- Execute multiple alternate jab cross punches.

Jab, cross, head butt

What is it?
A combination of hand strikes and a head butt.

Why do it?
This combination teaches moving in from mid, to close range striking using various striking tools.

How to execute the technique:
Execute a jab, cross combination as normal.

Step n drag forwards as you reach to grab the subject's head.

Execute a head butt as you carry out the 'drag' part of the step n drag.

The rhythm for this combination is:

1-2…1

Essentials:
- Execute a jab, cross combination.
- Step n drag and reach to grab the subject's head.
- As you 'drag' execute the head butt.

Lead regular kick, straights, knees, head to ground pull down, stomp

What is it?
A combination of strikes incorporating a takedown and a finishing strike

Why do it?
Incorporating takedowns into combinations, allows you to neutralise the subject quickly and clinically. It serves to teach forward pressure which is important to physically and psychologically put the subject on the back foot. It also reminds you to carry out a finishing move to prevent the subject from attacking again should this be necessary.

How to execute the technique:
Execute a lead regular kick to the subject's groin.

Carry out multiple straight punches whilst moving forwards, putting pressure on the subject.

Grab the subject in a proper clinch and execute knee strikes/skip knee strikes as appropriate.

Execute a head to ground pull to take the subject to the floor.

If necessary, carry out a stomp on an appropriate body target on the subject. For example, to prevent the subject from picking up a weapon that is close to hand, consider stomping on their arm. If you feel they will catch you if you try to escape, consider stomping on their ankle. If they pose an immediate deadly threat, then stomping on their groin/torso/neck/head may be necessary.

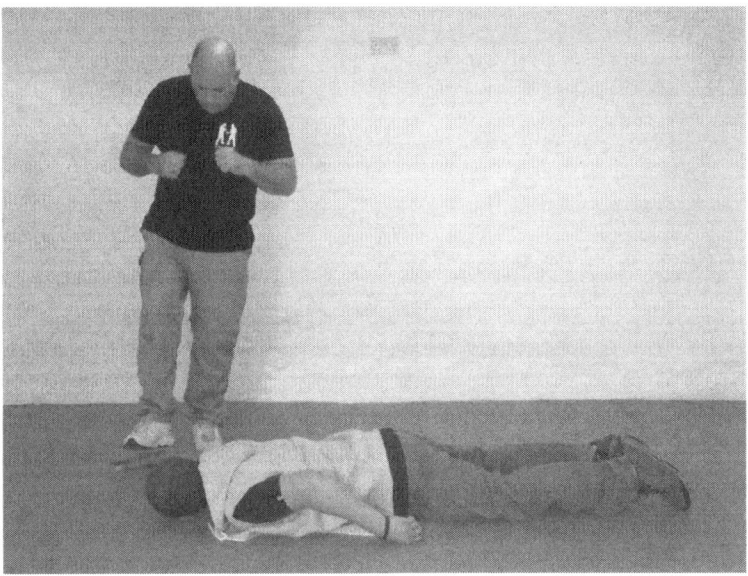

Essentials:
- Lead regular kick to the groin
- Straight punches
- Clinch and knee strikes
- Head to ground pull down
- Stomp, if necessary, on appropriate target

Toes out kick, jab, cross, lead hook, cross

What is it?
This is a combination of a kick and follow up hand strikes.

Why do it?
This combination can be used as a pre-emptive strike and follow up. It also helps to develop coordination with a mixture of strikes and movement.

How to execute the technique:
Carry out the toes out kick and recoil it so you land back into fighting stance.

Step n drag forwards if required and carry out the jab cross.

Step n drag forwards again and execute a lead hook punch.

Execute a second cross punch

The rhythm for this combination is 1…2,1,2,1

Essentials:
- Recoil into fighting stance after the kick
- Move forwards if necessary for the jab cross
- Move forwards again for the hook punch then execute the cross

Demonstration of your own combinations 5-10 strikes, long range to close range

What is it?
This is a combination of your own creation, starting from long range (kicking range), to close range (head butting, biting, elbowing, knee strikes etc.) but including mid-range (punching range) as you move forwards.

Why do it?
Refer to 'Demonstration of your own combination' described In Level 3.

Experimenting with moving forwards as you strike is important, as moving towards a subject demonstrates aggression and can physically and psychologically put them on the back foot. It also affords you a greater spectrum of targets.

How to execute the technique:
As before, these combinations are of your own creation and can be different every time.

However, you will find certain combinations or parts thereof, being used repeatedly. This is fine as you are working with your natural reactions and strengths.

You may also find that you use the same strike several times in succession – e.g. a rear forward hammer fist three times. This is fine too. Just remember that too frequent repetitions of the same strike will allow the subject to predict your next move.

It is still important to experiment though.

Each combination should be:

- Aggressive
- Flow together well
- Be moving to the dead side of the fighting arc
- Attempt to use high and low attacks to create confusion
- Try to keep the combination constant and without any pauses or hesitations
- Remember the overall guiding principles and incorporate them:

(Danger)
Attack
Move
Scan
Breathe

Refer to the principles of striking/combinations set out at the start of the book to make sure that you maintain effectiveness.

The following is an example using the 'Marking drill' (described in Level 3, 'Demonstration of your own combinations: 5-10 strikes') and shows a forward kick, landing forwards, jab, cross, lead hook punch, roundhouse knee, palm strike to the back of the head whilst moving out of the fighting arc:

Essentials:
- Experiment
- Minimum of 5 strikes starting from kicking range and moving through the ranges finishing with close range

- Don't repeat strikes too frequently
- Be aggressive
- Move forwards and to the dead side of their fighting arc, keeping them inside yours
- Try to create combinations that naturally flow well together
- Avoid pauses
- Mix high and low attacks where possible
- Use DAMSB mnemonic

Technique specific exercises:
Creating good combinations for counter attacking is arguably one of the most important parts of USP.

The reason we counter attack is so that once we have escaped a dangerous situation, we prevent it from happening again.

There are lots of different methods of practicing these combinations:

On a punch bag or realistic training mannequin.

Using a 'marking', or 'puppeting' drill.

Carrying out combinations in the air is another method – just make sure you are using your mind's eye as to where the targets on the subject are so you're not just throwing out wild strikes.

GROUND

Bicycle kick

What is it?
A violent repeated kicking out of the feet towards the subject.

Why do it?
These multiple rapid kicks are difficult to defend against but very simple to carry out.

How to execute the technique:
From the ground default position, simply carry out quick and repeated alternate forward kicks with both legs towards the subject until you gain an advantage.

Essentials:
- Forward kicks
- Alternate
- Repeated quickly

Technique specific exercises:
This is difficult to hold a pad for and dangerous if your training partner holds the pad with their knees facing towards your kicks. The kick shield should therefore be placed on the back of their leg, so their knee will bend in the correct direction when the pad is struck.

Punch bags and realistic training dummies can also be used. The bicycle kick can also be used when leaning back in a chair, so consider it's use during scenario training.

Defence against the guard

What is it?
A pain compliance method to escape a ground fighting position, where you are on your knees and the subject has locked their legs around your waist whilst lying on their back in front of you.

Why do it?
Of course, it could be argued that you are in a great position here to strike the subject. However, there may be other people trying to attack you and you need to escape the subject's legs. Even if there are not, ground fighting is never advisable and escaping to a standing position is always a priority – with their legs locked around you, it is very difficult to do so.

How to execute the technique:
Dig your elbows hard and fast into the inside of the subject's thighs, using your body weight to push downwards and parting their legs.

There are lots of nerves in this area and the pain caused should make them open their legs and release their grip.

You may need to move your elbows around slightly as you dig them in. Don't spend too long doing this as the subject will either get used to the pain and / or have time to come up with a counter move.

As soon as you get the desired reaction, hook your arm under the crook of one of their knees and throw their leg over your head so they lay on their side with their back to you.

Push down onto the subject to help you get up. This also keeps them in the disadvantageous position you have just put them in.

Be warned: as with all pain compliance techniques, they may not work on those who are intoxicated through drink or drugs, have mental health issues, have a high degree of determination or are conditioned to this sort of thing from Martial Arts or contact sport training. However, the surprise of a short sharp dig into the nerves of the thigh, will very often cause the subject to release their grip.

If this doesn't work, striking the groin is of course a valid alternative.

Essentials:
- Dig your elbows into the inside of the subject's thighs quickly
- Move the elbows downwards and parting the legs
- Swing their leg over your head when you achieve the desired reaction

Technique specific exercises:
This is simply a matter of having your training partner maintain the guard position as long as they can do whilst you execute the technique. It is painful though, so in training, it is recommended that you carry out the technique slowly until you achieve the desired result.

Low mount

What is it?
A ground fighting position.

Why do it?
This is a highly advantageous position when fighting on the ground as it allows you to dominate the subject and have easy access to get up off the floor.

It also negates the commonly used 'buck' or 'bridge' technique to remove someone carrying out a regular mount position.

How to execute the technique:
The subject is lying on their back and you are sat on their hips facing them.

Base your knees out to the sides for better stability.

Get your upper body close to theirs – i.e. chest to chest and carry out close quarter attacks, such as hook punches, head butts, thumb thrusts, ear grabs, head bouncing, spitting and biting.

To prevent being 'bucked' off, you need to keep your upper body as low as you can. The higher it goes, the more likely you are to get thrown off.

Essentials:
- Sit over their hips
- Base your knees out
- Get chest to chest
- Carry out close quarter attacks

Technique specific exercises:
A realistic training mannequin, a punch bag or a kick shield placed on the floor can be used to train this technique.

Of course it can be used in sparring too – just maintain sensible safety levels for contact.

Once you know some of the ground positions – high mount, low mount and side control, you can practice transitioning between these positions:

The key is to maintain contact with the subject – without this contact, they are likely to have enough space to escape. Use your training partner by feigning strikes in the various positions, whilst they try to throw you off, forcing you to maintain contact and good technique. Vary their resistance level – remember – simple to complex learning.

Side break fall

What is it?
A way of falling sideways safely.

Why do it?
It is perfectly possible for us to get tripped or knocked sideways during a violent confrontation.

The problem is, our natural reaction is to put our hands out to break the fall. This can cause all sorts of injuries to our hands, wrists, arms, shoulders or even collar bones.

If we don't use our hands, we can injure our ribs, arm and/or skull, so a safe method to fall sideways is very important.

How to execute the technique:
The fall is the same as the first part of a parachute landing.

As you fall, point your knees in the direction of the fall.

The aim is to get as many parts of the side of your body to touch the floor as you can, as you fall. I.e. the ankle can make contact, then the knee, then the thigh, then the hip/buttock, then the side of your waist, then your ribs.

It's like you are gradually 'unfolding' onto the floor rather than hitting the floor all at once. This should slow the momentum down.

As your ribs make contact, you should 'slap' the floor with the arm on the side of the direction of the fall – in much the same way as you do for a 'Backwards break fall' i.e. using the palm of your hand and your forearm, with a straight arm at around 45 degrees.

Keep your head tucked into your chin as you hit the floor to prevent it from whipping sideways and hitting the ground.

Once you have landed safely, get into 'Ground default' position.

Essentials:
- Point your knees in the direction of the fall
- Have the side of your body 'unfold' in stages onto the floor
- As your ribs make contact, 'slap' the floor with an open palm and forearm, with a straight arm
- Get into ground default position

Technique specific exercises:
If you have never done this sort of technique before, start by sitting on the floor. Roll sideways and splay your hand out to the side as described and keep your chin on your chest.

Do this a few times and when your feel comfortable, practice from a very low squat position.

Then build up the height as you become more proficient.

You can then practice this technique with your training partner shoving you.

Defence against kick to the face

What is it?
This is a method of protecting yourself and counter attacking when on all fours and having the subject kick you in the face.

Why do it?
This technique is designed to protect you from the kick and to be able to stand up as quickly as possible whilst counter attacking allowing you to escape.

How to execute the technique:
The kick is likely to be an upward kick, with a slight run up – a 'hooligan' type kick, as if they are kicking a ball.

As the kick comes in, if you are unable to get out of it's way, you will naturally use your arms to protect your face.

Their leg is stronger than your arms, so expect it to hurt. However, cross your forearms in front of your face and where possible, block to the very bottom of their shin. Whilst this is the fastest moving part of the kick, it is softer at the ankle joint than the shin bone.
As soon as you have blocked the kick, you need to stand up striking at the same time. There is no specific combination. You need to practice and see what works well for you. However, try to strike AS you're getting up and not wait UNTIL you've stood up. Move aggressively forwards towards them as you do so.

So the combination could be something like this:

- Punch their groin.
- Get one foot on the ground in a half kneel and punch the groin again.
- As you begin to stand, punch the solar plexus.
- As you reach full standing position, grab their neck in a proper clinch and execute knee strikes.

There is an alternate option of an 'ankle pick' take down. However, this leaves you on the floor for longer than the basic technique and is difficult, so should only be done when you are confident in its use, there is no other danger than the single subject AND the opportunity has presented itself – do not try to force this method.

The technique basically requires blocking in the same way but then quickly grabbing the subject's lower leg.

Wrap your arms tightly around the shin and drive your shoulder into their knee. Lean all of your body weight onto their knee and they SHOULD fall backwards. It is then up to you how you proceed. The suggestion would be to get up as soon as possible and perhaps carry out a counter attack so they are not able to get up and chase after you – perhaps an ankle stomp if appropriate.

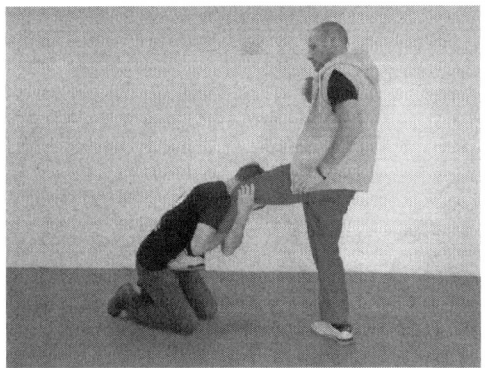 

Essentials:
- Block with both forearms
- Get up striking and moving forwards
- For the ankle pick takedown, block as before
- Grab their leg
- Drive your shoulder into their knee with your full bodyweight.

Technique specific exercises:
With forearm pads for you and shin pads for your training partner, the attack can be practiced quite realistically.

The striking whilst getting up is best done on a realistic training mannequin so you can make full contact strikes. Otherwise, the use of the marking drill from an 'all fours' position can also be used with your training partner.

Defence against prone mounted attack

What is it?
This is a method of protecting yourself and escaping, when you have found yourself in a prone (lying face down) position, with the subject sat on your back and striking you in the head/bouncing your head against the floor.

Why do it?
Real physical confrontations are incredibly dynamic and can very quickly end up in some strange and dangerous positions in the blink of an eye.

This is one of the more dangerous positions people sometimes find themselves in when fighting on the ground.

The subject is in one of the most advantageous positions they can be making you incredibly vulnerable to serious injury.

How to execute the technique:
Firstly, make a 'half push up', giving you space between the ground and your upper chest.

Fire your hand through this gap so your right arm is across your chest.

Continue moving in this direction with your whole body – in this case clockwise.

At the same time, try to bend your knee and drag it in line with your hips.

With your upper body twisting, push down with your knee against the floor to aid in the twist.

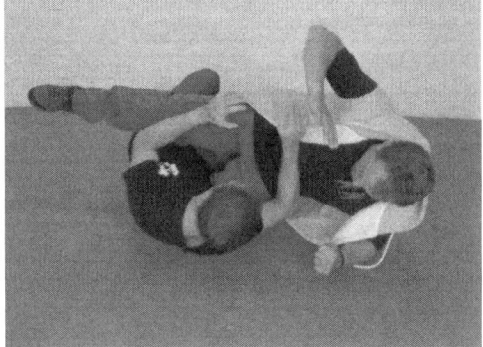

One of two things should now have happened:

1. You have rolled over so that you are face up, with the subject still mounting you.

2. As you rolled over, the subject has been thrown off your back.

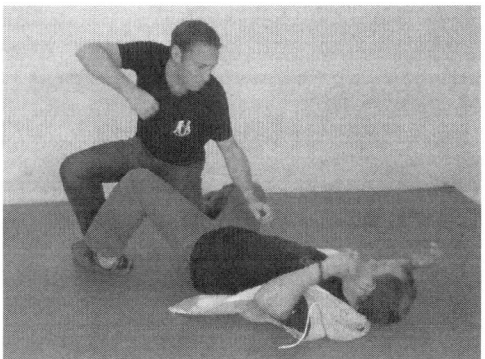

Both are better positions than the starting point. With position one, you can now use the table principle and/or take off wriggling to throw the subject off. You are also in a better position to defend against striking and counter attack.

With position two, you can continue the roll so you end up above the subject, counter attack and escape, or as you feel them being thrown off of you, roll in the opposite direction and stand up and escape.

Essentials:
- Half push up
- Drive your arm under your chest
- Bend your opposite knee and use to assist with twisting
- If they are still mounted, use the table principle/take off wriggling
- If they aren't, continue the roll and counter, or roll the opposite direction and escape

Defence against being tied up

What is it?
This is a method of protecting yourself from having your wrists restrained by a mounted subject.

Why do it?
The most common use for this attack is a sexual predator trying to tie a female victim's wrists together with rope or similar to make it easier to tear her clothes off and rape her. I.e. he can then control both her arms with just one of his, or even tie them to something freeing up both of his hands. Of course, this could happen for other reasons, but rape is the most likely.

How to execute the technique:
When mounted, take off wriggling and bucking violently should be employed to make it hard for the subject to balance.

You should keep your hands far away from each other because it is much harder to take control of them both when this is done.

You should also keep them moving to make it difficult to tie up. Shout "FIRE" repeatedly to try and obtain assistance.

If one wrist is caught and tied, keep the other as far away from it as you can.

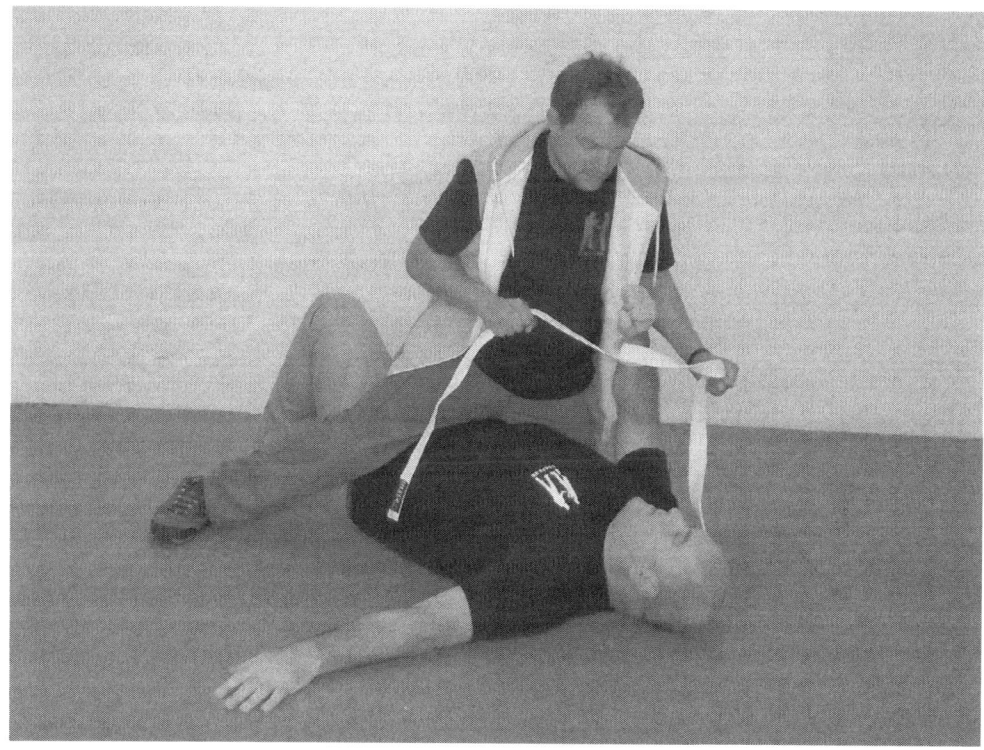

This must all continue for as long as possible or until the subject is thrown off/gives up. After all, a rapist is after an easy target and doesn't want to get caught. So the longer you struggle against them, the more likely they are to get caught and the more you struggle, the harder you are making their job to restrain you.

Essentials:
- Use take off wriggling and bucking violently and aggressively
- Keep your hands as far apart as possible
- Keep your hands moving
- Shout "FIRE" repeatedly

Technique specific exercises:
Have your training partner 'armed' with a karate belt – these are less likely to cause cuts and serious abrasions than rope etc. for this exercise.

Have them mount you for 20 seconds and try to tie your wrists together with the belt.

However, to develop the hand and arm movement, now try doing the exercise without using the take off wriggling or bucking methods.

SELF DEFENCE

Defence against a side bear hug (nearest arm free)

What is it?
An escape method from being held in a bear hug from the side. On this occasion your arm nearest the subject is free.

Why do it?
People attack from various angles and unfortunately, neither the front or rear bear hug defences will work with a side bear hug, although the principles are the same.

How to execute the technique:
With this attack, the subject's head may be in front of your body or behind it.

In either case, base out and drop your weight by bending your knees and parting your feet.

With the arm nearest the subject, execute a downwards elbow strike to an appropriate target on their back. Remember, striking the spine could cause more serious injury than striking the shoulder blade. However, if it is reasonable and necessary, strike the spine.

Then, if the subject's head is behind your body, turn and place the palm of your nearest hand against the side of their head and push it. This should force their head away making sure they release their grip. If not, it should give you some space to manoeuvre round so they are in your fighting arc enabling knee strikes etc.

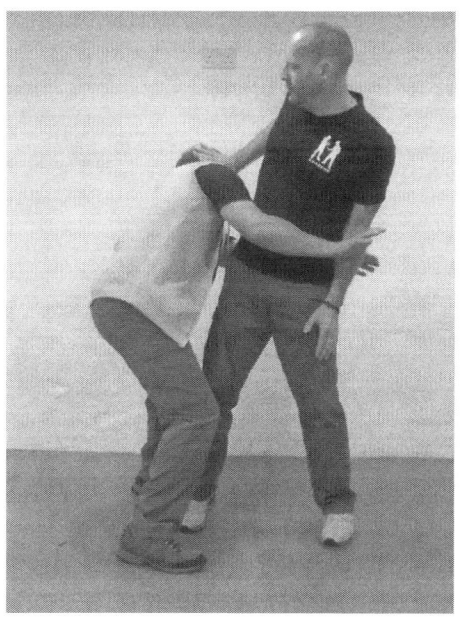

However, if the subject's head is in front of your body, use your nearest hand to reach over and carry out the 'Reverse head twist' (described earlier in Level 4) after the elbow strike instead.

Essentials:
- Drop your weight and base out
- Downwards elbow to the subject's back
- Face push/reverse head twist depending on subject's position

Technique specific exercises:
Carry out an eyes closed drill with a training partner so they randomly attack you with the side bear hug from the right or the left, with their head in front or behind your body. As per other eyes closed drills, as soon as you're attacked, open your eyes and carry out the correct technique.

Defence against a lifting bear hug front

What is it?
An escape method from being lifted using a front bear hug.

Why do it?
Often bear hugs are used to lift and throw people or to lift and move them somewhere else. Both are dangerous. Once you're off the floor, it is very difficult to gain any control, movement or striking. This method is used whether your arms are pinned or not, so you only have one thing to remember if you get caught in this situation.

How to execute the technique:
Simply draw your strong leg backwards and knee strike the subject's groin until they let you down.

Of course, if your arms are free you can also 'Thumb thrust' the subject's eyes.

Be ready for when they drop you so you don't fall over upon landing.

Essentials:
- Draw your leg backwards and knee strike the groin
- If your arms are free, thumb thrust the eyes
- Be ready for the landing

Defence against a front headlock

What is it?
An escape method from being held in a headlock. You will be bent at the waist, with the subject having you in a headlock – your head at their side facing behind them and your backside facing away from them. Sometimes referred to as a guillotine choke.

Why do it?
As mentioned before, it's very natural for fighters, trained or not, to grab the subject around the neck. This is one of the positions in which it can be done. The subject has you in a position of disadvantage, has a lot of control and could simply fall backwards, potentially driving your face into the ground as they do so. It is also quite possible to cut off your air supply with this headlock.

How to execute the technique:
Firstly turn your head in towards the subject. This will relieve some of the pressure from your windpipe.

With your arm furthest from the subject, hook their attacking wrist/forearm with your hand and pull downwards. Again, this helps to relieve pressure on your windpipe. It also helps you balance.

With your other hand, execute an open hand strike to the groin. This will hopefully bring their head forwards. At the same time, you can step forwards with the outside leg to assist with balance.

With the same arm, immediately execute a vertical back and upwards elbow to their chin. This will hopefully send their head backwards.

Then with the same hand, carry out a throat grab and push your fingers and thumb into their throat. This should cause them to release the hold.

If not, other options are to strike the groin again and consideration should be given to biting the subject at this stage.

Essentials:
- Turn head in
- Grab attacking wrist/forearm
- Groin strike and step forwards
- Elbow strike to the face
- Throat grab and push

Defence against a front headlock (being dropped)

What is it?
An escape method from being held in a front headlock, whilst the subject is leaning backwards in an attempt to drop to the floor and drive your face into the ground.

Why do it?
As per the front headlock defence.

How to execute the technique:
Initially, try to turn your head and grab the subject's wrist/forearm as per the front headlock defence. However, as soon as the subject starts to drop backwards you need to step across in front of them.

The aim is to land at a right angle to them, chest to chest, across their body.

As you fall, use your arm furthest from the subject to shield you from their legs hitting you in the fall.

This movement should ensure your face doesn't hit the ground, even if they manage to maintain their grip.

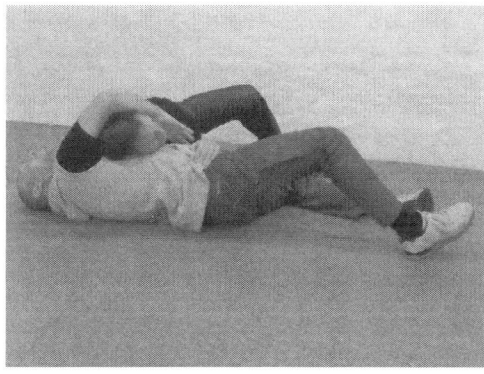 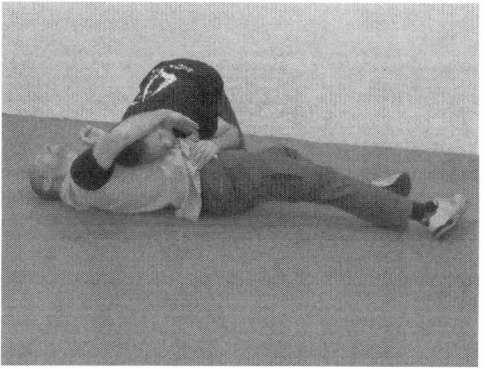

If they have managed to maintain their grip, apply pressure to their face with your forearm, sandwiching their head with the ground. Or carry out downward hammer fist strikes to their face. You can also grab their forearm with the other arm, and push it towards the floor as you pull your head towards the sky to help release the grip.

Essentials:
- Step across the front of the subject
- Use your outside arm to shield against their legs in the fall
- Land chest to chest at a right angle
- Attack the face
- Push their arm and pull your head back

Technique specific exercises:
This is very difficult to practice safely as gravity will not let you carry out the attack in slow motion. As such, it is suggested that a full size crash matt be used for both parties to fall on. If none is available, then the 'subject' should release their grip on your head prior to hitting the floor.

Defence against clothing grabs

What is it?
This is a method to defend against lapel grabs.

Why do it?
A lapel grab will almost always be followed by pulling you in and striking you. It's a common attack. This technique ties in with other grab defences such as the hair grab and bag snatch as the principles to follow are the same, thus making it easier to learn and retain.

How to execute the technique:
If the subject grabs you with one hand, they are likely to punch you with the other. If they grab you with two hands, they are likely to head butt you.

This technique aims to cover both eventualities.

Counter grab the subject's grabbing hand – your left hand should grab their right hand or vice versa. This is to prevent them from avoiding your counter attack.

At the same time as the counter grab, drop your chin to protect your face in case the strike they use is a head butt.

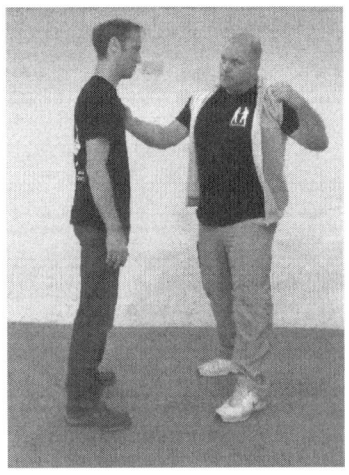

Or, if they have grabbed you with two hands, then use your non-dominant hand to counter grab.

Whichever grab type they have used, execute an open hand strike to their face with your other hand. This is a pre-emptive distraction strike, but is also important to block either an incoming punch if the subject grabs with one hand, or a head butt if they grab with two.

At the same time, step sideways. Stepping sideways allows you to move away from the subject's punch if they are only grabbing you with one hand. If they are grabbing you with two hands, this sidestep can still help to either get out of the subject's fighting arc or turn them off balance.

Kick at the subject's knees with toes out kicks (or execute knee strikes to the groin if the subject is too close) until they release.

Essentials:
- Counter grab
- Drop your chin
- Sidestep away from punching hand and palm strike
- Kick at the subject's knees until they release

Defence against being cornered by a dog

What is it?
These are tactics to use when a dog (be it stray or otherwise) is barking/growling at you angrily preventing you from being able to escape.

Why do it?
Regardless of breed, almost any size dog when it attacks a human is incredibly dangerous and very difficult to deal with.

How to execute the technique:
Firstly, take a step back slowly to keep away from the dog's snapping jaws. This also demonstrates you are non-threatening to the dog.

Lots of noise and fast movement are what excites a dog, so your movements should be slow and only shout as suggested below.

Adopt the following defensive position:

- Drop your chin – this helps to protect your throat as some attack dogs are trained to attack this area.

- Put your weak arm out in front of you between your throat and groin height. This is to 'offer' the dog should it attack you – it is less likely to go for your throat or groin if you do and a bitten arm is more survivable than a bitten throat or groin.

- Make your hands into fists to prevent your fingers from getting bitten off too easily.

- Stand bladed – this helps to protect your groin too.

- Don't make eye contact with the dog as this it may see this as a threatening gesture.

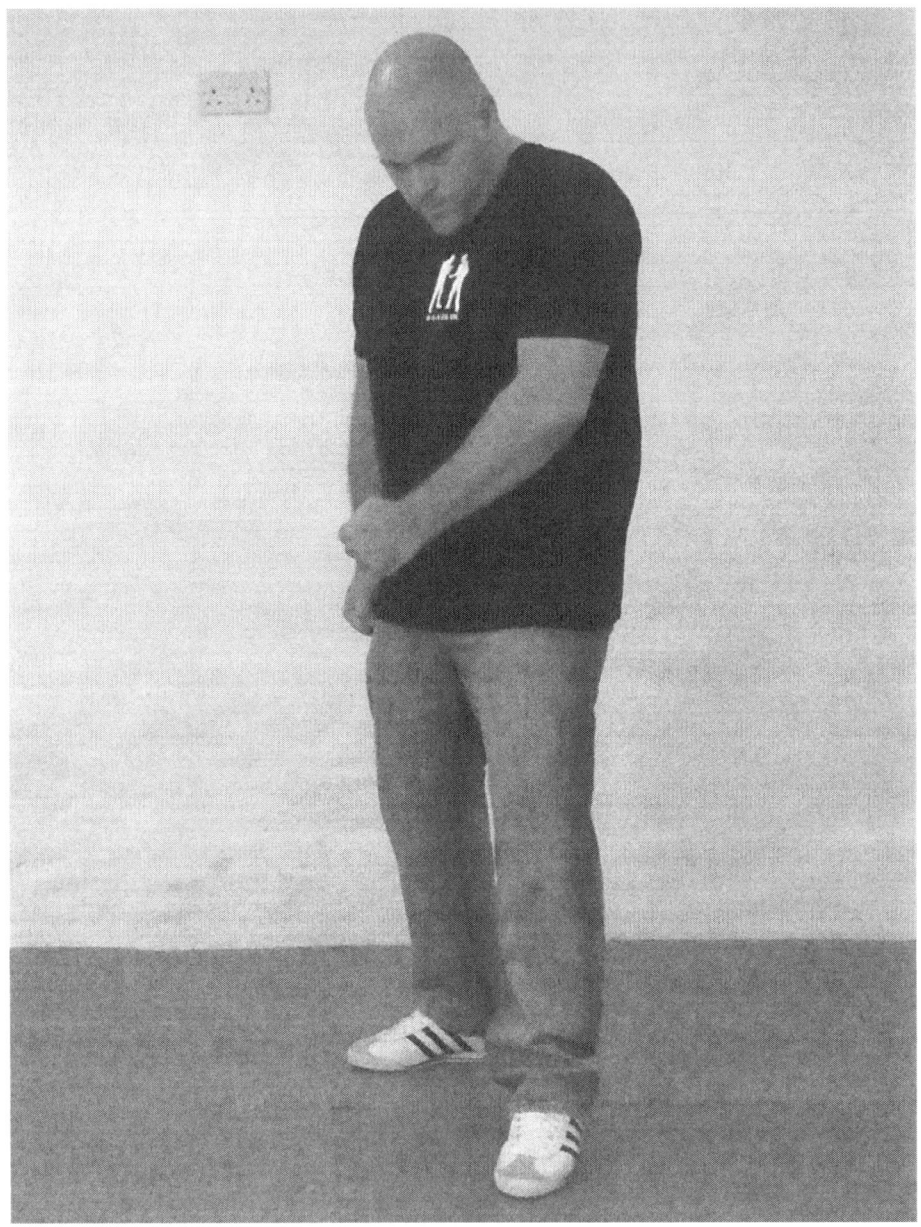

Don't run – dogs love to chase and they are guaranteed to be faster than you are.

Shout phrases the owner might use such as "NO", "SIT" or "HEEL". This may cause the dog to back away or stop what it's doing. However, don't repeatedly shout at it over and over again as lots of noise will excite the dog.

Regardless, try to wrap something like a jacket or similar around your weak arm to afford it some protection, should the dog bite it.

If the dog won't leave, consider throwing an object such as a bag away from you, to tempt them to approach it and investigate, giving you some space.

Back of slowly putting objects such as cars or walls between you wherever possible. Make your way towards somewhere that has a closing door – for example a car, or a shop. Once inside, keep the dog out by shutting the door.

Essentials:
- Don't make lots of noise or fast movements
- Take a step backwards
- Adopt the defensive position – drop chin, stand bladed, offer your weak arm, make fists, don't make eye contact with the dog
- Don't run
- Try shouting verbal commands it may recognise
- Try to wrap something around your arm to protect it
- Try to throw something away for the dog to investigate
- Back off slowly and try to keep objects between you and the dog
- Make your way towards somewhere that has a door

Technique specific exercises:
Please refer to exercises described in 'Defence against being threatened with a dog'.

WEAPONS

Defence against long distance knife attack from the rear

What is it?
The attack is when the subject is moving towards you from the rear with a knife. The technique uses a kick to keep them from getting close enough to stab you.

Why do it?
Your best option if you see someone moving towards you with a knife is to run. Perhaps in a zigzag or to put a large object between you and them. However, there may be times you cannot run away as discussed before – the most obvious being when you are with loved ones, or trapped in a confined area. This technique will hopefully prevent the subject from getting too close to use the knife.

How to execute the technique:
As the subject gets close enough, execute a backward stomping kick to their chest without telegraphing whilst leaning forwards and away from them.

USP doesn't normally endorse high kicks, but on this occasion a little higher than the pelvis is useful as it hits the subject's centre mass for maximum stopping power and it prevents them from leaning forwards during the kick giving them better reach with the knife.

As previously mentioned, when this is taught, someone usually says "I'd just slice your leg". But these people are only thinking about the physical aspect of the incident.

The fact is, the subject is not expecting you to fight back. Secondly, the kick being sent towards them – even if it doesn't make contact – is normally enough to cause them momentary hesitation and concentrate on defending themselves against being kicked - the OODA loop.

Timing is crucial as is getting a good base when the kick lands as you are meeting force with force. Both will take some practice.

In reality, you may only land a glancing kick, so be ready to change tactics if it doesn't go according to plan.

Essentials:
- Get the timing right
- Don't telegraph your kick
- Have a good base
- Back kick the middle of their chest

Technique specific exercises:
Your training partner can walk / jog / run towards you holding a kick shield in one hand and a rubber knife in the other so you can practice this technique. Make sure there's nothing hard to fall back on as you may well do so on the first couple of goes.

They will struggle to continue to run onto your kick without hesitating, but they must try.

To make this more realistic, a decent chest guard can be used instead of the kick shield. The author often wears more than one during this exercise because the force on force impact is very powerful.

Get your training partner to try and 'stab' you, or 'slice' your leg etc.

Defence against a knife threat to the throat

What is it?
This is a method of escape when the subject is behind you and reaches around your neck, placing a knife edge against your throat and threatens you/makes demands of you.

Why do it?
This is a common method to threaten someone with a knife.

Remember, it is best not to get into any physical contact with someone who has a knife. If they want money, your phone or your handbag – give it to them.

However, there are times when you must fight back:

- If they are forcing you to move to a different location or to get you into a vehicle.
- If they try to tie you up, gag you or blindfold you, or something else that puts you in a more vulnerable position such as kneeling.
- If they try to force you to comply with being assaulted, especially a sexual assault.
- If they try to force you to perform a sexual act on them.
- If you feel they are going to attack even if you comply.

Generally speaking – don't fight for property, but do fight for your physical well-being.

This technique is for when you are on your own as it requires a hit and run tactic. If you are with a loved one, running away would leave them defenceless. The 'Defence against a frenzied knife attack' would be the appropriate response under these circumstances.

How to execute the technique:

Act as you are being compliant and try to humanise yourself with the subject. If they think of you as a human being they are less likely to try and kill you. This means you perhaps tell them that you have a family and your children's names etc. This humanisation turns you from a piece of 'meat' that can be sacrificed into a real life person. This is why executioners often cover the persons head with a sack or similar – because a person's face and particularly their eyes, is what makes them seem human.

As you do so 'sneak' your hands up the front of your body to a better position to be able to take hold of the subject's arm. This means keeping your hands close to your body and stopping at around nipple height. This should ensure they don't see this tactical positioning.

When you are ready to act, ask a question as an OODA distraction.

Around half a second later carry out the following with aggression speed and no hesitation:

Hook one of your hands around the blade of the knife and the other around the wrist of the subject.

Although you are likely to get cut fingers grabbing the blade, it ensures that your throat (a far more vulnerable target) is shielded from the knife edge during the manoeuvre.

Pull the knife and the subject's wrist sharply down a couple of inches and pin it to your chest with both hands. Do not pull the knife forwards and away from your body, keep it close and slide it downwards to this position.

Turn your entire body by stepping forwards towards the subject's knife wielding arm, straightening it, whilst maintaining the knife and their wrist being pinned to your chest.

Once you have turned out of this grab, side stomp the subject's knee and 'throw' their knife and arm away from you as you run.

Essentials:
- Humanise yourself and appear compliant
- Sneak the hands up the front of your body

- OODA question
- Grab the blade and the wrist
- Sharply pull both downwards and pin to your chest
- Step and turn towards the subject's arm
- Side stomp their knee, throw the arm away from you and run

Technique specific exercises:
Your training partner can move you around shouting at you once they have you in this position with a training knife and then try to 'slash' your throat if they detect a defensive move. They should also offer you feedback if they can see your hands when you sneak them up your body.

Defence against frenzied knife attack (seated)

What is it?
This is a method to fend off a frenzied knife attack when you are seated. This could be on a train, bus or sat in a coffee shop for example.

Why do it?
Criminals tend to attack their victims when they are most likely to succeed. As you are in a position of disadvantage by being seated with less mobility than standing, the subject has a greater chance of achieving their goal.

How to execute the technique:
If someone approaches you and you feel they may be a potential threat – even if you simply don't know who they are and they make eye contact – then raise your closest hand to them to 'scratch' your nose as if you have an itch. This positions your hand ready to defend an attack but doesn't telegraph your intentions. If they don't attack, then it appears that you have simply scratched your nose.

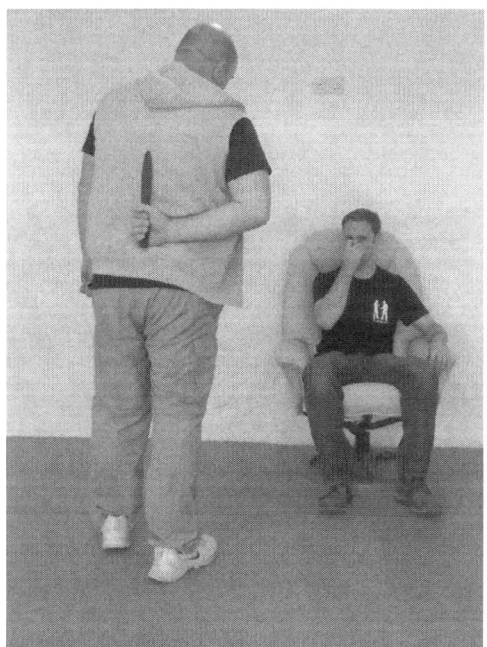 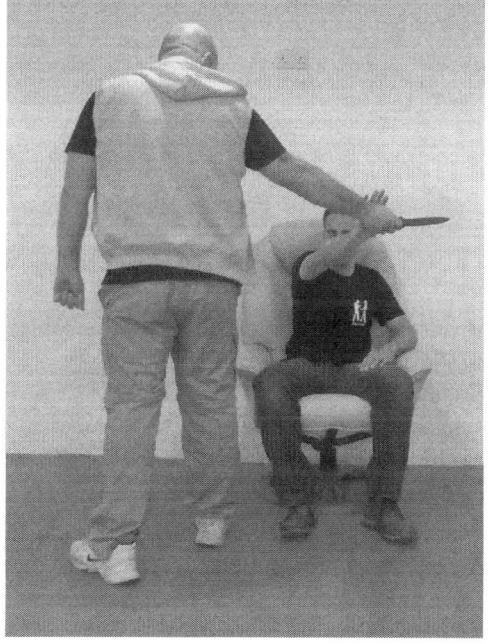

If they attack, use your hands and arms to instinctively deflect the knife, to protect your head, throat and torso.

As you do so, lean your upper body away from them.

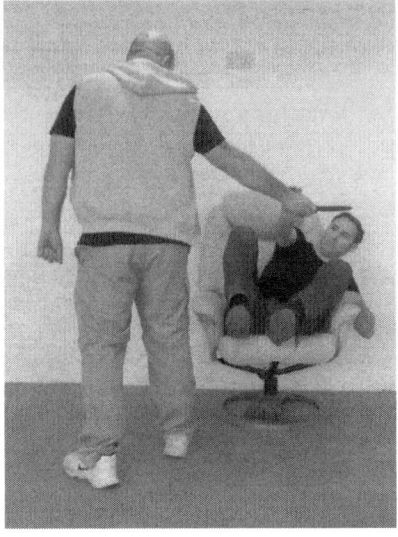 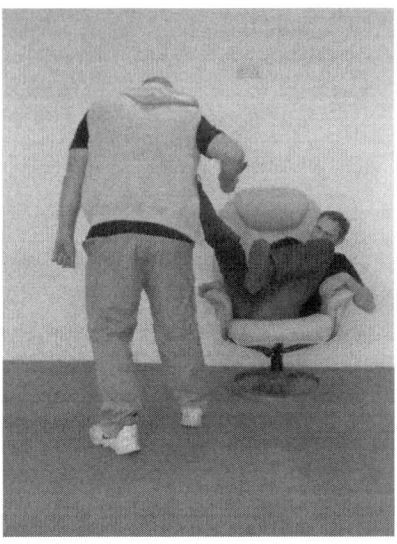

Get your knees up to your chest and bicycle kick the subject until they give up, help arrives or you manage to utilise a pause in conflict to stand and fight/escape.

 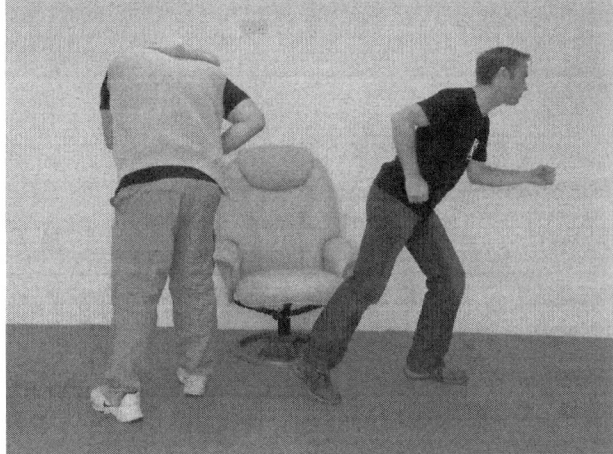

Essentials:
- Itch your nose
- Deflect the knife with your hands and arms
- Lean your upper body away from the subject
- Bring your knees to your chest and bicycle kick them

Technique specific exercises:
Try drilling this on different types of seating – e.g. comfy sofa, wooden bench etc. and with other training partners sat next to you. Use a marking training knife to see how well you are able to defend the attack.

Long gun disarm front

What is it?
This is a method to deflect, control and disarm a long gun such as a shot gun or rifle, when the subject is stood in front of you and threatening you with it.

Why do it?
In many countries, it is far easier to legally obtain a shotgun or rifle than any other type of firearm. As such, it is prudent to learn an effective defence in case you are ever threatened with one.

How to execute the technique:
Remember that as with any threat with a weapon, do not fight for property, but do fight for your well-being.

Carry out the deflection and technique as soon as you see the gun.

The exception is if it's slightly out of range and/or it's obvious the subject is not immediately going to shoot. In which case:

Place your hands with palms facing the subject at the same height as the gun in a submissive posture. This is to give the appearance of compliance, but keeps your hands close to the weapon so that as you execute the defence, you do not have to move your hands too far.

The subject may well speak to you to tell you their demands.

If you judge that you have time ask them a question to engage their brain. Use the same question in training every time as trying to think of something on the spot puts you at a disadvantage.

Wait for around half a second to a second and then explosively and without telegraphing, deflect the barrel of the gun with your hand. This should be done with the hand that will cause the muzzle to be pointing at you for the shortest time and as such depends on positioning of the muzzle ON YOUR BODY in the first place. It means that you may move to the live side or the dead side of the subject.

At the same time as the deflection, turn your body sideways and out of the line of fire just as you did with the knife threat defence.

The deflection is a momentary parry.

With your other hand and arm, under hook the barrel of the gun.

Move aggressively forwards and grab the subject in a bear hug, ideally using a gable grip.

The muzzle should be pointed upwards and the subject should not be able to move it.

Execute knee strikes to the groin, then slide both hands/arms around the gun and yank it violently out of the subject's grip.

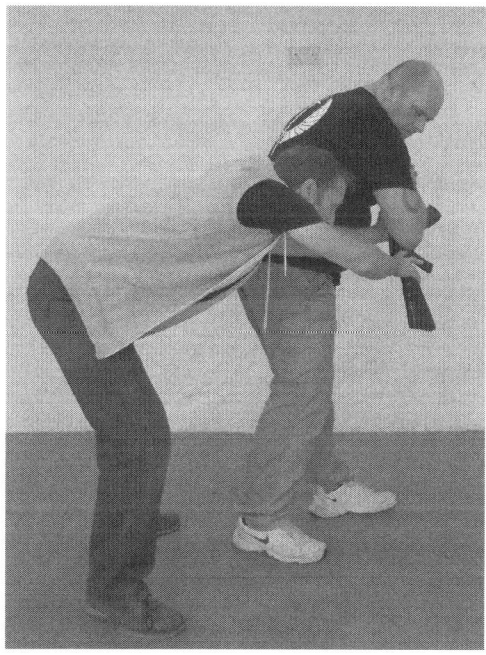

Remember, at any point during the struggle it could discharge and shoot you, so you must maintain the deflection of the barrel.

Direct the subject to prone position as learnt previously.

If the subject is larger than you, you would be better bear hugging the subject's arms and the gun.

If the subject is holding the gun at hip height, you would be better bear hugging around their upper arms.

Essentials:
- Deflect immediately unless the weapon is out of reach or you are sure the subject will not fire immediately
- If this is the case, raise your hands to gun height
- Ask an OODA question
- Parry the muzzle and move out of the line of fire
- Under hook the barrel
- Bear hug the subject
- Execute knee strikes to the groin
- Disarm

Technique specific exercises:
An airsoft rifle can be used with appropriate safety equipment to check the speed of your deflection. PLEASE REFER TO SECTION ON BB GUN TRAINING BEFORE CARRYING OUT THIS DRILL.

The muzzle can be positioned in different areas of the front of the body/head.

Defence against an out of reach firearm threat

What is it?
A method of escaping the threat of a firearm when it is not close enough to enable a disarm.

Why do it?
You may be threatened with a pistol or rifle (or any other type of remote injury weapon such as a Conducted Electrical Weapon that fires electrified barbs or crossbow) without it being close enough to reach. Your only option may be to run to safety. The following method gives you the greatest chance of survival, should the subject begin shooting at you.

How to execute the technique:
Remember that as with any threat with a weapon, do not fight for property, but do fight for your well-being.

Carry out the technique as soon as you see the weapon.

The exception is if it's obvious the subject is not immediately going to shoot. In which case:

Place your hands with palms facing the subject in a submissive posture. This is to give the appearance of compliance.

The subject may well speak to you to tell you their demands.

If you judge that you have time, ask them a question to engage their brain as per previous firearms techniques.

Wait for around half a second to a second and then carry out the technique.

There are two options depending on the environment you are in:

Zigzag run to cover.
2 second run to cover.

If your nearest cover (cover explained in Level 1) is more than 2 seconds away, OR it is close to the centreline (in front or behind you) the zigzag run should be employed.

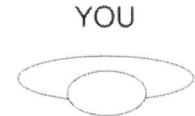

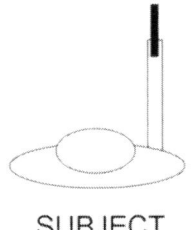

COVER

YOU

SUBJECT

COVER

YOU

SUBJECT

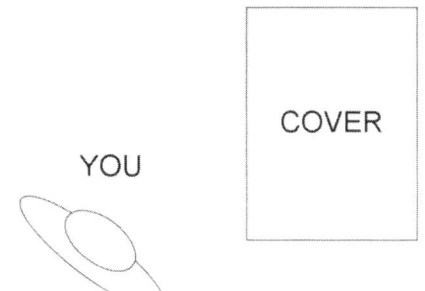

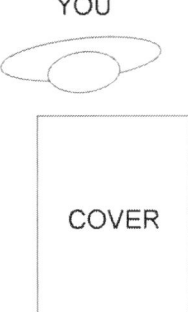

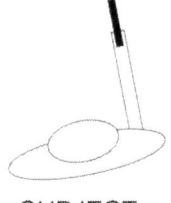

If however, you have nearby cover at roughly a right angle to the centreline between you and the subject, then you can use the 2 second run to cover.

2 seconds is how long the average shooter can get a fix on a target moving at a right angle to them, hence your cover needs to be a distance no further than 2 seconds from your position.

Turning to the side and running at this right angle, also reduces your target profile and any projectiles are likely to hit your arm as opposed to your body.

COVER

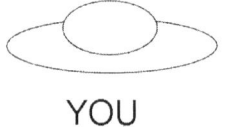
YOU

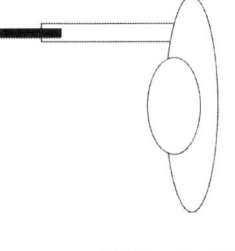
SUBJECT

COVER

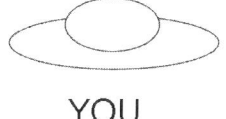
YOU

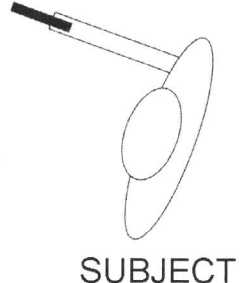
SUBJECT

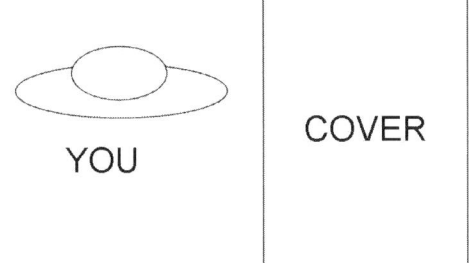

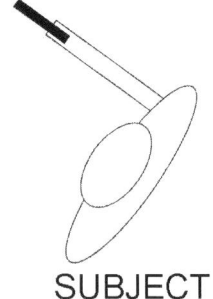

Remember, if you are with a loved one, running away and leaving them to face the subject alone is not really a viable option. In this case, you should either try to engage the subject in conversation and get close enough to reach the weapon or if you have no choice but to run, get between your loved one and the subject to offer body cover and guide their running using the zigzag or 2 second run method.

Essentials:
- Appear compliant and use an OODA question IF you're sure the subject won't fire immediately
- If cover is available within 2 seconds and at or around a right angle to you, run to it
- If cover is not available within 2 seconds OR it is not at or around a right angle to you, execute the zigzag run

Technique specific exercises:
If you are being shot at whilst running, you are very likely to flinch. Try running in the flinch position to get used to this.

An airsoft gun can be used with appropriate safety equipment can be pointed at you by your training partner. As the gun is raised, you can perform one of the techniques. As you begin to do so, your training partner should try to shoot at you. You will feel if and where you have been hit. PLEASE REFER TO SECTION ON BB GUN TRAINING BEFORE CARRYING OUT THIS DRILL.

You can also use the airsoft gun to test the 2 second theory. Within a large hall, designate several areas of 'cover' perhaps a stand up punch bag could represent a tree and a table turned on its side could represent a car engine block for example. You will need to run from behind one area of 'cover' to the next whilst being shot at with the airsoft gun. Then run to the next and so on. The areas of 'cover' can be set at different distances to so you get a flavour of realistic distances you could cover in real life. PLEASE REFER TO SECTION ON BB GUN TRAINING BEFORE CARRYING OUT THIS DRILL.

Remember though, a real subject is unlikely to be expecting you to run, your training partner is. As such, you will have a slight advantage of surprise in a real life encounter……but of course the disadvantage of real bullets!

Staff use - grip

What is it?
A safe and effective method for holding an improvised weapon which has the characteristics of a staff approximately 4-6 foot in length. For example:

- Broom
- Stick
- Pool cue
- Large spirit level
- Garden rake or hoe
- Folded tripod
- Crutch
- Scaffolding pipe

(For training, we generally use a rattan Jo or Bo staff and soft versions thereof).

You should make it a habit to spot these types of objects when you are out and about. For example, in your place of work is there a mop you could pick up and utilise?

Each object should be considered for it's individual characteristics. For example, pool cue is light and easy to handle, but may break easily on the first strike. A metal hospital crutch may be made stronger and can withstand more strikes, but it is not balanced well due to the handle and arm brace. That is not to say that you should look for the perfect object for the specific situation as time is of course, of the essence. But you should have some idea of the differences in characteristics and a good way to do this is to handle these various objects as part of your training. This will help weed out objects you think would be effective, but actually may be of little use to you in a conflict.

Please also consider the law when using an improvised weapon and how it fits into the 'Conflict resolution model' described in Level 1.

Why do it?
A staff weapon can greatly improve your chances of surviving an attack as it gives you advantages of distance, force, posturing and shielding type defences. Staff weapons of opportunity are plentiful and are generally very easy and simple to use to good effect.

How to execute the technique:
The method of holding the staff is with two hands. Grip the staff with one hand. Then with your other hand make a fist grip around the staff around one and a half foot (depending on the object and your physiology) further along the staff. The strong hand will be in an overhand grip and the other hand will be in an underhand grip, just as if you were holding a rifle. This is for the following reasons:

- It is easy from here to block with the staff and make a strong bayonet type attack.
- For those used to carrying a rifle as part of their job, this uses a grip that they are already used to, keeping things as simple as possible.
- A mixture of overhand/underhand grip is important as the weakest point in the grip, is where the fingertips and thumb meet. If both hands are in an overhand grip and the subject tries to yank the staff from you, then it is easy to break the grip of both hands by pulling sharply in one direction only. However, the overhand/underhand grip allows one of the hands to maintain purchase on the staff under the same circumstances, making it less likely to be pulled from your grip.

Your stance should be strong side back to maintain weapon retention.

Keep the front of the staff above your waist.

The staff should be across your body, with the rear of it pulled in slightly and the lead pushed forwards slightly.

Essentials:
- Use an overhand/underhand grip
- Strong side back
- Front of staff above your waist
- Staff should be across your body, rear pulled in slightly, lead pushed out slightly

Staff use - blocking

What is it?
A method used to stop the subject's attack from making contact with you. Be this an attack using their body weapons or other weapons.

Why do it?
To block an attack means stopping it from injuring you which of course is a good thing. It is even more important when you are attacked with a weapon. However, as per our guiding principles, we should counter attack as soon after blocking as possible. The staff weapon blocking method is exactly the same as with an impact weapon – a stick – as described in Level 2 and as such is a buy one get one free technique.

How to execute the technique:
When holding the staff, it can be used exactly the same way as you would use your arm for a 360 blocking defence. It just means you have a safer distance from the subject and a harder blocking surface. Block to the centre of the stick where possible.

360 blocking with a staff in two hands initially will seem easier with a double overhand grip, but as discussed before, the overhand/underhand grip is advantageous for weapon retention. With a little practice, it is easy enough to carry out 360 blocking with a staff in the overhand/underhand grip.

Inside blocks can be carried out against straight attacks too, using the staff as you would with your hands.

Essentials:
- Use the staff as you would use your forearms in 360 blocking
- Block to the middle of the stick in both grips

Technique specific exercises:
Your training partner should have a soft stick and you should have a solid staff e.g. a Bo or Jo staff. Your partner should carry out light outside attacks exactly as they would for 360 blocking, but using the stick. You can then block the stick with your staff. Your training partner can then build up the speed and power.

You can also do a similar drill against straight attacks.

Staff use - 10 Angles

What is it?
Strikes using an improvised staff-like weapon.

Why do it?
The use of an improvised weapon is a force multiplier, meaning that smaller weaker defenders will have a greater chance of neutralising larger and stronger subjects. Staff like objects are readily available in everyday life, whether it's a walking stick, a pool cue or a broom.

How to execute the technique:
In all but the forwards and backward angle strikes, try to strike the target with the end quarters of the staff. The tips of the staff will always be moving the fastest, but to strike a target with such a small area takes accuracy which will likely not be present in the heat of the moment. As such, using end quarters is sufficient to keep distance from the subject, allows a powerful strike and most importantly gives a greater margin for error. All strikes are carried out with a two handed grip.

Targets need to be considered when striking them, so please refer back to the 'Conflict resolution model'.

Forwards angle –as per stick like weapon, using a bayonet attack motion, thrust the lead tip of the staff into the subject's sternum. Carry out a drop step as you begin to carry out this strike, then pivot on your rear foot as you complete the strike.

Backwards angle - Hold the staff in one hand and look over your shoulder (remember that by looking over your shoulder, you will lose depth perception as you will effectively have only one eye on the target). If you are in a passive stance, take a step backwards and thrust the rear tip of the staff into the sternum of the subject. Pivot on your lead foot as you do so.

Horizontal plane, both angles – use one end quarter of the staff to swing from right to left and the other to swing left to right on the horizontal plane in a similar motion to rowing with a double ended paddle. Pivot on the balls of your feet as you would for hook punches.

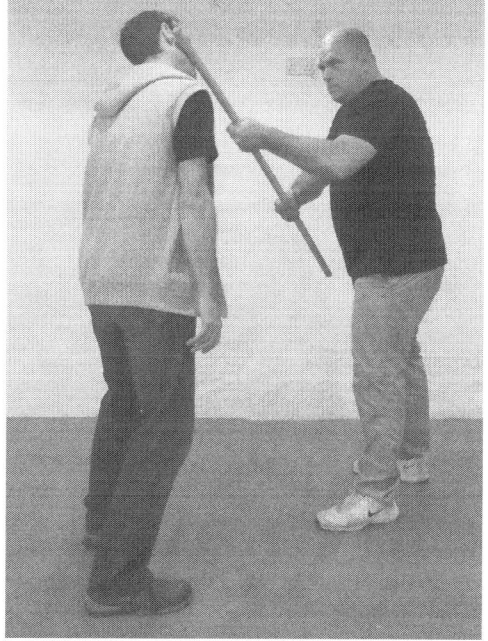

Vertical upward angle – if the staff is short enough, you can carry out the same strike as with the stick on this angle. If not, you can swing the rear quarter of the staff up and along the vertical plane on the centre line, pivoting on your rear foot.

Vertical downward angle – raise the lead quarter of the staff up and back. Swing the lead quarter of the staff straight down the centre line on the vertical plane. This may be to target the head in a serious attack or perhaps a limb in a less dangerous incident. Drop your weight as you make contact with the target.

Diagonal angles – all of the diagonal angles use the same technique as the horizontal plane angles. The only difference is the path the two end quarters of the staff move along an imaginary 'X' on the subject's body. Downward diagonal strikes are particularly useful for targeting areas of the subject's leg for a lower level of force. The paths of the striking area of the end quarters of the staff are described below:

Diagonal down, right to left
Diagonal down, left to right
Diagonal up, right to left
Diagonal up, left to right

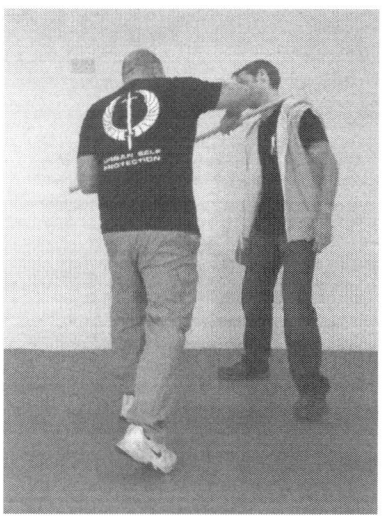
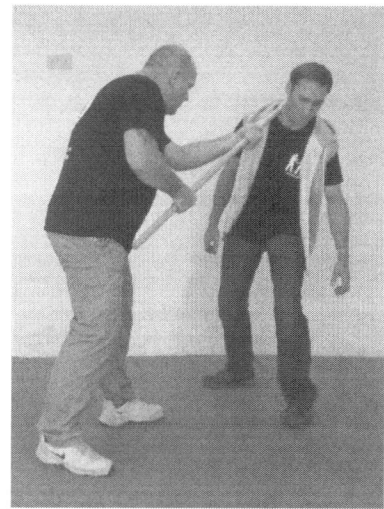

Technique specific exercises:
To gain power and skill, a Jo or Bo staff used against a punch bag is very useful. However, anything struck with a staff can cause it damage, so you could consider adding some protection to the bag by taping an off cut of thick carpet to it where you are likely to strike it. Old tyres make a great striking surface for staffs too, provided you can position them appropriately.

Use of a realistic training mannequin is good too as it assists with target acquisition.

Use of a soft staff against a padded training partner makes for a more dynamic training scenario, particularly once you have learnt all of the staff weapon strikes.

Staff use – push

What is it?
Use of a staff-like weapon to 'shove' a subject and gain some space.

Why do it?
This technique can be executed very quickly in close quarters and can knock the subject off balance very easily.

How to execute the technique:
Hold the staff in an overhand/underhand grip.

Use the middle portion of the staff to strike the subject's chest, throat or face (depending on the circumstances) and push forwards with both hands extending your arms at the same time as stepping forwards, just as you would if you were to push them with two hands in the chest.

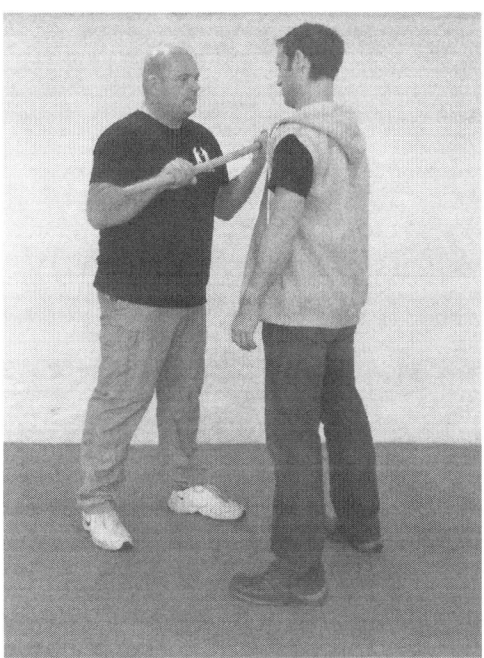 

If you start in a passive stance, step forward with the lead leg like a drop step as you do so.

If you start in fighting stance, take a drop step forwards pushing off of the rear leg.

Essentials:
- Hold the staff in an over/underhand grip
- Use the middle portion of the staff to shove into the subject
- Step forwards/drop step as you do so

Technique specific exercises:
Using a Jo or Bo staff on a realistic training mannequin is ideal to train this technique. A punch bag could also be used.

You could also step up the pressure by having your training partner hold a kick shield covering their chest, throat and face area and have them constantly walk towards you, whilst you repeatedly execute the technique to keep them away from you. Either use a soft stick for this, or be very careful with a Jo or Bo staff.

Staff use – rifle butt strike

What is it?
A jabbing strike with the butt of a staff-like weapon.

Why do it?
This is a close quarter strike against someone behind you.

How to execute the technique:
This technique is very similar to when the butt of a rifle is used to strike a subject.

Hold the staff in an overhand/underhand grip.

It is important to look over your shoulder before you carry out this technique as striking out indiscriminately could mean you injure an innocent party.

The shoulder you look over, should be the same side as the hand holding the staff at the lower end.

If you are in a passive stance, take a step backward.

Then raise the rear quarter of the staff slightly and thrust the rear tip downwards and backwards into the subject's sternum.

If you were already in a fighting stance, then do as above, but you will not have to take a step backwards although you may need to adjust your stance for balance.

148

This strike can be used forwards. Imagine you have an overhand grip with your right hand and underhand grip with your left and that you are in passive stance. You can take a step forwards with your right foot (which would place you in a right fighting stance) and use the (now lead) end of the staff to strike forwards and downwards in the same motion.

This is called a rifle butt strike because it resembles the use of rifle butts by the military to strike their enemy in close quarters.

Essentials:
- Overhand/underhand grip
- Look over your shoulder
- Step back if in passive stance
- Raise the rear tip of the staff slightly
- Thrust the tip of the staff into the sternum of the subject
- Can be used forwards too

Technique specific exercises:
A realistic training mannequin, punch bag or partner with a kick shield are again useful to train this technique.

Staff use – choke hold

What is it?
The use of a staff-like weapon to restrain a subject around their neck. This can also be used as a choke hold.

Why do it?
The use of a staff simply increases the effectiveness of a choke hold, but it can be more dangerous as it is more likely to damage the throat and/or neck area than your arm would. However, it can cause more pain, so pain compliance could be used as an effective control/restraint tool without causing excessive damage to the subject's throat or having to choke them into unconsciousness.

How to execute the technique:
From behind the subject, place the staff across the throat.

Place the lead half of the staff in the crook of your other arm.

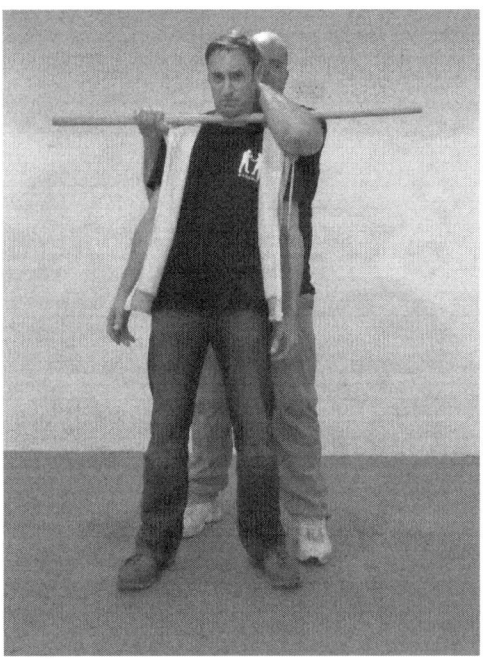 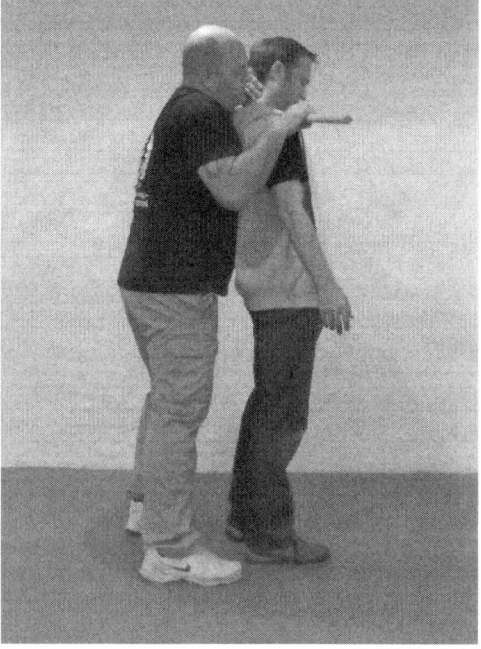

Place your free hand on the back of the subject's head.

Pull backwards with the hand holding the staff and inflate your chest to obtain the desired result.

Essentials:
- Approach from behind
- Place the staff across the throat and into the crook of your other elbow
- Place your free hand on the back of their head
- Pull back with the staff
- Inflate your chest

Technique specific exercises:
A realistic training mannequin should be the only way your practice this with a Jo or Bo staff.

A soft stick can be used slowly on a training partner making sure they are aware of the 'tap-out' rule.

Staff use – spear poke

What is it?
A jabbing strike with the tip of a staff-like weapon.

Why do it?
This is a method of using the length of a staff to your advantage to keep the subject away from you.

How to execute the technique:
Hold the staff in an overhand/underhand grip.

However, make the underhand grip loose enough for the staff to slide through it. The overhand grip is at the very end tip of the staff, so that roughly two thirds of the staff is in front of your lead hand.

The tip of the staff should be moved around randomly in small movements at head height and pointing roughly at the subject's face. This is to distract them so they find it difficult to block the strike.

Then quickly with the rear hand, thrust the staff so it slides through the lead hand. The tip of the staff should strike the subject in the face.

With a little practice on a realistic training mannequin, you will soon become quite accurate by using your lead hand as the guide.

As with all strikes, retract quickly.

Essentials:
- Overhand/underhand grip
- Rear hand grips the rear tip of the staff
- Lead hand allows movement of the staff
- Move the tip of the staff around face height
- Slide the staff through the lead hand so the tip strikes the subject's face

Technique specific exercises:
A realistic training mannequin, or a punch bag are again useful to train this technique.

FIRST AID

Dealing with an unconscious casualty who is not breathing normally

What is it?
A set of jump start commands which will remind you how to prioritise your actions when dealing with an unconscious casualty who is not breathing normally.

Why do it?
First aid is useful for all sorts of situations. When it comes to self-protection, we are really thinking about giving our friends or loved ones the best care possible after an assault until help arrives.

How to execute the technique:
As per DRSAB learnt in Level 3, but this time, the patient is not breathing normally when you check.

Someone who isn't breathing 'normally' is either not breathing at all, or they may be taking 'agonal' breaths. These are short irregular gasps for breath and common after a cardiac arrest. The following procedure is the same whether they are not breathing at all or are taking agonal breaths:

DRSAB(C) stands for:

Danger

Responses

Shout for help

Airway

Breathing

Circulation

Circulation, is a reminder for you to do two things:

1. Check for catastrophic bleeding
2. Carry out CPR

Checking for catastrophic bleeding means a very quick look over the patient to see if there is severe bleeding. If there is, there is no point carrying out CPR until there is pressure on that wound / tourniquet applied as you would simply be pumping blood out of the patient.

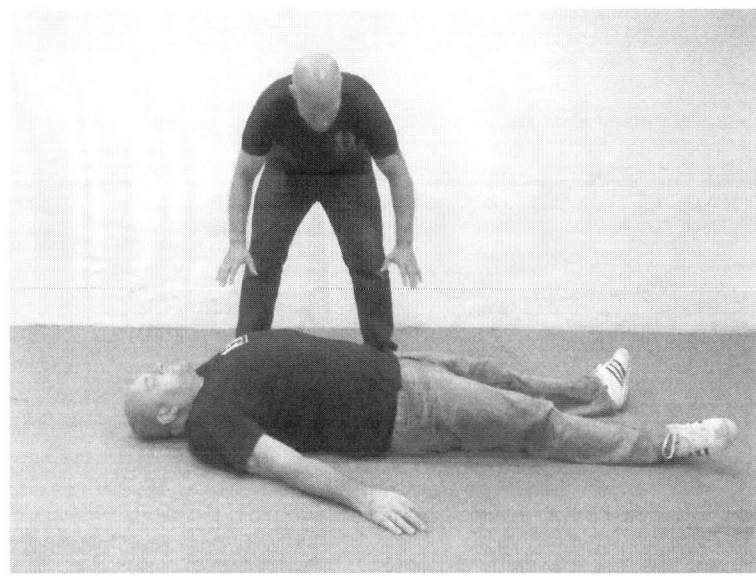

CPR stands for Cardio Pulmonary Resuscitation.

CPR is a mixture of chest compressions to help the heart pump blood around the patient's body and mouth to mouth ventilation breaths which help to oxygenate the patient's blood.

However, recent research has shown that carrying out only chest compressions and no ventilations may be just as effective. This is because the compressions themselves also cause the lungs to deflate, excreting carbon dioxide, thereafter re-inflating with air through the airway.

If you are unable or unwilling to give rescue breaths (perhaps because of injury to the patient's jaw or out of concern of contracting a communicable disease) then carry out chest compressions only, until you are no longer able to, Paramedics arrive and tell you to stop or the patient recovers (highly unlikely without advanced medical intervention).

If however, you are able and willing to carry out rescue breaths, then start with 30 chest compressions and follow with 2 rescue breaths at a rate of roughly 100-120 compressions per minute. The speed and rhythm for this is the same as the song 'Nelly the Elephant'. 30 compressions are equal to two repetitions of the first verse:

For those who don't know the first verse……

"Nelly the elephant packed her trunk and said goodbye to the circus, off she went with a trumpety trump, trump trump trump."

A chest compression is executed by kneeling at the side of the patient at chest level and placing the palm heel of one hand in the centre of their chest. You then place the palm heel of the other hand on top of the first then interlock your fingers. Your arms are kept locked and you lean over the patient, so your shoulders are above their chest.

Push straight down onto their chest to a depth roughly a third of the way down. Release the pressure completely between compressions but maintaining contact with their chest.

Compressions should be carried out with the patient lying on their back on a firm flat surface.

Repeat this until you are no longer able, Paramedics tell you to stop or the patient recovers.

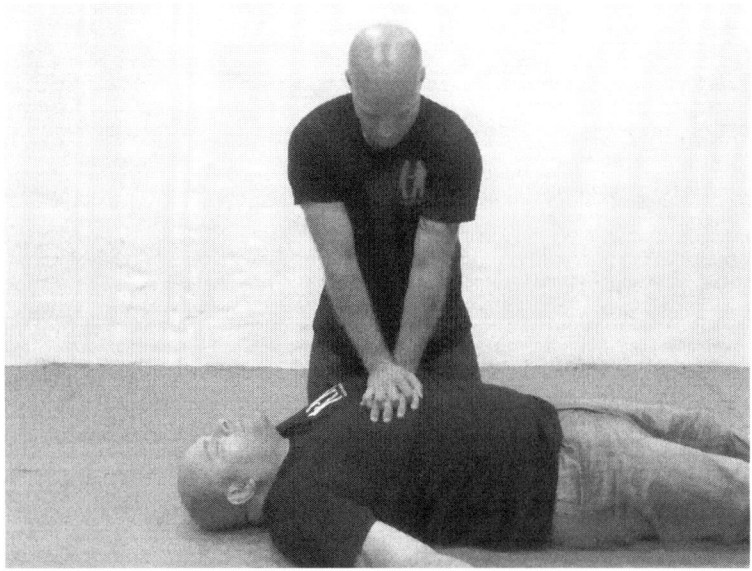

Rescue breaths are carried out by placing the patient's head in the same position as when you were checking their airway. Pinch their nose with one hand and open their mouth with the other. Take a normal breath, seal your lips around their mouth and blow steadily until the chest rises. A common mistake is blowing with such speed and force, that the patient ends up vomiting. The breath is gentle. Once the chest has risen, release the nose and keeping the airway open, let them breathe out. Carry out a second breath. Wherever available, barrier masks should be used.

The guidance given above is for an adult who appears to have collapsed for any reason other than drowning. For a suspected drowning victim, give the breaths at the start and then carry on with CPR as before. This is because they may have no oxygen in their system because of the type of incident and carrying out chest compressions first means you'll be pumping around blood that hasn't yet been oxygenated.

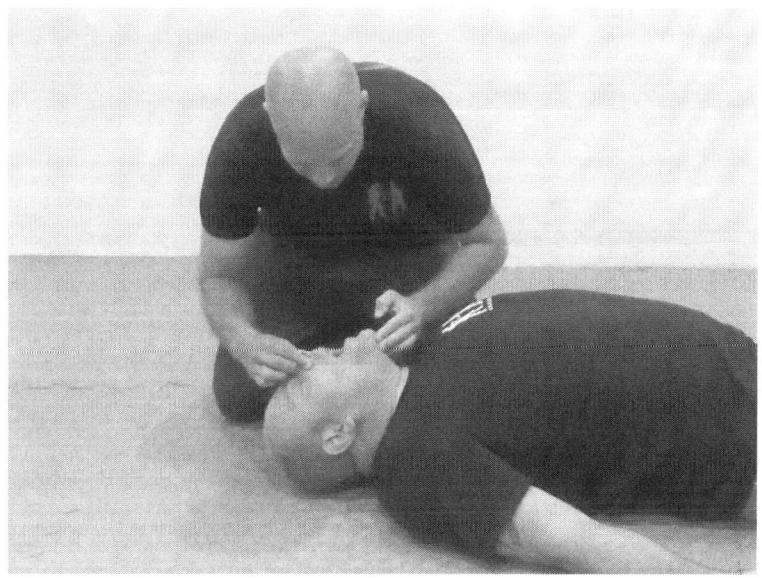

For children use one hand instead of two for the chest compressions. The breaths need to be more gentle and have less volume than breaths given to adult patients.

For babies, 5 breaths must be given first every time. Use two fingers for the chest compressions. To give breaths, place your mouth over their nose and mouth and use only a small amount of breath – even less than you would for a child.

Essentials:
- DRSAB first
- Check for and deal with severe bleeding first
- Carry out CPR at a rate of 30:2 or just compressions if you are unable/unwilling to carry out breaths
- Rate of 100-120 compressions per minute
- Chest compressions to the centre of the chest, to a third of it's depth
- 2 handed for adults, 1 handed for children and 2 fingered for babies
- Breaths until the chest rises
- Breaths first for drowning victims/babies, compressions first for everything else

Technique specific exercises:
Your training partner can simply play an unconscious breathing patient whilst you work through the DRSAB acronym. However, do not use them to practice CPR. Use a purpose made first aid mannequin.

It is wise to obtain additional training in first aid as the methods are refined regularly.

CONFLICT KNOWLEDGE

LEAPS model of verbal diffusion

More often than not, physical confrontations start with an argument and escalate. This method is designed to prevent this escalation, thus removing any risks that come with a physical confrontation.

LEAPS stands for:

Listen
Empathise
Ask
Paraphrase
Summarise

These are all things you should try to do when you have a subject arguing with you. We are simply trying to take the wind out of their sails and calm them down.

Listen:
This means actually taking in what they are saying, not preparing in your mind what you want to say.

It means making eye contact and nodding at relevant moments without butting in. Quite often, this, in itself, is enough to allow the other person to vent and calm down.

Empathise:
This does not mean 'sympathise' with them. If you sympathised and said 'I know exactly how you feel mate' they would very likely say 'No you don't, how could you?' and become more, not less, frustrated.

Empathise means to try to imagine yourself in their position and recognise their emotions, perhaps by saying something like 'If I was in your position, I'd probably feel pretty angry too'.

Ask:
Ask questions about what they are talking about at appropriate moments.

This demonstrates you are trying to understand what they are saying and will allow you to gain enough information to try and resolve the issue.

Paraphrase:
To paraphrase, you simply sum up in a few words what the other person has been saying.

This again demonstrates you are trying to understand them. It also allows the other person to correct you if you haven't received the right message from them and lastly it highlights the main issues so something can be done about it.

So it could be that you accidentally cut the other person up in a car park and they have spent the last few minutes ranting at you about this.

You might say something like 'So you're saying that when I turned in here, I wasn't indicating and I drove in front of you causing you to slam your brakes on'.

Paraphrase periodically through the encounter.

Summarise:
To try and resolve the issue you may want to round things up to prevent a never ending conversation/discussion/argument.

You should include their point of view, your point of view, if you choose to apologise or not and to try and come to some sort of agreement – even if that's agreeing to disagree. Something like:

'Okay, I don't want to argue with you about this – you say I cut you up and didn't indicate. I feel it was my right of way but I appreciate I should have indicated so I apologise for that. Can you accept my apology regarding the indicator and agree to disagree about who's right of way it was?'

If someone refuses to agree with you and tries to pursue the argument, you are best returning to the broken record method learnt in 'Protecting personal space'.

Simply by repeating 'I'm not prepared to argue with you about this anymore' and begin to remove yourself from the area.

Obviously if they begin to follow, then you may need to consider other options.

Try to project a confident demeanour when using this method and control your emotion. See the section on 'Controlling fear' and 'Command presence' for more details.

Essentials:
- Listen – eye contact, nod, don't but in, take notice of what they are saying
- Empathise – try to imagine their position and recognise their emotions
- Ask – ask clarification questions when required
- Paraphrase – sum up in a sentence what you think the other person has been trying to tell you
- Summarise – their point of view, your point of view, any apology, some sort of agreement to end the discussion on
- Use broken record method if this fails

Technique specific exercises:
Scenario training doesn't have to involve physical techniques. Have your training partner try to argue with you about a fictitious incident that you both set out before hand and see if you are able to use LEAPS to take the wind out of their sails.

Dealing with being followed

To prevent yourself from being followed when on foot:

Walk on the side of the road that faces traffic. This is to prevent someone driving along behind you and then pulling up next to you to attack.

How to detect if you're being followed when on foot:
If you suspect you are being followed, turn and face the person. If they make eye contact and suddenly turn away, they are probably following you. This might be enough to deter them as you have demonstrated awareness and confidence, making you a harder target.

Evading the person following you on foot:
Once you feel you are being followed, just after you turn the next corner, run. By the time the person following you gets to the same corner, you will have a decent head start if they try to chase you.

You could also try getting onto public transport or go to wherever there are lots of people. This may not stop the person from following you, but it will most likely deter any sort of attack and give you time to call the police for help.

Altering your appearance when out of the subject's sight can also help you lose them. For example taking your jacket off and putting a hat on quickly.

Detecting vehicles following you when driving:
If a vehicle behind is too close to you, this is one indicator they may be following you, as is making the same lane changes as you.

Drive around a roundabout and leave it so you drive back in the opposite direction. If they do the same, it is highly likely you are being followed.

Evading a vehicle that is following you when driving:
There are several options. The first is the best and safest option:
Drive to a safe location, be it a Police station, Fire station A&E room or a petrol station and summon help there.

Another option is to cut across lanes to make an exit on a motorway or dual carriageway. This is a dangerous manoeuvre and should really only be considered if you are already in danger from the following vehicle – perhaps they have been trying to ram you off the road or even firing a gun at your car. This requires you to be in lane two, overtake a vehicle in lane one just before an exit ramp, then pull across lane one straight onto the exit ramp at the last moment. This will hopefully cause the following vehicle to continue along the motorway/dual carriageway having overshot the turn off.

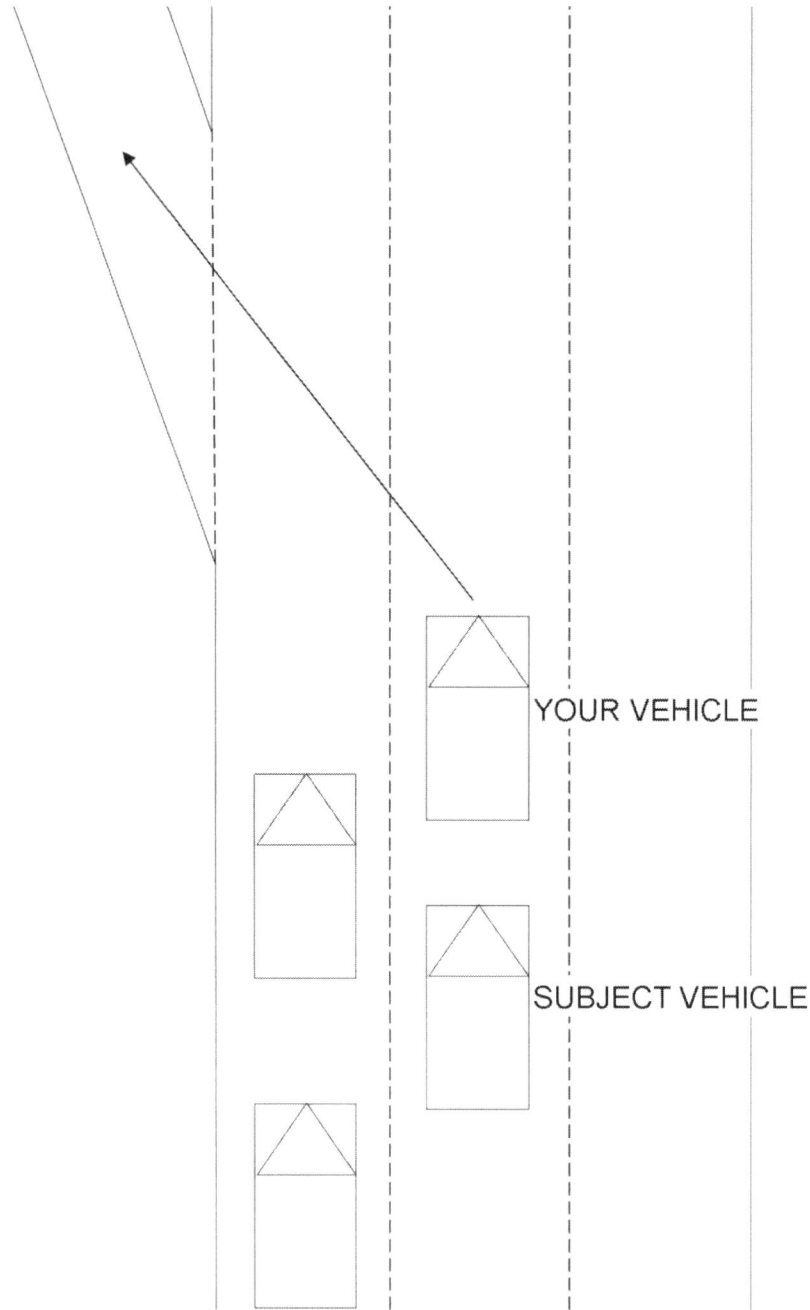

(This illustration shows a UK 3 lane motorway – UK citizens drive on the left. Mirror for countries whose citizens drive on the right). This will likely be seen as dangerous driving, but there is a defence in law if you were under duress at the time. 'Duress' is decided by the courts, so you need to refer to the 'Conflict resolution model' again to articulate your reasons should you be asked to account for your behaviour.

A similar – and equally as dangerous - manoeuvre is when you are driving on a two way road with traffic approaching in the opposite direction. You quickly turn right into a junction by cutting across in front of the oncoming traffic just before it gets to you, thus the oncoming traffic blocks the path of the following vehicle.

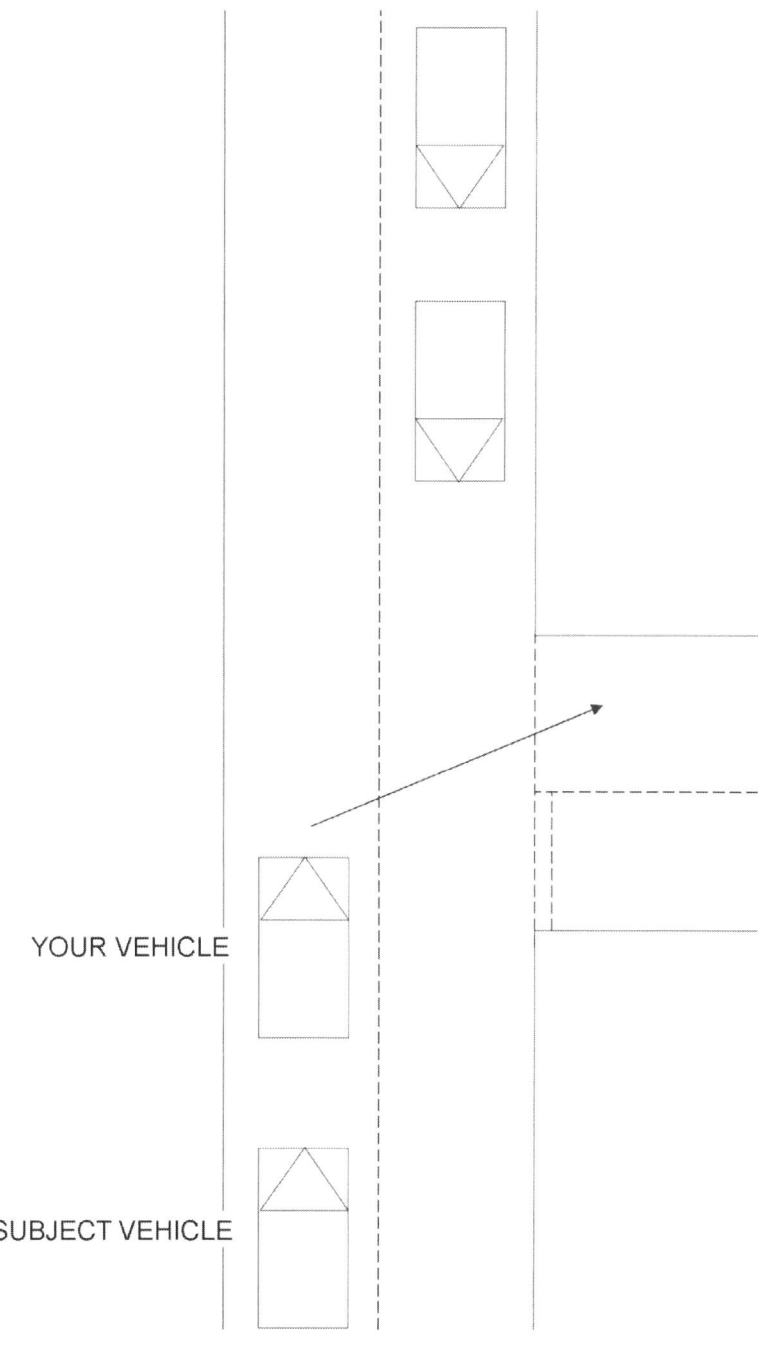

Again, this illustration depicts a road in the UK where citizens drive on the left. Mirror for countries where citizens drive on the right.

Essentials:
- Walk facing oncoming traffic
- Turn and face the person to detect a follow
- Evade by running just after turning a corner, using public transport, going to where there are lots of people or quickly alter your appearance when not in view
- If a vehicle is close behind you and/or making the same lane changes, this may indicate a follow
- Drive around a roundabout 180 degrees to see if the vehicle follows you
- If you are being followed, drive to a safe location
- If you are under duress, consider cutting across lanes to make an exit on a motorway/dual carriageway or if you are on a two way road, consider turning right into a junction across the path of oncoming vehicles

Concealed weapons

If you can spot that a subject is carrying a weapon early on, your chances of avoiding it or dealing with it successfully are improved. Someone who wants to use a weapon on you is likely to use the element of surprise in order to do so by concealing the weapon until the last second. As the saying goes: 'A stabber won't usually show and a shower won't usually stab'. The key word there is USUALLY.

You should always assume that the subject is armed, so scan their hands during a confrontation as described in 'Alert stance'. Can you see both the subject's hands? Can you see all of their fingers/thumbs? If not, why not? Are they concealing a weapon?

Look out for nervous behaviour: erratic eye movement, a pale face, wide open eyes or a trembling hand.

Indicators of a concealed weapon:

Subject moves one hand behind him out of your sight.

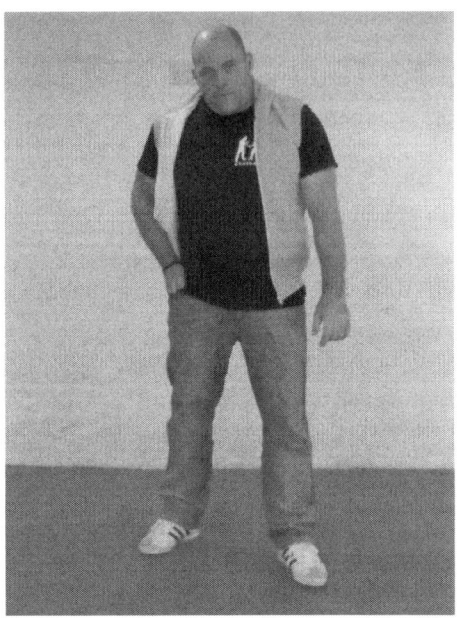

Subject conceals his hand with clothing (e.g. in a pocket, under a hoody etc)

One hand reaches into the front of his waist band which is hidden by clothing.

The subject 'guards' or 'protects' an area of their body. This is often done subconsciously.

The subject frequently feels over or inside their clothing as if to reassure themselves that whatever they are carrying is still there. This too, is often done subconsciously.

If the knife is already at hand: It could be 'palmed' – pressed against the thigh with a cupped hand or the blade being held in the palm of the hand obscured from view.

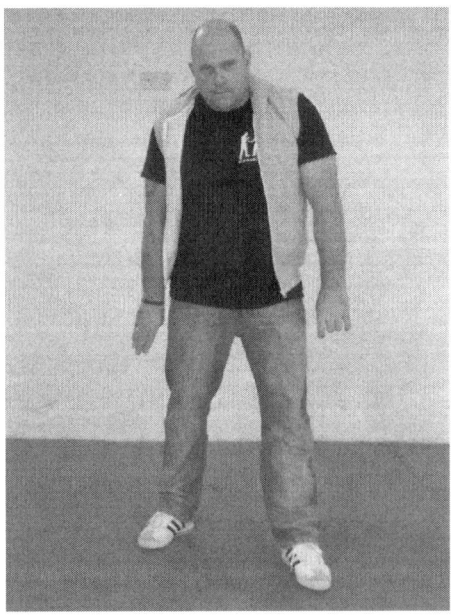
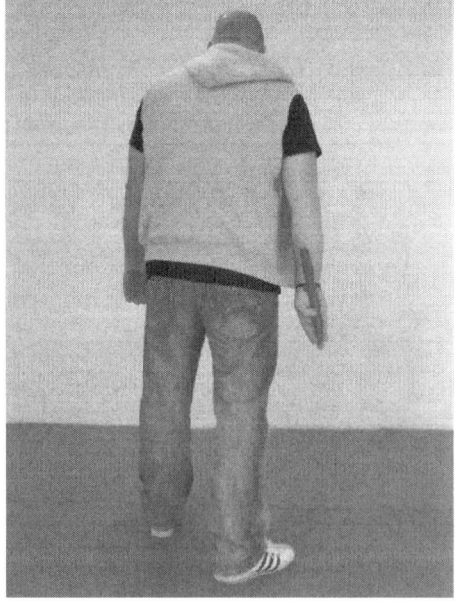

It could be 'thumbed' – using an open hand only the thumb holds the knife against the palm of the hand with knuckles pointing towards you so you are unable to see it.

The non-weapon hand will often display some kind of deceptive body language to misdirect you.

Likely locations on the body for concealed weapons:

- Pocket
- Waist band
- Sock/boot
- Under a hat
- Taped/strapped to limbs or front/back of torso

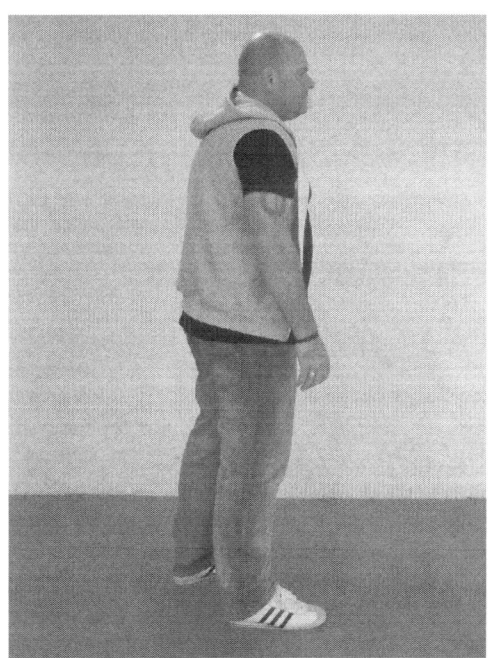
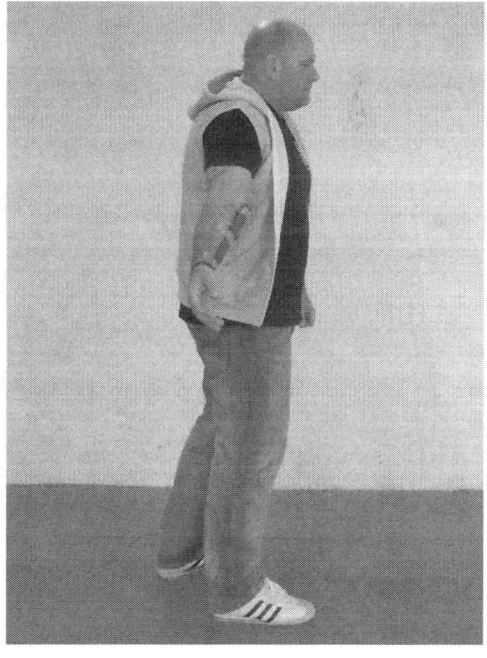

How to respond:

If the subject approaches you with their hand behind their back, in a pocket, hidden by clothing, or using another concealment method, you should gain space in an open hand fighting stance and demand they show you their hands.

If you feel they are about to draw a weapon, immediately execute the 'Frenzied knife defence' (described in detail in Level 3) by grabbing the subject's weapon arm, closing the distance, attacking, shoving and running.

The above assumes you cannot run for one reason or another, as this is of course the preferred option.

Essentials:
- Scan the subject's hands
- Look for nervous behaviour
- Make sure you can see all fingers and thumbs on both hands
- Look for hands hidden by clothing
- Look for subject guarding an area of the body
- Look for the subject feeling over a part of the body
- Look for a hand moving to likely carrying areas
- If you can't run and are being approached - open handed fighting stance, gain space and demand to see the subject's hands
- If you can't run and you feel a weapon is about to be drawn, execute the frenzied knife defence

Technique specific exercises:
Have your training partner conceal a training knife somewhere on their body using the likely concealment locations/methods detailed above.

Stay within arm's length and stand in an 'Alert stance'. Your training partner should slowly go for the weapon and exaggerate their movements when they do so. This allows you time to recognise the movement and carry out your response. This of course can be sped up and exaggerated less as you become more proficient at spotting the cues. You can include role play and padded suits to increase realism.

Eventually, you should have your training partner try to conceal the training knife and be fully committed to drawing it and 'stabbing' you with it.

The chase instinct

This is a natural human behaviour relating to conflict and occurs when one or other of the parties shows weakness – either by running away or by showing they are hurt. This causes the other party to fight more aggressively in order to finish the fight. It could also be described as 'blood lust'.

It is important to learn about this because you can train yourself to show no weakness so you don't become a victim of a more aggressive attack.

Equally, if the subject shows weakness, it MAY be excessive to carry out further attack especially when it is likely to be a more aggressive one. For example, you have hit the subject in self-defence and they become dizzy as a result and are unable to fight back. If you continue to hit them repeatedly afterwards, it could well be seen as excessive, but your 'Chase instinct' may be to blame. The animal inside us wants to finish the fight. This however, is not an excuse in law.

The 'Chase instinct' of one party kicks in when the other 'displays' that they are hurt or tired.

This can be instantly recognised and capitalised on by either party.

The instant the subject recognises you are hurt either by you saying 'ouch', guarding a certain area on the body or grimacing for example, then their brain automatically reacts by attacking even more aggressively as they now assume they are winning and this burst of aggression is to finish the fight.

Be aware that you may also have this reaction, but you must control yourself and only use force that is reasonable –i.e. to stop the subject or enough to escape.

To train yourself not to show weakness, anytime you hurt yourself – for example, if you stub your toe, try to carry on as if it hasn't happened. Then deal with any injury. Another example is when your training partner gives you a 'dead leg'. You must carry on as if it hasn't happened. You can deal with the pain after the round is up. Obviously during training, if you are seriously hurt, you must stop and deal with the injury immediately to prevent further damage, but when defending yourself, you must carry on until the threat is neutralised/you can escape.

Essentials:
- Do not show weakness by grimacing, saying 'ouch' or guarding a certain area when engaged in a physical confrontation
- Practice a 'poker face' when you hurt yourself in everyday life
- Do not allow the chase instinct to take control of your actions – use only force that is reasonable

Command Presence

What is it?
'Command presence' is a behaviour one can adopt to persuade the subject they have picked on the wrong person.

Why do it?
This method employs no physical contact, so provided it works, you will be able to survive an encounter without having to risk injury by fighting. The common reaction to 'Command presence' is the subject back-peddling and making some aggressive face-saving comment.

How to execute the technique:
We've all come across characters who walk into a room and just ooze a certain type of presence which seems to command the attention of the room. This is the person who instantly makes you say to yourself 'I wouldn't want to mess with them'. Sometimes described as the 'Alpha' presence and is usually achieved through confident speech and body language.

To use 'Command presence', you must stay cool and unflustered in the face of aggression – this will portray you as a 'veteran' to violent encounters and will put off all but a few.

To be able to do this, you should use your knowledge of fear and breathing exercises, both described in the section 'Dealing with fear'.

Use of realistic acting by training partners and carrying out scenario training will also help you to become desensitised to aggression, thus helping to achieve the calm state you are trying to portray.

The intention is to scare the subject into leaving you alone without having to make contact with them.

Be prepared to fight if you have to.

Essentials:
- Become desensitised to aggression in training
- Use confident speech and body language to portray an 'Alpha' presence to prevent any challenge

LEVEL 5: COMBATIVES

Open hand hooks

What is it?
This is an open handed version of the hook punch.

It is a close quarter strike which hits the target from the side instead of straight on by moving in a circular pattern.

Why do it?
Open hand hooks work at a close range where straight punches will not. They are very powerful and have the added benefit of being able move around the subject's guard.

How to execute the technique:
Open hand hooks can be executed with the lead or rear hand.

Open the striking hand and strike with the palm heel.

Your fingers should be pointed forward with your elbow at around shoulder height.

The power of the strike actually comes from the hips.

Turn your hips and shoulders in the direction of the strike and come up on the ball of your foot, your hand will naturally 'whip' round a split second afterwards.

The open hand moves in a circular motion at around shoulder height, (although the target is likely to be the subject's jaw) moving from the outside in and across the centre line.

Your elbow should be bent somewhere between 90 and 120 degrees, depending on the distance of the subject.

Strike aggressively and recoil quickly.

Essentials:
- Elbow and open hand at around shoulder height
- Strike with the palm heel
- Arm bent 90-120 degrees
- Circular motion inwards and across the centre line
- Turn your hips and pivot on the ball of your foot

Open hand groin strike

What is it?
This is an open handed strike to the subject's groin.

Why do it?
With your hands at their sides, they are ideally positioned for this shot. It can be used covertly, is very effective and incredibly simple.

How to execute the technique:
With your fingers pointing downwards and your hand open, strike the groin forwards and upwards with the palm and fingers.

The reason for striking upwards is because when striking a male, the top of the testicles hold the most nerves. This part of the testicle is then forced upwards and is stopped by the pubic bone hopefully causing the most amount of pain. The female groin is also shaped in such a way that striking in this way will also hit clusters of nerves.

This can be a great pre-emptive strike to allow you time to move behind the subject and apply a sleeper hold or similar.

Essentials:
- Fingers pointed downwards
- Open hand
- Hit forwards and upwards with palm and fingers

Skip knee

What is it?
This is a method to change position in order to carry out a rear knee strike.

Why do it?
When under the stress of a real life incident, we tend to default to what we feel most comfortable with. It maybe that your right handed, so your right rear knee strike is your preferred option for example.

However, you may be in a clinch with someone and have your right knee forwards in a right fighting stance. You may not feel comfortable carrying out a rear knee strike with your left knee and a lead knee strike isn't very effective. As such, you will want to quickly switch your stance so that the right knee can be used from a left fighting stance. The skip knee allows you to do this.

Another reason for learning this method is because you may be fighting in a clinch once more and decide to execute a couple of decent rear knee strikes. However, if you repeat this strike over and over again, the subject will work out your repetitive pattern and defend against it. So this technique allows you to carry out a couple of rear knees, then change positions quickly to execute more, keeping the subject guessing.

How to execute the technique:
From a clinch position, quickly switch into the opposite stance.

As soon as you land in the switched stance, execute a rear knee strike.

It maybe that you carry out two knee strikes, then skip and carry out another two with the opposite leg and so on.

You may also consider moving the subject between sets of knee strikes. Whilst you have the subject in a tightly gripped 'Proper clinch', step back with your lead leg and use the momentum to twist your hips and upper body to follow. This will allow you to yank the head of the subject to a different position. Then carry out another set of knee strikes and/or skip knees. This will disorientate the subject and make it much harder to defend against your strikes.

Essentials:
- Switch quickly to opposite stance and execute a rear knee strike from the new position
- Keep the subject guessing rather than too many repetitions of the same strike
- Move the subject by swinging your lead leg back and yanking them around in the same direction between sets of knee strikes/skip knees

Head twist

What is it?
A method of forcefully twisting the subject's head to control them and / or to escape a poor position.

Why do it?
This is a tool that can be used in many different positions in many different situations. It can be used when fighting on the ground, when trying to break free from certain holds and can be used to turn or move the subject. It can also be used to negate or mitigate biting and spitting.

Contrary to how movies portray fighting, it is actually very difficult to kill someone with a head twist. To do so requires the spinal cord to be damaged. To do this requires the supporting cervical joints and ligaments to be broken. Whilst it is possible, it is difficult.

With any physical defence technique, there is potential for injury to varying degrees and these, of course, need to be considered. However, potential injuries from twisting the neck are worthy of special mention. There are, of course significant dangers to the subject when applying this technique. It is possible to damage their spine and / or spinal cord as well as other parts of their neck and throat, causing unconsciousness, brain damage, paralysis or death.

The more serious injuries tend to be caused when applied with speed, maximum force and for longer periods of time. That said, the body is quite robust and can take a certain amount of abuse without permanent injury. It must also be mentioned that the injuries described being caused, can be completely reasonable under the right circumstances.

How to execute the technique:
The palm of one of your hands should have the subject's chin in it. This hand should have it's fingers pointing out to the same side.

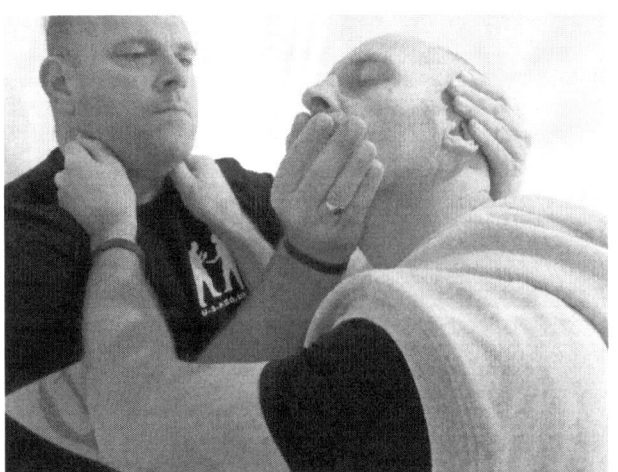
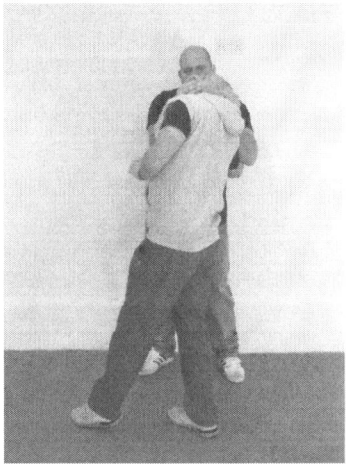

The left hand should have hold of the back of the subject's head – this could be with a hair grab should there be enough to take hold of. Pull with the hand on the back of the head and push with the hand on the chin, turning their head on a horizontal axis.

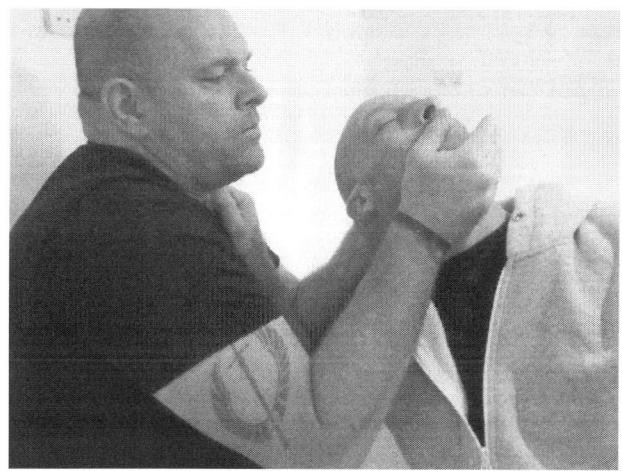 

Provided the subject is in a position to move their body as their head turns, the chances of serious injury are less likely as they will naturally turn to compensate. However, if their body is in a position where it cannot move to compensate (for example pinned to the floor or because the twist is too fast) then the chances of injury become greater.

For escape or control, the neck needs only to be turned slowly to it's natural maximum extension to cause pain compliance control – not forced beyond this.

Essentials:
- One hand on chin, fingers pointing out
- Other hand on back of head
- Push the chin and pull the back of the head to twist on horizontal axis

Technique specific exercises:
Never practice this quickly on a training partner and never force their neck beyond it's natural extension.

Practice in various positions – for example, to escape a bear hug, or being mounted on the ground.

The head twist can be a good way to turn a subject so that they are facing away from you. Practice transitioning into a rear headlock after the twist or other appropriate follow ups.

You can practice full power and full speed on a realistic training dummy, but remember to only use force that is reasonable under the circumstances in a real life situation.

Double arm restraint

What is it?
A method of controlling both of the subject's arms whilst stood behind them.

Why do it?
Control and restraint methods are notoriously complicated, but the double arm restraint is fairly simple and based on natural reactions.

Being able to control someone is often an appropriate use of force and can prevent escalation – for example, a drunken friend at a party is becoming angry and waving their arms around. To be able to take control of their arms and escort them outside or restrain them until they calm down would be advantageous.

It has to be said that trying to apply any control or restraint technique on a combative subject is incredibly difficult. This is for someone who is either compliant, weaker than you (even if that's by way of intoxication) or after softening them up with other techniques and is usually only successful when used as a surprise tactic without hesitation. Hesitation usually ends up with resistance from the subject.

How to execute the technique:
Approaching the subject from behind them, slide your arms around theirs at elbow height, as if you are bear hugging them both.

If they are flexible enough, cross your arms behind their back and grab the opposite triceps.

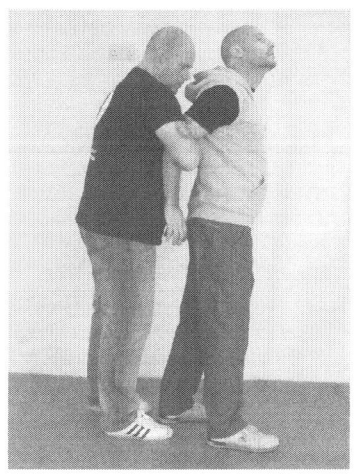 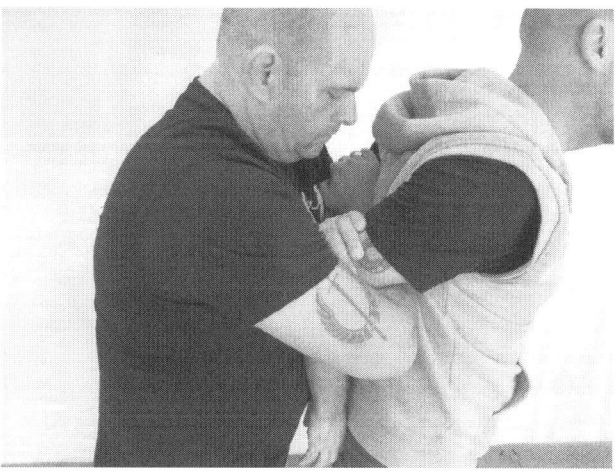

This is because without this grab, it is simple for them to lean forwards and raise an elbow to escape the hold.

If they are not flexible enough for you to reach the opposite tricep, then you need to try and get your upper body / shoulders over their elbows to prevent the raising of the elbow.

This is a temporary control method to allow you to pin them face first against a wall or to escort them away from the area.

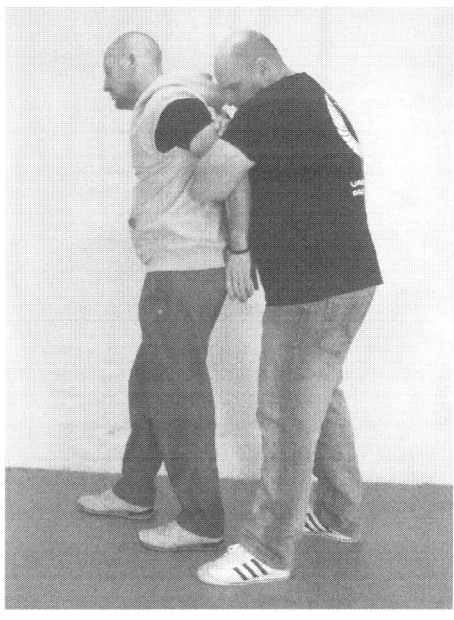 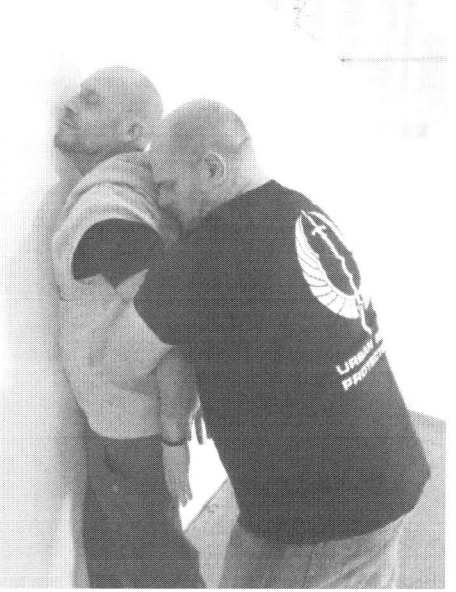

This is because there is no pain compliance to aid the control and the subject's hands could potentially grab at your groin. It is still worthy of learning because it is very simple and provided it is used quickly, the incident will not escalate and the subject will not have time to think of using their hands to grab you or be able to fight their way out.

The trick is to point turn them towards the direction you want them to go and then drive them forwards.

Pinning them against an object such as a wall or parked car means you may have enough control and time to talk to them to try and calm them down. However, as you pin them to the wall or car etc, remember, they cannot protect their face as you do so. If you lean hard enough against them, they may also be susceptible to positional asphyxiation (dying from being unable to breathe because of the position they are in) explained in more detail in the 'Ground pin' technique.

Essentials:
- Grab around both of their arms
- Cross your arms behind their back
- Grab the opposite triceps if possible
- If not, compensate to prevent their escaping the hold
- Turn them to point in the direction you want them to go and drive them forwards
- Either pin them to a wall or similar or move them out of the area

Arm snatch

What is it?
This is a method of pre-emptively closing distance and controlling a subject to set you up for a throw or perhaps a control method.

Why do it?
Being able to close distance quickly and pre-emptively can be very useful during an escalating verbal confrontation.

How to execute the technique:
This method can be used if the subject's arm is high (for example their hand on your shoulder) or if it is low (for example hanging at their side).

Firstly, use the hand opposite to the subject's that you want to grab. I.e. use your left against their right and vice versa.

If their hand is high, deflect it outwards slightly wrist to wrist, similar to a '360 block' (If their hand is low, you can skip this outside deflection).

Grab their wrist and yank it towards you and across your body.

 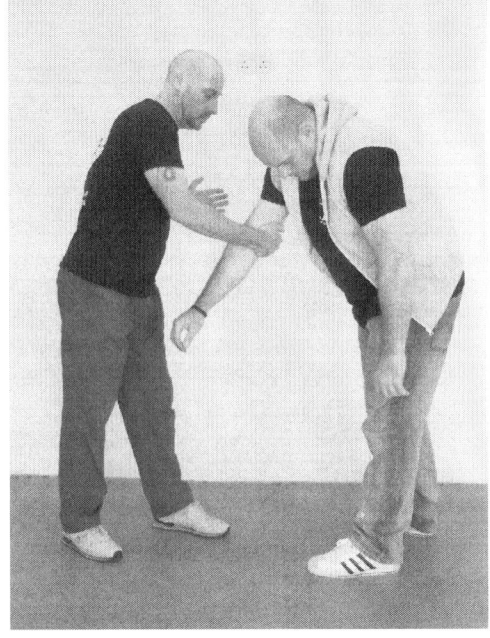

This motion is almost 'passing' the subject's arm to your other hand As you do so, release your grip and then, with your other hand, under hook and grab their tricep/upper arm and yank this further across your body and directly under your arm pit. If you are yanking their right arm, then it should end up under your right armpit and vice versa.

They should be close in your fighting arc, sideways onto you.

Now quickly use a 'Gable grip' to secure them in a low side bear hug. It doesn't matter if their arms are pinned or not.

You should now be in a position to execute a wrestling throw should you need to. Alternatively, you could use the bear hug as a restraint if appropriate.

Essentials:
- Use the opposite hand to grab theirs (your left to their right or vice versa)
- Deflect if their hand is high
- Yank the arm forwards and across, passing it to your other hand
- Under hook the tricep with your other hand and guide it under your arm pit
- Use a gable grip to bear hug

Rear double leg takedown

What is it?
A method of approaching a subject from behind and taking them to the floor in a surprise pre-emptive use of force.

Why do it?
This technique is most likely to be employed when protecting a third party from someone threatening them.

For example, the subject is threatening the third party with a knife. The rescuer approaches the subject covertly from behind them and takes them to the floor, face first, with a quick, violent act.

This will likely lead to them protecting their face by instinctively letting go of the weapon and putting their hands out towards the floor to reduce the impact.

If they don't let go of the weapon, the impact with the ground will likely render them unconscious.

How to execute the technique:
Remember:

1. Only execute a takedown if a good opportunity arises. I.e. do not force a takedown to happen in difficult positions or circumstances – it should pretty much be a 'sure thing'.
2. Only execute a takedown if you are proficient in it's use.

Covertly approach the subject from behind and squat down when you're close to them.

Reach around the outside of both their shins with both of your hands and hook the lower part of the shin.

Violently snatch their shins backwards and upwards (similar to the movement of emptying a wheel barrow) whilst simultaneously standing up straight.

 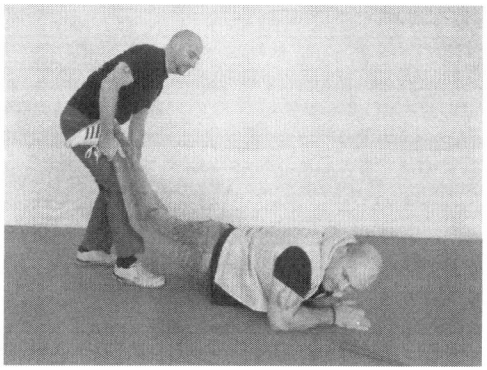

The subject's face should be the first thing to hit the ground. If they are rendered unconscious, then secure the weapon. If not, be prepared to escape with the third party or neutralise the subject further.

Remember, if the weapon is a firearm, it is dangerous to run. The weapon should be controlled and the subject disarmed.

Essentials:
- Covertly approach from behind
- Grab the lower shins
- Pull their lower shins backwards and upwards violently
- Be prepared to continue fighting if necessary

Technique specific exercises:
Your training partner must be competent at 'Forward break falls' before practicing this technique.

You must also have an appropriate crash matt for them to land on.

You must also pull the shins upwards in increments. Meaning that on the first attempt, you don't pull the shins higher than the height of your knees. Then build up progressively.

Once you are proficient, your training partner could hold a training weapon and when taken down, they should recover and try to use it as soon as possible. Your job is of course to decide the best course of action and take it.

Hip throw

What is it?
A method of throwing a subject onto their back from a close quarter position.

Why do it?
This is a very effective throw and relatively simple. When in a close quarter position, it can neutralise a subject quickly.

However, it is not a practical throw for a small person to execute against a large person. The defender needs to be of similar or larger build. Unless you are highly skilled at this technique – for example an expert Judo player – then this technique requires a certain degree of strength, hence the warning.

How to execute the technique:
Remember:

1. Only execute a takedown if you have 'softened up' the subject first. I.e. you have hurt them enough that they would be less likely to resist.
2. Only execute a takedown if a good opportunity arises. I.e. do not force a takedown to happen in difficult positions or circumstances – it should pretty much be a 'sure thing'.
3. Only execute a takedown if you are proficient in it's use.

This technique can be used from the following positions:

- 50/50
- Grabbing the subject's clothing at the lapel
- Having the subject in (or close to) a side head lock

From 50/50, lift your under hooking arm upwards (raising the subject's shoulder) and with your opposite hand, pull the subject's other arm down and back.

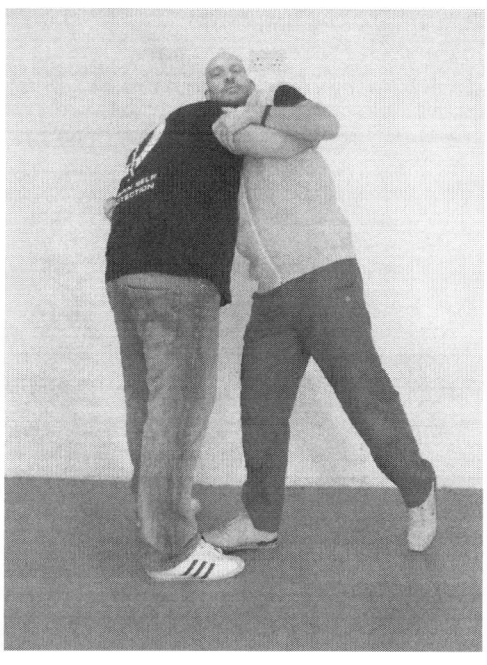

Step across in front of the subject and bend at the knees, so your back and buttocks are into their lower stomach, just past the centreline.

Straighten your legs so that effectively, your buttocks and hips lift subject, raising their centre of gravity, possibly even their feet off the ground.

Throw them over your hip to the ground.

If you have the subject by the lapel (bearing in mind that clothing can rip), then skip step one and continue by stepping across as before.

If you have the subject in a side headlock, your opposite arm would ideally grab the subject's outside arm at the tricep (as per a 50/50 grip). Skip step one and continue by stepping across as before.

Essentials:
- From a 50/50, raise the under hook arm and pull on the other
- Then from this or other described grips, bend your knees and step across the front of the subject so your hips and buttocks are into their lower stomach
- Your hips should be just past the centre line
- Straighten your legs lifting the subject
- Throw them around your hip

Technique specific exercises:
Your training partner must be competent at backward break falls before practicing this technique.

You must also have an appropriate crash matt for them to land on.

You can practice timing for this technique by carrying out vertical grappling and trying to gain the first part of the throw (stepping across and lifting your training partner) but without actually throwing them.

COMBINATIONS

Toes out kick, rear roundhouse kick

What is it?
A kick to the knee followed by a powerful kick to the leg.

Why do it?
To neutralise the subject, the first kick may not be enough. This combination prepares you to follow up if necessary with further strikes. The kick may cause the subject to step backwards. If this is the case, then you can follow up quickly with a longer ranger strike – the rear roundhouse kick.

How to execute the technique:
From a fighting stance, execute the toes out kick with the rear leg, targeting the subject's knee.

Retract it quickly to the original stance and execute a rear roundhouse kick.

Essentials:
- Kick with the rear leg
- Retract it quickly
- Execute a rear roundhouse kick with the same leg

Forward kick, straights, knees

What is it?
A kick, followed by punches, followed by knee strikes.

Why do it?
This combination teaches you how to continue striking whilst moving from a long range, to a medium range, to a close range.

This forward momentum is aggressive and more likely to overwhelm the subject.

It also teaches you to fight from your non dominant stance.

The strikes are simple gross motor skills making it quite simple.

How to execute the technique:
From a fighting stance, execute the forward kick with the rear leg, landing forwards in an opposite stance.

As you land, use the 'marriage of gravity' principle by executing a jab with your lead hand (this started as your rear hand, but you are now in an opposite stance).

Then carry out alternate jab and cross punches.

Reach forward and grab the subject in a 'Proper clinch' as you step forward slightly with your lead foot.

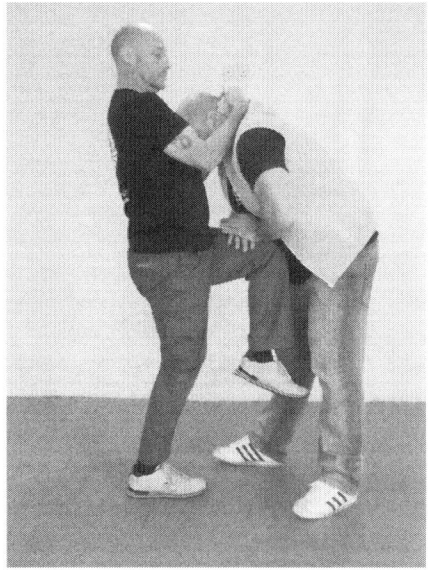

Execute multiple rear knees. You can continue from hear into skip knees if appropriate.

Essentials:
- Carry out a forward kick, landing forwards in an opposite stance
- As you place your lead foot, execute a jab, then continue with alternate straight punches
- Reach forwards into a 'Proper clinch'
- Execute knee strikes

Demonstration of your own combinations 5-10 strikes, close range to long range

What is it?
This is a combination of your own creation, starting from close range, (head butting, biting, elbowing, knee strikes etc.) to long range (kicking range), but including mid-range (punching range) as you move away from the subject.

Why do it?
Refer to previous 'Demonstration of your own combination'.

Experimenting with moving away from the subject as you strike is important, as movement keeps the subject guessing and you may need to get out of their fighting arc or perhaps they are particularly effective at grappling or punching range. It also affords you a greater spectrum of targets.

How to execute the technique:
As before, these combinations are of your own creation and can be different every time.

However, you will find certain combinations or parts thereof, being used repeatedly. This is fine as you are working with your natural reactions and strengths.

You may also find that you use the same strike several times in succession – e.g. a rear forward hammer fist three times. This is fine too. Just remember that too frequent repetitions of the same strike will allow the subject to predict your next move.

It is still important to experiment though.

Each combination should be:

- Aggressive
- Flow together well
- Be moving to the dead side of the fighting arc
- Attempt to use high and low attacks to create confusion in the subject
- Try to keep the combination constant and without any pauses or hesitations
- Remember the overall guiding principles and incorporate them:

(Danger)
Attack
Move
Scan
Breathe

Refer to the principles of striking/combinations set out at the start of the book to make sure that you maintain effectiveness.

An example:

Essentials:
- Experiment
- Minimum of 5 strikes starting from close range and moving through the ranges finishing with long range
- Don't repeat strikes too frequently
- Be aggressive
- Move away and to the dead side of their fighting arc, keeping them inside yours
- Try to create combinations that naturally flow well together
- Avoid pauses
- Mix high and low attacks where possible
- Use DAMSB mnemonic

Technique specific exercises:
Creating good combinations for counter attacking is arguably one of the most important parts of USP.

The reason we counter attack is so that once we have escaped a dangerous situation, we prevent it from happening again.

There are lots of different methods of practicing these combinations:

On a punch bag or realistic training mannequin.

Using a 'marking drill', or 'puppeting' drill.

Carrying out combinations in the air is another method – just make sure you are using your mind's eye as to where the targets on the subject are so you're not just throwing out wild strikes.

GROUND

Two leg shove

What is it?
This technique is a strike with both feet simultaneously, whilst on the ground.

Why do it?
The kick is powerful because you're using both legs simultaneously. It should allow you to gain space between you and the subject (who is stood up and attacking you) affording you time to stand up.

How to execute the technique:
You are on your back on the ground.

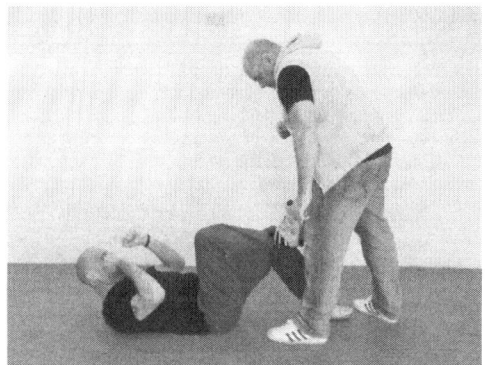 

Pull your knees back to your chest to chamber the kick.

Drive both your heels towards the target (hips, buttocks or torso of the subject) with your feet together, whilst driving your hips off the ground.

Essentials:
- Bring your knees back to your chest
- Fire both your heels towards the target at the same time
- Lift your hips as you do so

Technique specific exercises:
A punch bag or realistic training mannequin are both ideal for this.

If your training partner is holding the pad for you, the best way is across their buttocks with knees bent, ready to absorb the energy of the kick by hopping forwards.

Defence against attack in the guard/rape position

What is it?
This is a technique to escape a position where you are on your back and the subject is facing you, lying or kneeling between your legs.

Why do it?
This position is a common position for rapists but can also be one you end up in during a fight on the ground regardless of the subject's motives.

Obviously rape is a horrific crime that no one would want to be subjected to. Even without the rape element though, this position is a dangerous one as it is, because the subject has the dominant position with gravity and the ground assisting them.

The technique is the same for a high or low attack. High meaning your face and chest has space between the subjects' face and chest – perhaps they are strangling you with their arms straight, or knelt up trying to punch you. A low attack would be where you are chest to chest with the subject – perhaps they are biting you or whispering verbal threats close to your ear in an attempt not to make a noise. As the defence is the same for both, this is a 'buy one, get one free' technique.

How to execute the technique:
If the subject begins the attack in a 'low' position, then execute a thumb thrust to their eyes driving their head back into a 'high' position. This will give you space to manoeuvre.

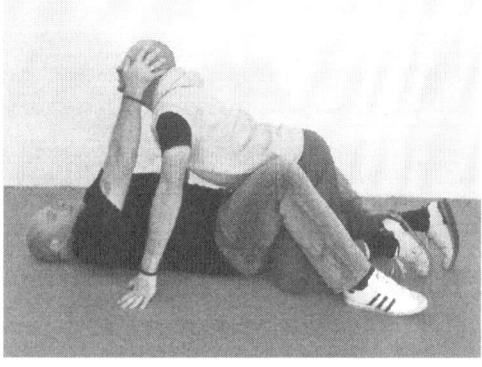

If the subject begins in a 'high' attack position then you will already have the space to manoeuvre, which means the thumb thrust will not be necessary.

'Shrimp' to one side.

When on your side, get the knee that is not on the ground against the chest of the subject.

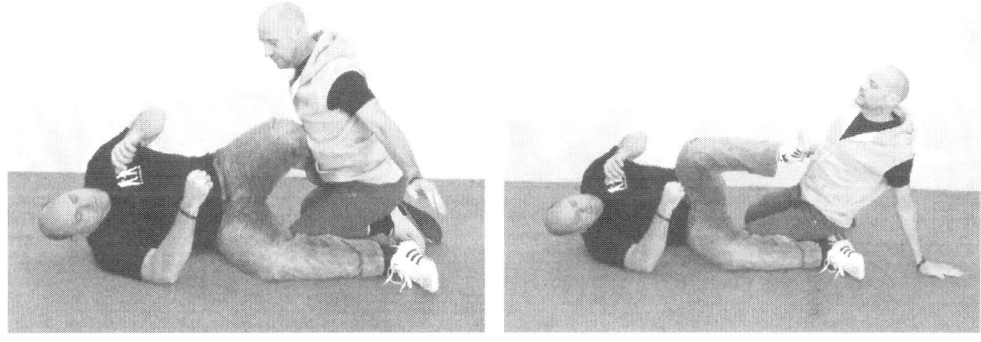

Use this leg to push them back to gain more space.

Then return to your back and execute bicycle kicks to their chest/face.

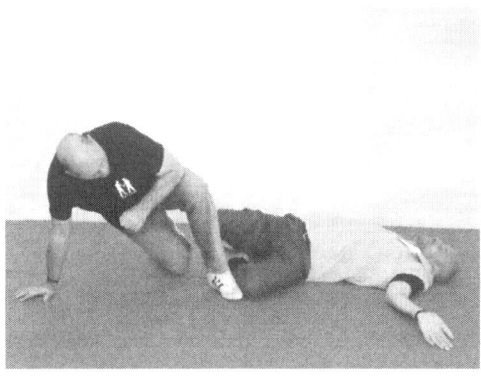 

Essentials:
- If a low attack, gain space using a thumb thrust
- Once the subject is in a high attack position, shrimp
- Get your knee against their chest
- Push the subject backwards
- Bicycle kick

Defence against kick to the ribs

What is it?
This is a method of protecting yourself against a kick to your ribs whilst you are on the ground on all fours.

Why do it?
It's quite possible that you could end up in this position during a confrontation. Unfortunately, it is all too common for subjects to kick people when they are down. This defensive technique allows you to protect your rib cage and stand as soon as possible.

How to execute the technique:
You start on your hands and knees.

The subject is at your side.

As they try to kick you, bring your knee that's closest to them forwards to meet your elbow on the same side of your body.

In doing so, you create a blocking surface in a similar way to a standing 'Leg jam' described in Level 2.

The blocking leg's foot should now be on it's ball. This allows you to tense your lower leg to absorb the kick effectively, but also prepares you to stand quickly.

As soon as the kick has made contact, stand up, striking the subject as you do so and moving forwards to neutralise them.

Essentials:
- Bring the knee closest to the subject, to your elbow
- Be on the ball of your foot and get up attacking

Technique specific exercises:
Your training partner can wear heavily padded shin and instep protection in order to safely carry out a more realistic kick.

Gouging

What is it?
This is a method of causing pain to the subject when you are grappling with them.

Why do it?
Gouging can cause the subject to flinch or change position during grappling which can give you an advantage in terms of preventing attack or gaining space etc. It is also very useful for smaller/weaker people as even a light person can exert a great deal of pressure using this method.

How to execute the technique:
The principle behind this method is essentially to focus weight and pressure through a small hard area, thus causing pain.

A simple analogy can help clarify the principle:

If a ten stone person was to wear flat soled shoes on soft ground, they would likely only make a large but shallow depression in the ground when walking.

However, if they were to wear stiletto heeled shoes, the stiletto is likely to dig deep into the ground leaving a small but deep depression.

This is because the flat shoes have a wider surface area which dissipates the ten stone, whereas the stiletto has a very small surface area, but still has ten stone above its point, thus all of the weight is focussed into a small area.

So, you need to use a small bony part of your body and exert pressure behind it, against a vulnerable target area.

Some examples are:

The point of your elbow pushed into the rib cage or sternum of the subject.

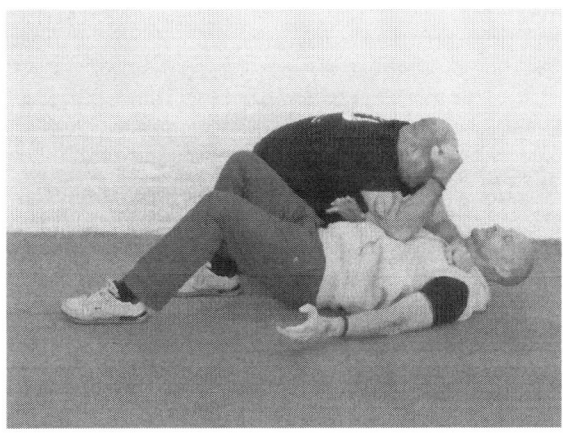

One of your knuckles pushed into the face of the subject.

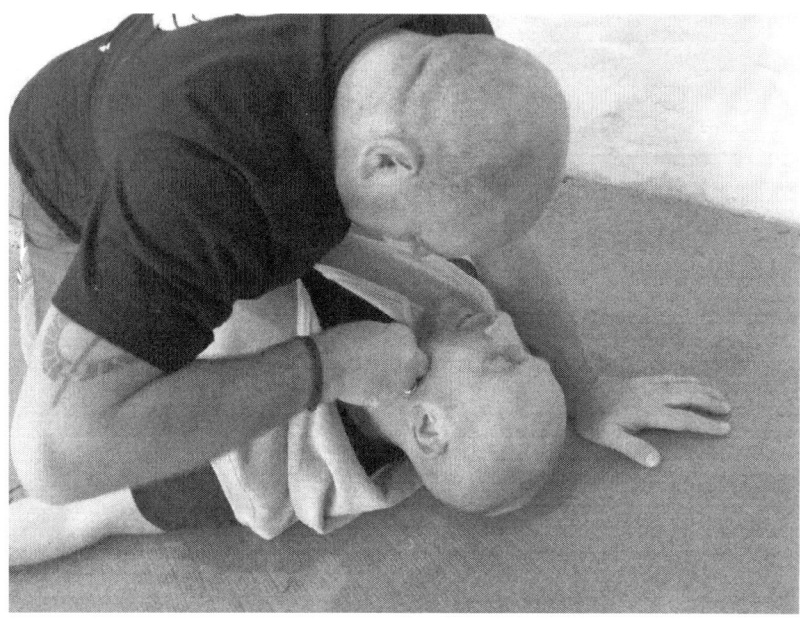

The tip of your thumb pushed into the bicep of the subject.

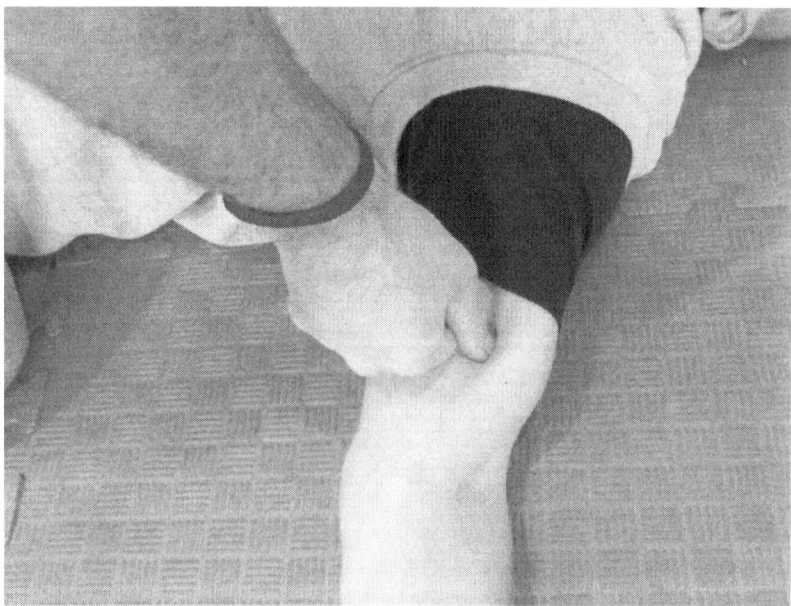

Your knee pushed into the groin of the subject.

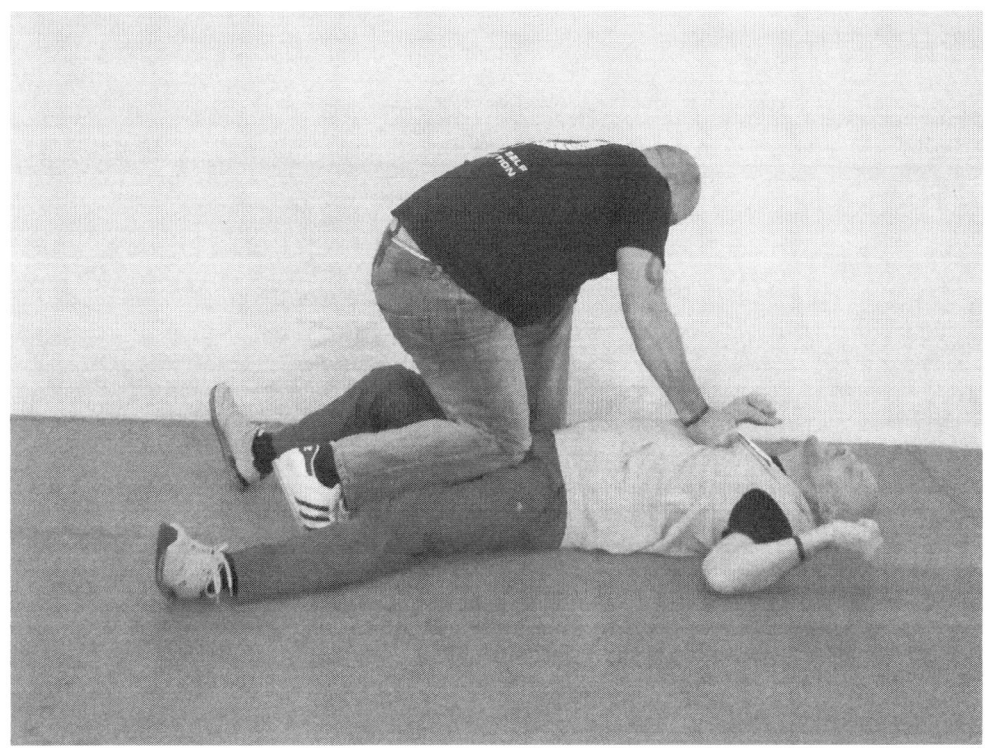

Gouging is most effective when you have gravity to assist you. This could mean that you are on top of the subject being able to lean your weight over the top of the body weapon you are using, or, the subject could be on top of you leaning their weight onto your body weapon.

Essentials:
- Use a small hard body weapon
- Target vulnerable areas
- Use gravity to assist where possible

Technique specific exercises:
The technique should be used during any form of sparring when appropriate and when drilling self-defence techniques, perhaps as contingencies, should the initial technique not work.

Side mount

What is it?
This is an advantageous ground fighting position.

Why do it?
When engaged in a fight on the ground, your goal should be to get up as soon as possible giving you manoeuvrability and to help mitigate dangers of the environment, weapons and multiple subjects. However, you still need to be comfortable and competent on the ground when grappling.

This method is a variation of most ground fighting systems' methodology, which, whilst not as effective at pinning the subject as these other systems, it does allows for more manoeuvrability, striking and the ability to stand quickly. This is because our goal is to counter attack and escape the situation rather than pin the subject and score points.

How to execute the technique:
The subject is on their back and you are knelt at their side.

You should be chest to chest with them and have your knees as wide apart as possible and pushed up against the subject's side. Your knee closest to their legs should be against their hip. You should be on the balls of your feet to maintain your knee's position's and to allow you to get up quickly. Being chest to chest reduces

their ability to move, as does having your knees against their side. Your knees being spread helps to balance you should the subject try to throw you off of them.
Your elbow closest to their legs should be tight into the opposite side of the subject, ideally against their hip, again, reducing their ability to move.

Your other forearm should be applying pressure across their face/throat.

From here, you have various options:

- You can strike (described in next technique)
- Transition to low/high mount
- Disengage

To transition to a low mount position, slide your knee closest to the subject's legs, across their stomach, maintaining contact. The contact is essential to prevent the subject from manoeuvring underneath you. Many people who are trained in ground fighting systems will cross their legs to prevent you from transitioning in this way, however, you can normally simply push their knee downwards to give you space to transition.

To disengage safely, slide your knee closest to the subject's legs onto their stomach. Press your knee and shin into their stomach and come up onto your other foot. Lean your weight into your knee to maintain pressure. From here, strike if appropriate, stand and move quickly to prevent your legs from getting caught by the subject.

Essentials:
- Knees spread wide and close to the subject
- Elbow close to hip
- Forearm across face/throat
- Chest to chest
- Options – strike, transition to low mount or disengage

Technique specific exercises:
This transitioning drill is a great way to ensure you maintain pressure on the subject and can change positions quickly and effectively.

Your training partner starts on their back and you start in a side mount. Your training partner tries to get off of their back whilst you try to transition to low mount. From low mount, transition to high mount, then back to low mount, then to the opposite side mount. All the while, your training partner offers resistance. To start with, this should be a low level of resistance and build up progressively using the simple to complex learning method.

You can also use a punch bag lying on the ground, a large kick shield or realistic training mannequin instead of a training partner.

Striking from the side mount

What is it?
Various effective strikes from the side mount position described in the previous technique.

Why do it?
Our goal is to counter attack and escape the situation rather than pin the subject and score points, as previously mentioned. However, we need to be able to strike effectively and maintain a solid position until we are ready to transition/disengage.

How to execute the technique:
Remember that when in a side mount, you are trying to prevent the subject from moving. Moving one of your arms or legs in order to strike the subject, may give them an opening to escape. As such, execute a maximum of two strikes at a time before checking your position again.

Elbow to the side of the head: Use your elbow closest to the subject's head to execute a downward vertical elbow strike to the side of their head.

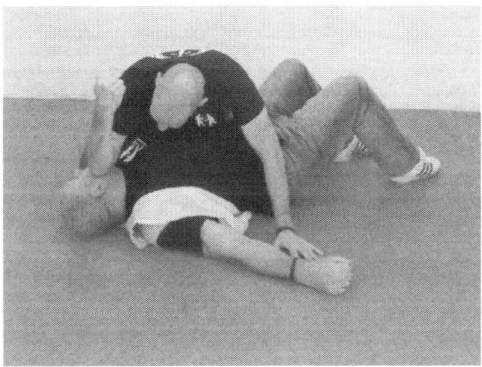 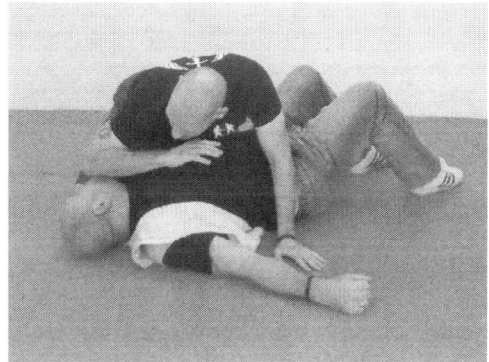

Elbow to the face: Use your elbow closest to the subject's head to execute a forward horizontal elbow strike to their face.

 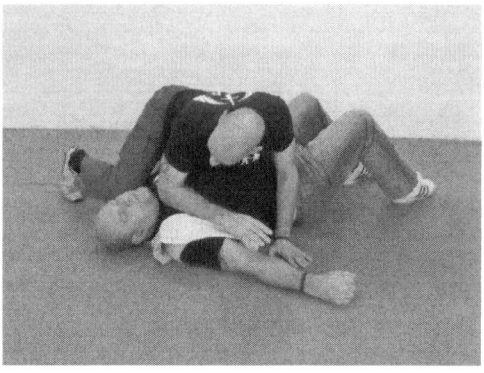

Knee to the head: Bring your knee closest to the subject's head back and raise your leg. Drive the knee into the side of their head.

Knee to the body: Bring your knee closest to the subject's legs back and raise your leg. Drive the knee into the side of their body.

 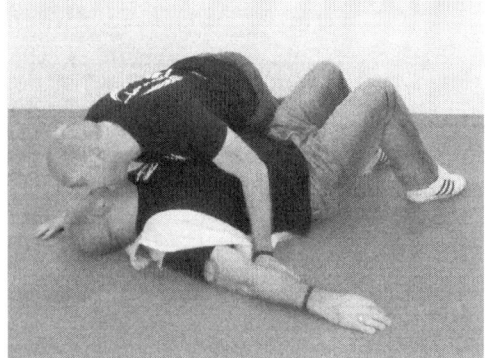

Head butt: As per standing 'Head butt'.

Bite: Described later in more detail, but essentially biting vulnerable targets.

Claw: As per standing 'Claw'.

 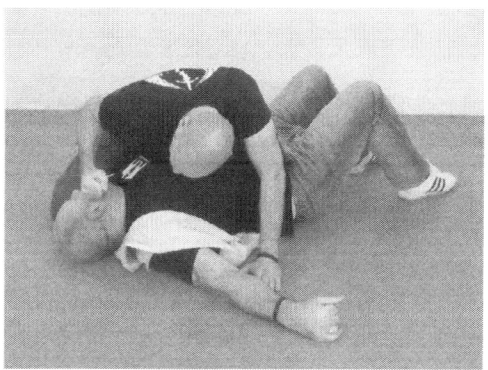

Hammer fist to face or groin: As per 'Forward/Downward vertical hammer fists'.

Essentials:
- Two strikes and check position
- Elbow to side of head
- Elbow to face
- Knee to head
- Knee to body
- Head butt
- Bite
- Claw
- Hammer fist to face/groin

Technique specific exercises:
These strikes can be feigned and incorporated into the transitioning drill described in the side mount use. You can also incorporate feigning ground and pound strikes when in low/high mount during the same drill.

You can also use a punch bag lying on the ground, a large kick shield or realistic training mannequin instead of a training partner in order to carry out full contact strikes.

Ground pin

What is it?
A method of restraining a subject in the floor.

Why do it?
This technique is a method of restraining someone. Therefore, it is particularly useful for Law Enforcement Officers and Security Operatives. However, there may well be other circumstances where you may wish to restrain someone using this method. For example, you may have overpowered a burglar in your home and are confident you can hold them until the Police arrive. Or perhaps an aggressive subject needs to be held in place whilst they calm down.

This method has the subject in a position of disadvantage, whilst you are in a reasonably good position in terms of opportunity to disengage, to tie the subject in a restraint device (specifically made or improvised), use one of your hands to use a phone to call for help and be able to visually monitor your surroundings.

This position is also designed to reduce the chances of the subject suffering from positional asphyxiation.

How to execute the technique:
The subject is in a prone position on the floor – i.e. face down. This could be because you have physically forced them into this position, they have got themselves into this position, or they have complied with your commands to assume this position because you have threatened them with an improvised weapon.

Kneel with your inside shin across their shoulder, whilst on the ball of your foot. Your knee will be just beyond their armpit. You will be facing towards their feet.

The outside knee will be on the ground again whilst on the ball of your foot.

You will be on the balls of your feet to enable you to disengage quickly should you need to.

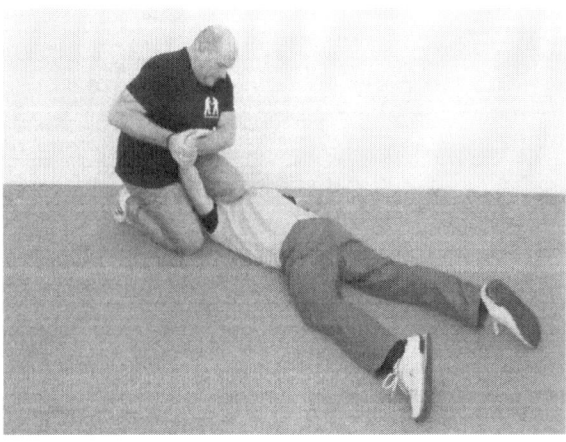

The subject's arm should be straight having had their wrist turned and folded over so their finger tips are pointing in towards their body. The right wrist must turn anti clockwise and the left wrist clockwise, otherwise pain cannot be inflicted and the subject will easily escape the hold.

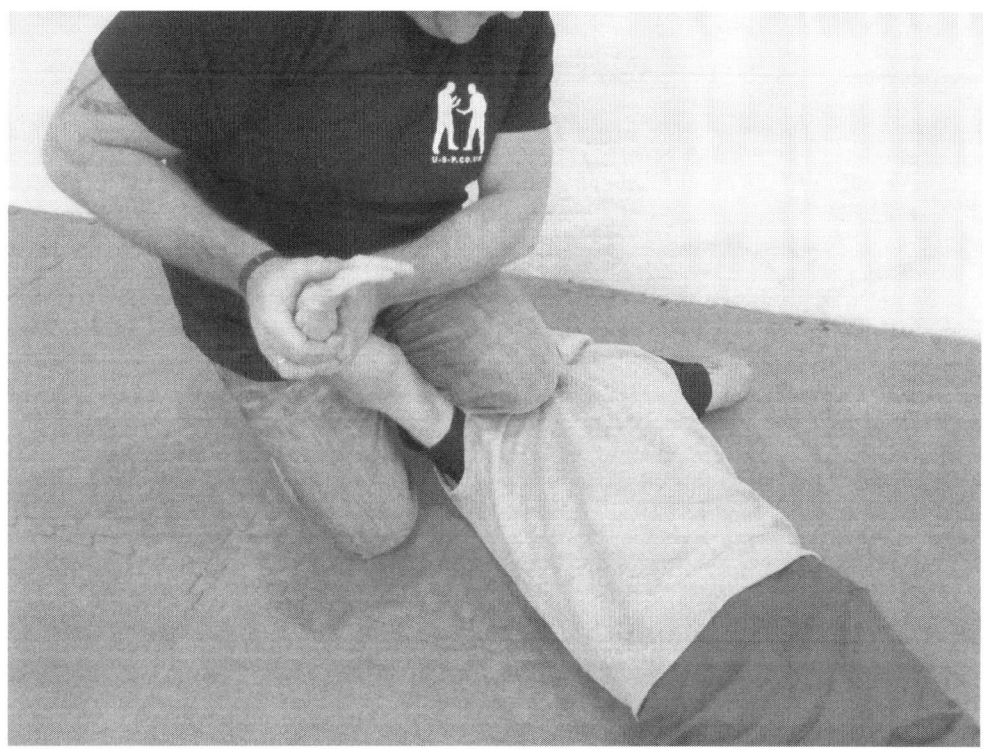

Their arm should be between your legs and pulled into your groin.

Squeeze your knees together.

Have a strong grip of the subject's hand.

Should they resist, pull their arm back towards you whilst leaning your upper body back slightly. This will inflict some pain. Give loud verbal commands so they know what you want them to do for example "STOP RESISTING".

This pain compliance method should be kept on for only a few seconds as it can cause a dump of adrenaline in the subject. This allows them to get used to the pain so it is no longer effective and can give them additional strength etc. Obviously if they comply with what you have commanded them to do, then release the pressure.

Keep an eye on their mouth in case they try to bite you – tell them to turn their head away from you. Keep an eye on their other hand too in case they try to reach for a concealed weapon. Get them to cross their ankles and raise their heels to their backside. This allows you plenty of time to react should they try to kneel and then stand.

Any position where the subject's chest is put under pressure has the potential to kill them via a phenomenon known as positional asphyxiation, essentially, by preventing them from breathing properly as a result of their position.

The ground pin can easily be a position that causes this phenomenon. There are very few circumstances where killing someone like this, even by accident, would not land you in prison for a long time. There are cases where someone has been so violent and had access to weapons that a member of the public has had no choice but to hold the subject down eventually killing them. This is where knowledge of the conflict resolution model is essential.

However, this method and knowledge of the phenomenon and exacerbating factors should steer you clear of accidental / unlawful killing.

Firstly, your shin across the shoulder is important. If you apply your knee to the subject's back instead, you are more likely to be applying pressure to their chest.

From this position, you should be close enough to monitor the subject's breathing by sight and sound.

Subjects struggling for breath, may well resist violently at this point. Our natural response would be to apply more pressure to match the violence offered. However, this is most likely a sign that they are fighting for their lives. As such, you need to consider disengaging, or at least adjusting your position to allow them to breathe.

Another sign is the subject gasping and/or stating they can't breathe. Our natural response may be to answer with "If you can speak, you can breathe". However, they may have literally used their last breath to say this.

A further sign is the subject going limp, particularly after they have struggled violently. This is likely to be the subject having lost consciousness through lack of oxygen to the brain. You must consider not only disengaging, but administering first aid at this point if appropriate.

However, you must also make sure you are safe even if you think the person is demonstrating signs of positional asphyxiation. So when disengaging, make sure to do so tactically so you gain space quickly and escape if necessary.

If you need to adjust their position, consider restraining their wrists and turning them on their side. This allows them to breathe with far less effort and the restraints maintain your safety.

Factors that exacerbate positional asphyxiation – i.e. make it more likely are:
- The subject is out of breath – from running or struggling for example.
- The subject is panicking/choking/suffering from an allergic reaction.

- The subject has a breathing condition (not easy to tell unless you know the subject).
- The subject is overweight – their stomach will be pushed into their torso putting pressure on the lungs when in a prone position.
- The subject is intoxicated with drink/drugs or both.

This list is not exhaustive.

Being in a prone position is not the only position a person can die in this manner. For example, they may be slumped over, drunk or unconscious and the weight of their head is closing their windpipe. Or the subject is slumped over in a kneeling position – their knees applying pressure to the internal organs including the lungs. Or when you execute a choke hold, headlock or throat grab for too long.

Lastly, make sure you are very aware of what's going on all around you as a second subject could attack you from behind. You need to be particularly aware as you are in a position of reduced mobility and will need to stand to be able to escape or engage with a second subject.

Essentials:
- Subject prone
- Inside shin across their shoulder
- Outside knee on the floor
- On the balls of your feet facing the subject's feet
- Be mindful of their mouth, hands and legs
- Have their right arm straight and squeezed between your thighs against your groin
- Their right hand should turn anti clockwise, left clockwise
- Their fingertips should be pointing towards their body, wrist folded over, knuckles up
- Maintain a strong grip on their hand
- Use pain compliance for short bursts when required
- Be aware of positional asphyxiation and adjust position/disengage if needed
- Be aware of your surroundings

Head bouncing

What is it?
This is a method of using your environment to your advantage by thrusting the subject's head into something hard.

Why do it?
You can knock the subject unconscious, cause pain and/or injury and concussion. All of which may help to neutralise the subject thus ending the incident.

It is easy to use something hard in the environment such as a wall, the ground, furniture a car door etc. and will be less likely to injure you (for example by breaking or wounding your hand by punching the subject).

How to execute the technique:
Of course, hitting someone's head on something hard is potentially very serious so as with all techniques, you must use only force that is reasonable, necessary and proportionate in the circumstances. Again, the 'Conflict resolution model' can help you decide what is and what isn't reasonable.

The technique is simply pushing the subject's head quickly against a hard surface. This could be used when fighting on the ground and you use one or both hands to shove the subject's head against the hard floor. When stood up and in a clinch, a wall may become a viable striking surface for the subject's head.

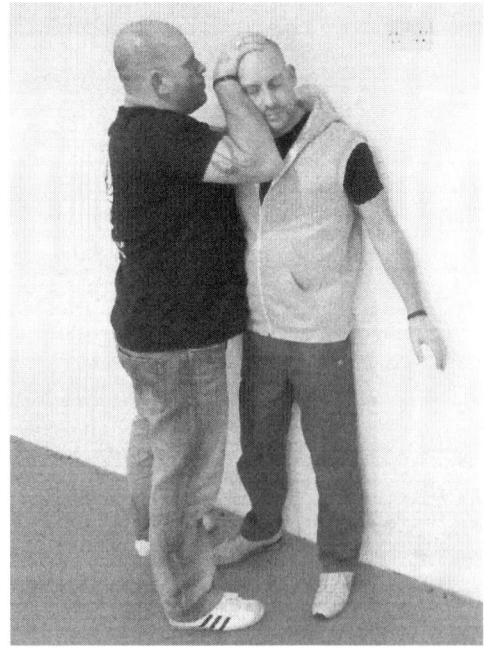 

221

The technique works best when there is a gap of around 2-6 inches between the subject's head and the hard surface. Any more than this and they will be able to brace themselves and reduce impact. Any less than this and you will not build up enough velocity to be effective.

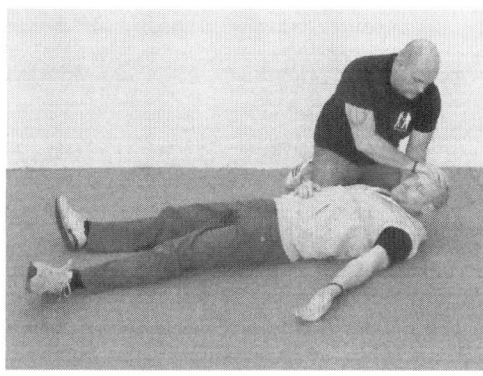 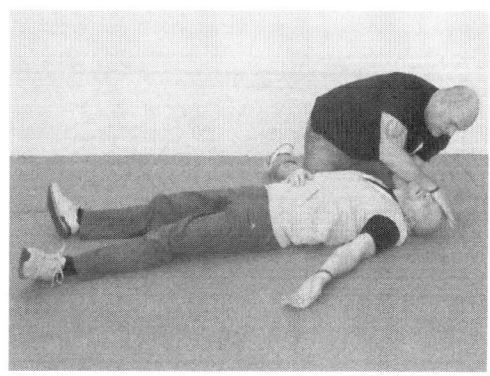

Essentials:
- Have 2-6 inches between the subject's head and the hard surface
- Shove their head quickly against the surface

Technique specific exercises:
When ground sparring on a matted surface, gently executing this technique against the matt with your training partner's head, is a good way to keep the technique in your mind.

For full contact training, a realistic training mannequin is ideal.

SELF DEFENCE

Defence against a side bear hug, near arm/both arms pinned.

What is it?
This is a method of escaping a bear hug from the side, whilst your arm closest to the subject is pinned by the grab. This method also works if both arms are pinned.

Why do it?
A bear hug with your arm(s) pinned could mean you are thrown without having your arms free to break your fall or that you are restrained whilst the subject's friends strike you.

How to execute the technique:
Drop your weight and base out.

As you do so, use your hand nearest to the subject to strike their groin with a 'Testi tap' (described in more detail elsewhere in Level 6) by flicking the groin area with your fingertips. This is to distract and hopefully obtain some space when the subject flinches.

Lean away from the subject in order to give you some room to pull your nearest arm out of the hold.

Raise your nearest elbow straight up under their chin. The main goal is to get your arm out, but if you can connect with the elbow, then all the better.

If the subject's head is behind your body, turn and place the palm of your nearest hand against the side of their head and push it. This should force their head away making sure they release their grip. If not, it should give you some space to manoeuvre round so they are in your fighting arc enabling knee strikes etc.

If the subject's head is in front of your body, use your nearest hand to reach over and carry out the reverse head twist technique.

Essentials:
- Drop your weight and base out
- Execute a 'Testi tap' at the same time
- Lean away and quickly move your nearest elbow up under the subject's chin
- Push their face away or execute the 'Reverse head twist', depending upon their position

Technique specific exercises:
Carry out an eyes closed drill with a training partner so they randomly attack you with the side bear hug from the right or the left, with their head in front or behind your body. As per other eyes closed drills, as soon as you're attacked, open your eyes and carry out the correct technique.

Be very careful with raising your elbow under your training partner's chin. It would be wise for your training partner to wear protective equipment for the chin and groin as both can easily be struck by accident during training of this technique.

Defence against a lifting bear hug rear

What is it?
An escape method from being lifted using a rear bear hug. You can use this technique whether your arms are pinned or not.

Why do it?
Often bear hugs are used to lift and throw people or to lift and move them somewhere else. Both are dangerous. Once you're off the floor, it is very difficult to gain any control, movement or striking. This method is used whether your arms are pinned or not, so you only have one thing to remember if you get caught in this situation.

How to execute the technique:
If the subject is strong and / or you are light, they may be able to move you around violently once they've lifted you. To avoid this, use your weaker leg to 'grapevine' the subject's leg by wrapping around the outside of it. This should give you some stability and restrict their movement a little too.

Then raise the heel of your other foot straight into the subject's groin repeatedly until they let you down.

Of course, if your arms are free you can also stabilise yourself by gripping their arms.

Be ready for when they drop you so you don't fall over upon landing.

Essentials:
- Grapevine the subject's leg
- Kick their groin with the back of your heel on the other leg
- If your arms are free, stabilise yourself by gripping their arms
- Be ready for the landing

Technique specific exercises:
As per other bear hug defences, you can use eyes closed and overlap drills to pressure test.

Defending yourself whilst on a push bike – subject blocking your path

What is it?
A method of protecting yourself when on a push bike and a subject is purposely blocking your path.

Why do it?
Many people ride push bikes. Push bikes are desirable items for theft and in many ways immobilise you or at least make defending yourself difficult.

This method is to deal with a subject blocking your path - perhaps they intend to steal your bicycle or attack you.

How to execute the technique:
As soon as you realise your path is being blocked on purpose, you should of course try to cycle safely away in another direction.

However, if you are unable to do so, then immediately stop your bicycle and get off of it. This gives you a better chance of defending yourself – you have access to your body weapons and your balance will be far better.

As soon as you have gotten off of the bicycle, place it between you and the subject sideways on. This helps you maintain your personal space as discussed in 'Protecting your personal space'. Use the same principles – broken record technique for someone pestering you, assertive body language and voice for 'Warning signs' and act quickly (escape or fight) when 'Danger signs' are displayed.

If the subject displays 'Danger signs', topple the bicycle towards them and either escape on foot or execute a pre-emptive attack.

Essentials:
- Cycle in another direction if possible and escape
- If not, stop the bicycle and get off of it as soon as possible
- Place the bicycle sideways on between you and the subject
- Use the 'Protecting personal space' principles
- If 'Danger signs' are displayed, topple the bicycle towards the subject and escape on foot or execute a pre-emptive attack

Technique specific exercises:
Obviously using a real push bike is the best way to train this, but remember the additional dangers of a hard training surface, any members of the public nearby (on foot or in vehicles) and the various metal parts that could strike you or your training partner.

Ideally, use an open space such as a park in a quiet spot.

Defence against being rushed by a dog

What is it?
These are tactics to use when a dog (be it stray or otherwise) is charging at you.

Why do it?
Regardless of breed, almost any size dog when it attacks a human is incredibly dangerous and very difficult to deal with. Dogs are incredibly fast and there is no way you could out run one.

How to execute the technique:
Adopt the defensive position described in previous dog defence techniques:

- Drop your chin – this helps to protect your throat as some attack dogs are trained to attack this area.

- Put your weak arm out in front of you between your throat and groin height. This is to 'offer' the dog should it attack you – it is less likely to go for your throat or groin if you do and a bitten arm is more survivable than a bitten throat or groin.

- Stand bladed – this helps to protect your groin too.

- Don't make eye contact with the dog as this it may see this as a threatening gesture.

- Keep your fists closed as your fingers will be better protected – these can be torn from your hands by the dog easily.

Don't run – dogs love to chase and they are guaranteed to be faster than you are.

Shout phrases the owner might use such as "NO", "SIT" or "HEEL". This may cause the dog to back away or stop what it's doing. However, don't repeatedly shout at it over and over again as lots of noise will excite the dog.

Kick the dog hard and fast when it is approaching. Due to the speed, you may have to start your kick early on.

A roundhouse kick to the ribs or forward kick to head can be effective. Hopefully this will send them away in pain. However, be prepared that this may not work and you may have to use other techniques. A further technique regarding a dog bite is described later.

Essentials:
- Adopt the defensive position – drop chin, stand bladed, offer your weak arm, don't make eye contact with the dog, make fists with your hands
- Don't run
- Try shouting verbal commands it may recognise
- Kick the dog to the ribs or the head

Technique specific exercises:
This is very difficult to practice realistically. The author is lucky enough to have a friend who is a dog handler and has been able to carry out training drills with his dog. However, with just a training partner and some pads it isn't going to be very realistic.

But, you can drill the scenario using a kick shield where the dog would likely be. You could add dog barking sound effects on a CD or MP3.

USP has it's own YouTube channel, on which is a video made with the help of the author's dog handler friend. It is filmed from the perspective of the defender being attacked/threatened with a dog and should be watched to help give you a flavour of the reality of such an incident.

WEAPONS

Using a bag as a shield

What is it?
This is a method of utilising a bag to defend against a close quarter weapon such as an edged weapon, e.g. a knife or an impact weapon, e.g. a stick.

Why do it?
Edged weapons and impact weapons are both dangerous to deal with empty handed.

A bag (suitcase, rucksack, holdall etc.) is an item carried by most of us a lot of the time and has the characteristics of a shield:

It can mitigate the damage strikes from edged and impact weapons can cause due to the relatively large area the bag covers. The density of the bag (and its contents) can also help dissipate the energy from an impact weapon and help prevent penetration from an edged weapon.

As such, it makes sense to learn how to use a bag to mitigate the amount of injury these weapons can cause.

How to execute the technique:
As soon as you are attacked with the weapon, try to put the bag between you and the weapon.

This is to prevent injury whilst you gain your balance and composure.

You should then drive the bag forwards into the face of the subject whilst moving aggressively forwards yourself – distracting/unbalancing the subject and engaging their OODA loop.

This should then give you an opportunity to escape. You may well find releasing the bag at this stage helpful as the bag may be cumbersome and impede your ability to run.

However, there may be various situations in which you are unable to make an escape – perhaps you are cornered in a room or you may have loved ones with you who you need to stay to protect.

In which case, in a similar method to 360 blocking, you should continue to move the bag with each strike so it is between you and the weapon every time. Doing so at arm's length gives you the best protection; however, this will depend on the size/shape/weight of the bag.

If you are with loved ones, you should try and manoeuvre yourself between them and the subject at the same time shouting at your loved ones to run.

If you are cornered in a room, then you should try to manoeuvre around so you have access to an exit.

Essentials:
- Take the first strike on the bag
- Thrust the bag into the face of the subject and move aggressively forwards
- Release the bag when you have done so, so as not to impede your escape

- If you cannot escape, keep the bag at arm's length (if practicable) and block each strike with the bag
- Manoeuvre to protect loved ones/gain access an exit

Technique specific exercises:
To start with, have your training partner use a rubber knife or soft stick to attack you with. You should have a kick shield to use as your 'bag'.

Practice the basic technique of blocking, then thrusting the bag into the face of the subject.

Then drill the non-escape technique by having your training partner try to strike you with the weapon repeatedly for twenty seconds before you can escape.

It is wise to then practice with the bag you carry most often to see where it is best to carry it and how well it can be manoeuvred.

Lastly, practice with different types of bags. The author will, for example, practice with a suit case a few weeks before he goes on holiday as it is what he will be carrying around airports etc. Other times he will practice with the rucksack he uses every day.

Defence against close in knife threat – problem solving

What is it?
This is a set of principles to adhere to when held at knife point.

Why do it?
If a subject threatens you with a knife in close quarters, it could be positioned anywhere. Up to this point in USP we have already learned defence against a knife threat from the front, back, side and held to the throat from behind.

However, whilst these are by far the most common threats you might encounter and as such the most important to learn first, there are countless other possibilities. As such, using a few basic principles and practicing them in all manner of close in knife threats, should allow you to adapt to an unusual threat.

For example, the subject may stand in front of you and hold the knife horizontally across your throat. They may hold it pointing upwards under your chin, or even very close in next to your groin. They could rest the point on your face millimetres from your eye ball, or perhaps under your arm pit next to your artery.

How to execute the technique:
The first thing to consider is how the knife could injure you in the position that the subject has chosen. If you or the subject moved, would it stab you or slash you?

Then you must move the vulnerable body part the knife is resting on, away from it without causing the injury you have considered. For example, if the edge of the knife is placed horizontally against the front of your throat, then moving sideways may well cause a slash injury to your throat. The obvious thing to do is move your throat backwards away from the blade. If the blade is under your arm pit, then the best body defence would be to swing your arm up and away from the knife.

However, to offer a 200% defence, a hand defence is also required, i.e. deflecting or controlling the knife. For example, if the edge of the knife is resting horizontally across your throat, you would pull your head back (body defence) and then slap the knife to the side (hand defence). If the knife is pointed upwards under your chin, you might consider that pulling the subject's wrist downwards and pinning it to your chest (hand defence) whilst at the same time throwing your head backwards (body defence) is the most effective method of dealing with the threat.

If you deflect with your hand defence (i.e. slap the knife away) then your follow up is likely to be the same as 'Defence against knife threats to the front/back/side' – kick the subject and run.

Three examples follow – one per page:

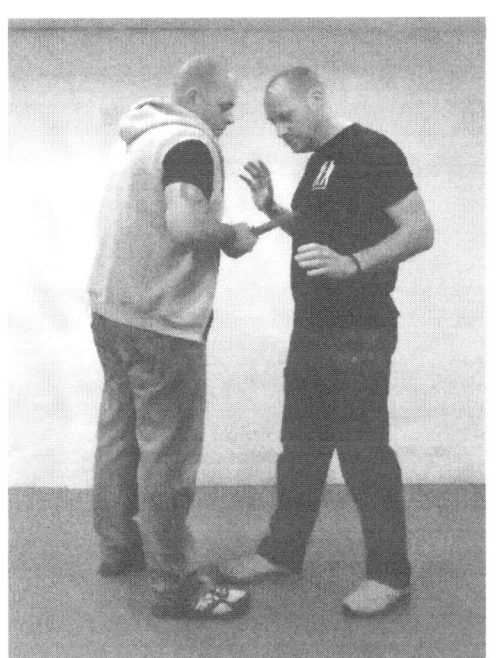

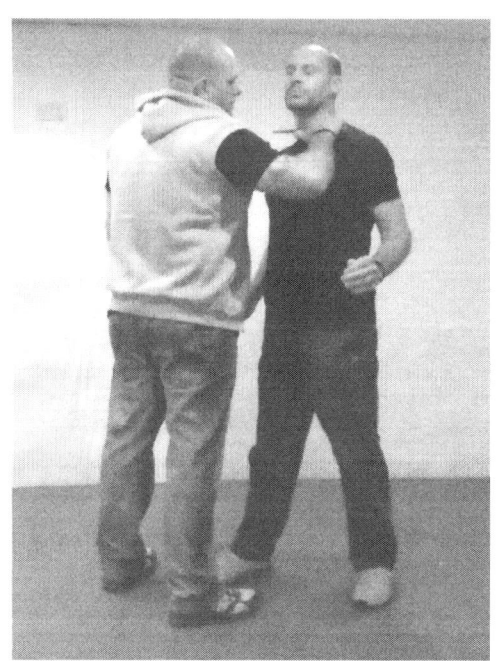

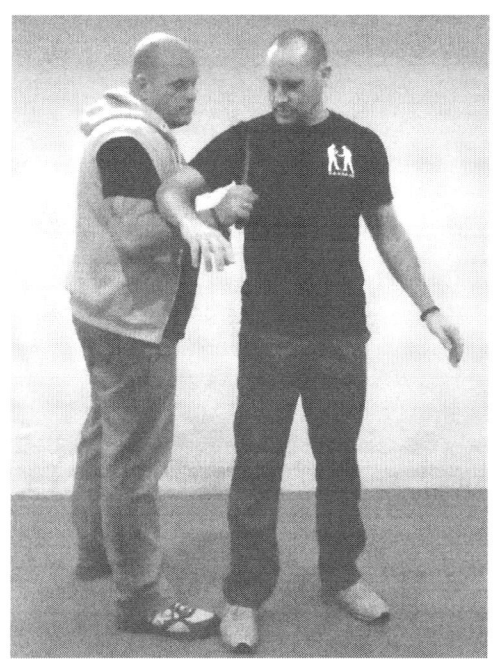

If you have to control the knife as your hand defence because of the position you are in, then your follow up is more likely to be as per 'Defence against a frenzied knife attack' – grab, close the distance, attack, shove and run.

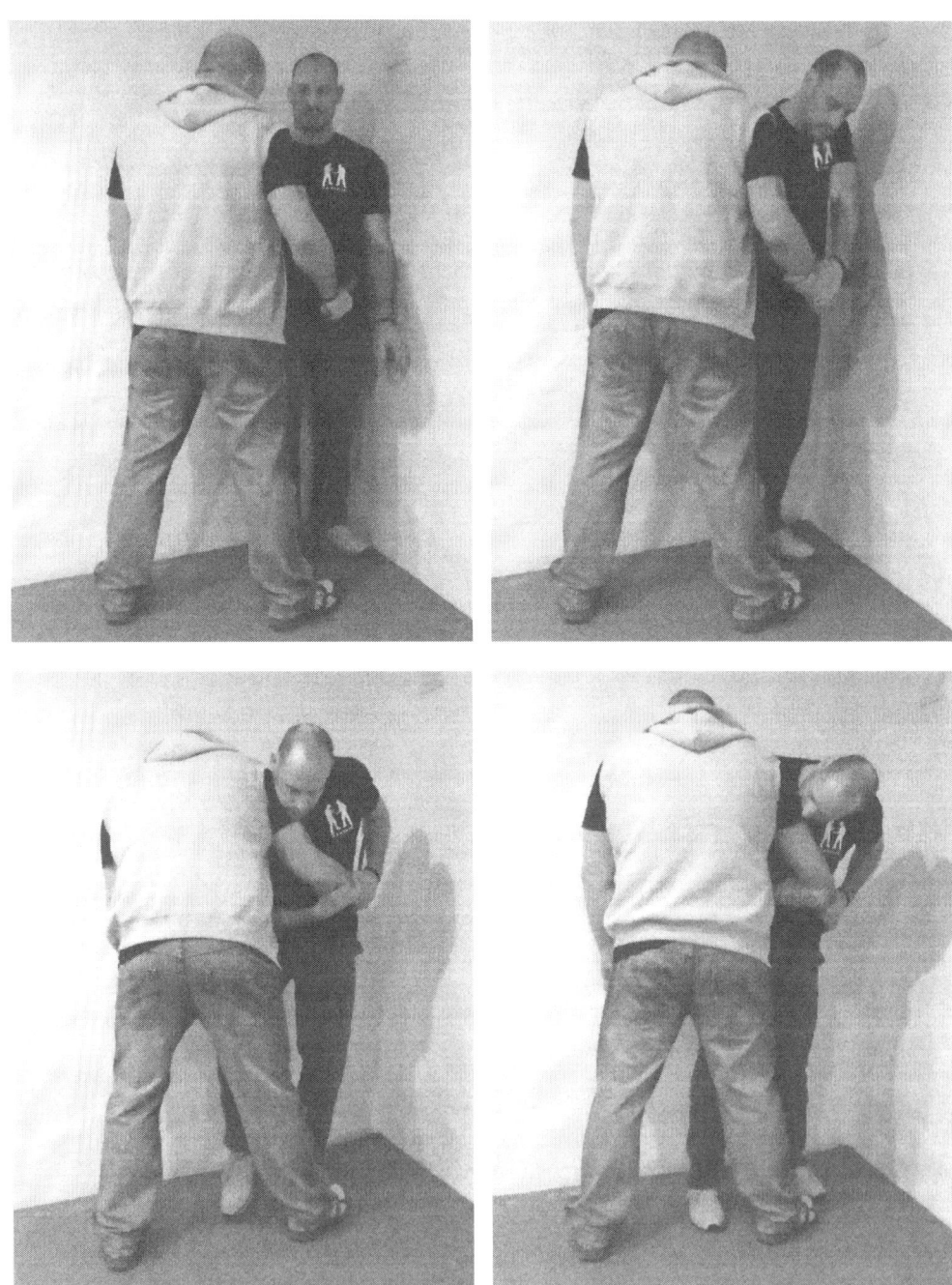

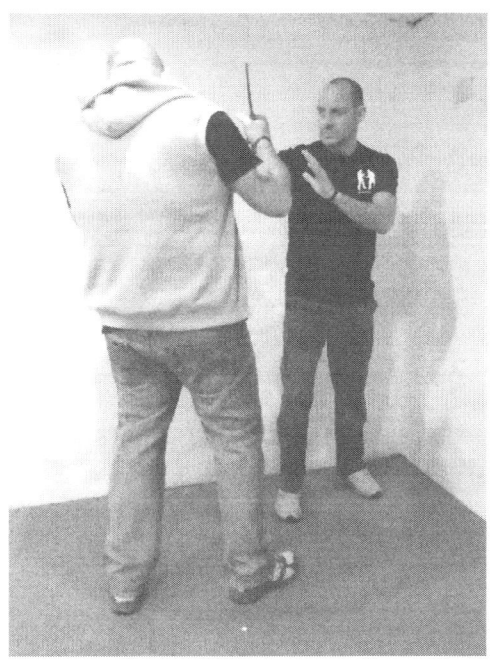 

Obviously if you feel it is appropriate, you can try to humanise yourself to the subject as per defence against a knife threat to the throat. You can also consider distracting the subject by asking a question before you execute your physical defence.

Lastly, there may be positions that are incredibly difficult / impossible to defend yourself against. In these cases, you should ACT your way into a better position. For example, you could act as though you are begging for your life and turn slightly in order to do so. This turn may give you a much better position to defend yourself in.

Essentials:
- Consider the potential method of injury when you move – stab or slash
- Execute a body defence
- Execute a hand defence (deflect or control)
- Follow up with kick and run for a deflection, or 'Defence against frenzied knife attack' principles for control
- Consider humanising yourself and/or distracting the subject
- If you are in a particularly difficult position, consider acting your way into a better position

Technique specific exercises:
This is something that needs to be approached in a slow, considered and methodical way. Your training partner should hold a safe training knife in various different positions. Each time, you should go through the principles slowly to solve the problem. Sometimes there may be more than one way to solve the same problem. As you spend time experimenting with different problems and different methods to solve them using the principles, you will eventually find methods and

positions that suit you best. Your thinking time will also reduce enabling you to react more quickly.

After spending sometime experimenting slowly in this way, try carrying out the same drill, but with your training partner acting aggressively and reacting if they spot you beginning a defence. Your defences should be full speed now.

Should a defence not work at full speed, take it back to slow time experimenting and solve the problem before moving back to full speed practice.

Defence against a knife attack when seated in your car

What is it?
This is a defensive technique to mitigate the injuries and escape from a subject who has either opened your car door and carried out a frenzied knife attack on you or done so through an open or broken window when your car is stationary (perhaps you've just got into your car in a car park).

Why do it?
Your mobility is hindered when sat in a car. More so when your seat belt is on. As such, if you are attacked in your car, you are in a very vulnerable position.

It may be that the subject simply wishes you harm, or they may be trying to car jack you. All modern cars are required to have an immobiliser system meaning the car cannot be started without its own key. No longer can car thieves 'hot wire' cars or drive a screw driver into the ignition barrel to start it. However, criminals still want to steal cars. This means they need the key so they will obtain this either by burgling your house or mugging you for it.

How to execute the technique:
Use your nearest arm to deflect the initial attack(s) and lean your upper body away from the attack. Both of these are fairly natural responses anyway.

Then grab the subject's forearm/wrist and pin it to the car with both your hands. This may be against the steering wheel, the door pillar or the roof of the car.

They will find it nearly impossible to break free from this for at least a few seconds and will likely be suffering from weapon focus.

Once you have the subject's arm well pinned, use your furthest hand from the subject to grab your seatbelt (if it is already on). Slide your hand along the belt until you find the buckle, then unclip it.

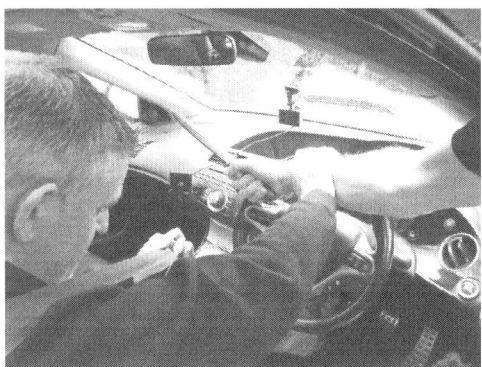 

Now lean and move further away from the subject, bring your knees to your chest and bicycle kick them violently. Obviously you will have to release their forearm in order to do so.

This will at the very least keep your upper body away from the attack and make it extremely difficult for them to continue an effective attack.

If you are unable to turn and kick due to the confines of the vehicle, bite the subject's thumb joint hard until they release the knife instead.

In either case, they are likely to run off at this point. However, if they don't, your goal will be to exit the car on the opposite side. You should then have the vehicle acting as an obstacle and have an escape route.

Essentials:
- Deflect with the nearest arm and lean away
- Pin the subject's forearm/wrist
- Grab your seatbelt and slide your hand to the buckle in order to release it
- Lean further back, bring your knees to your chest and bicycle kick the subject
- If you are unable to turn and kick, bite the subject's thumb joint hard until they release the knife

Technique specific exercises:
You must practice this in a car. The driver's seat is the hardest place to execute the technique from as the steering wheel hinders movement.

Practice with the door open, then through a (fully) opened window.

Use appropriate safety equipment and carry out a risk assessment within the vehicle before you start training – consider if there are any sharp objects in the car, is it possible to accidentally knock the car out of gear and turn the handbrake off? If so, park on the flat and chock the wheels. Don't have the engine on. Consider also that you could damage the car you're training in – the rear view mirror could be pulled off for example. Keys in the ignition could be snapped off.

This is not an exhaustive list. Remember, you are responsible for your own safety in training and those you are training with. You are also responsible for any damage to the vehicle you are training in.

Long gun disarm rear

What is it?
This is a method to deflect, control and disarm a long gun such as a shot gun or rifle, when the subject is stood behind you and threatening you with it.

Why do it?
In many countries, it is far easier to legally obtain a shotgun than any other type of firearm. As such, it is prudent to learn an effective defence in case you are ever threatened with one.

How to execute the technique:
Remember that as with any threat with a weapon, do not fight for property, but do fight for your well-being.

Firstly, look over your shoulder so you can see what you are dealing with. This is a natural reaction anyway, so should not cause the subject to feel threatened.

Carry out the deflection and technique as soon as you see the gun.

The exception is if it's slightly out of range and/or it's obvious the subject is not immediately going to shoot. In which case:

Place your open hands at the same height as the gun in a submissive posture. This is to give the appearance of compliance, but keeps your hands close to the weapon so that as you execute the defence, you do not have to move your hands too far.

The subject may well speak to you to tell you their demands.

If you judge that you have time ask them a question to engage their brain. Use the same question in training every time as trying to think of something on the spot puts you at a disadvantage.

Wait for around half a second to a second and then explosively and without telegraphing, turn out of the line of fire and in towards the subject. The forwards momentum towards the subject is designed to give you a psychological advantage, it gets you further away from the muzzle of the gun and you may well put the subject off balance too.

If possible, you should turn to the side that will cause the muzzle to be pointing at you for the shortest time and as such depends on positioning of the muzzle ON YOUR BODY in the first place. It means that you may move to the live side or the dead side of the subject.

At the same time as the turn, your nearest arm should deflect the barrel of the weapon by under hooking it and the subject's arms.

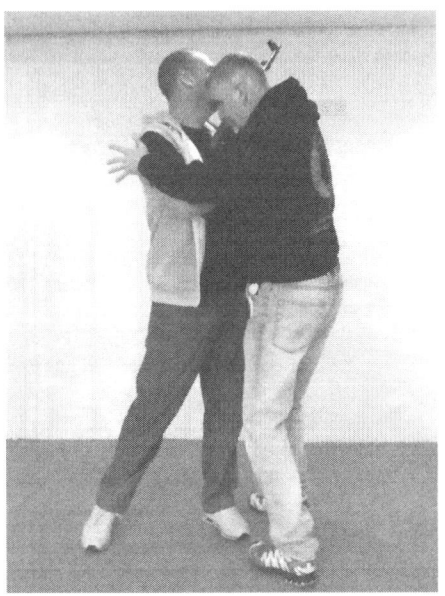 

Bear hug the subject from their side, using a gable grip if possible. The muzzle should be pointed upwards and the subject should not be able to move it.

Remember, at any point during the struggle it could discharge and shoot you, so you must maintain the deflection of the barrel.

Attack the subject with knee strikes if you are in a position that allows this, or stomping their instep and/or biting their neck, ear or face/head butting them.

Once the subject is 'softened up' grab the gun with both hands and yank it violently from their grip.

Carry out the post disarm procedure learnt with handgun defence.

If the subject is larger than you, you would be better bear hugging the subject's arms and the gun.

If the subject is holding the gun at hip height, you would be better bear hugging around their upper arms.

Essentials:
- Look over your shoulder
- Deflect immediately unless the weapon is out of reach or you are sure the subject will not fire immediately
- If this is the case, raise your hands to gun height
- Ask an OODA question
- Turn out of the line of fire and move forwards towards the subject
- Deflect the barrel by under hooking it
- Bear hug the subject from the side
- Attack the subject but maintain control of the gun
- Disarm

Technique specific exercises:
An airsoft rifle can be used with appropriate safety equipment to check the speed of your deflection. PLEASE REFER TO SECTION ON BB GUN TRAINING BEFORE CARRYING OUT THIS DRILL.

The muzzle can be positioned in different areas of the front of the body/head.

Defence against being held hostage at gun point

What is it?
This is a method to deflect, control and disarm a hand gun, when the subject is stood behind you and threatening you with it by holding it to the side of your head.

Why do it?
This is a common way to hold a person hostage with a handgun. Perhaps they are trying to kidnap you, or you are being held hostage whilst Police try to negotiate with the subject.

How to execute the technique:
Remember that as with any threat with a weapon, do not fight for property, but do fight for your well-being.

Grab the gun and execute the technique as soon as you see it.

The exception is if it's obvious the subject is not immediately going to shoot. In which case:

As per knife to throat threat, act as you are being compliant and try to humanise yourself with the subject. If they think of you as a human being they are less likely to try and kill you. This means you perhaps tell them that you have a family and your children's names etc. This humanisation turns you from a piece of 'meat' that can be sacrificed into a real life person. This is why executioners often cover the persons head with a sack or similar – because a person's face and particularly their eyes, is what makes them seem human.

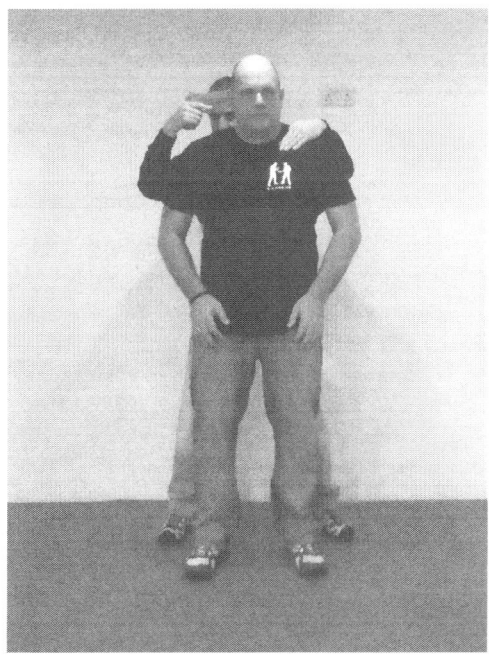
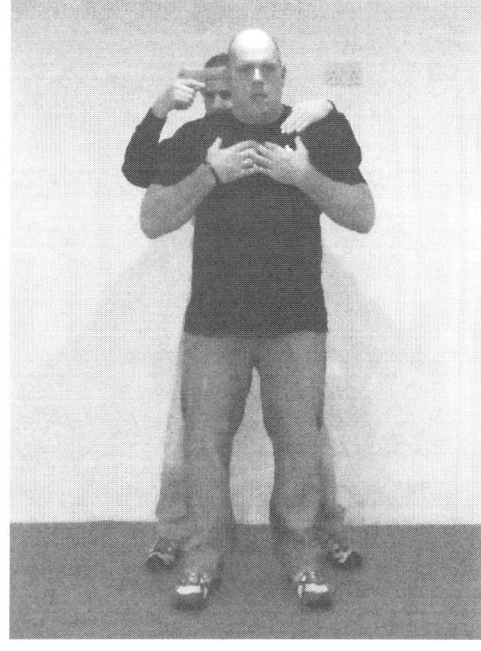

As you do so 'sneak' your hands up the front of your body to a better position to be able to take hold of the gun. This means keeping your hands close to your body and stopping at around nipple height. This should ensure they don't see this tactical positioning.

When you are ready to act, ask a question as an OODA distraction.

Around half a second later carry out the following with aggression speed and no hesitation:

With your hand that's on the side of the gun, reach up and grab the barrel, palm facing behind you.

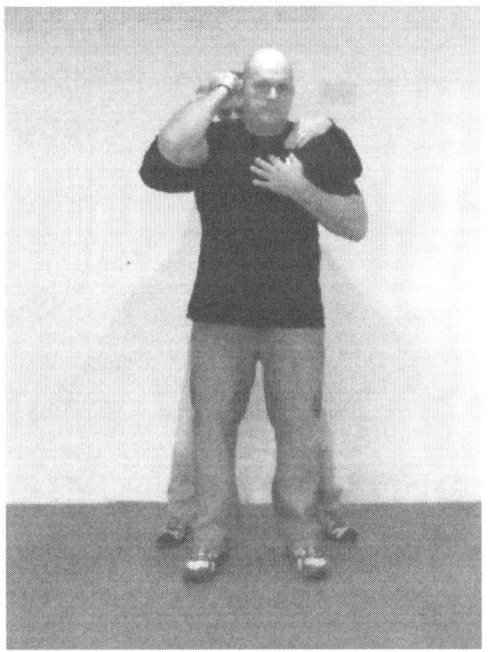 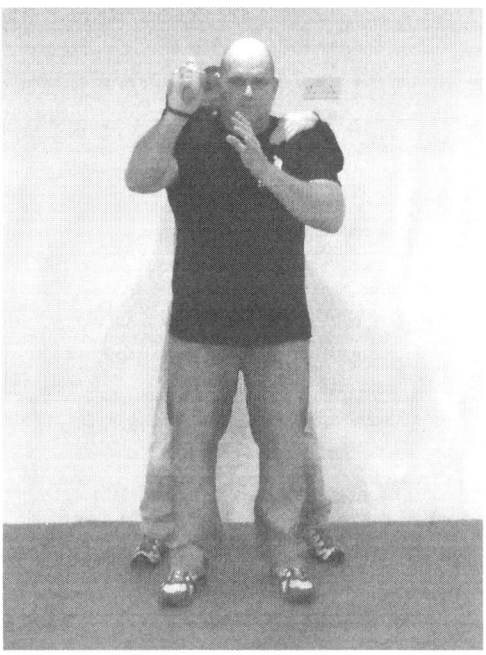

Pull the barrel forwards and turn it 90 degrees so it is pointing ahead of you.

Continue to pull the barrel forwards and with your other hand, push the hammer (rear end) of the gun away from you and straighten both of your arms. This will help to turn the gun another 90 degrees and push the weapon from the subject's grip.

As you carry this part of the technique out, fire your backside backwards into the subject to obtain space and distract the subject, as well as putting them off balance.

Carry out post disarm procedures as per front handgun threat.

Essentials:
- Deflect immediately unless you are sure the subject will not fire immediately
- If this is the case, humanise yourself and sneak your hands up to your chest
- Ask an OODA question
- Grab the barrel of the gun and pull it forwards turning it 90 degrees
- Push the hammer end of the gun with the other hand pushing it out of the subject's grip and turning it another 90 degrees
- Fire your backside backwards into the subject at the same time
- Carry out usual post disarm procedure

Defence against gun point robbery out of reach

What is it?
This is an escape method in case you are threatened at gun point with demands for money and the weapon is out of reach – preventing you from carrying out a disarm.

Why do it?
As with all weapon threats, the option to comply with the subject may be available and may be the safest thing to do. However, the guiding principle is to comply with any 'reasonable' request. You may not feel it's 'reasonable' to hand over your wallet or keys to your car. However, if you are sure this is all the subject wants, then the safest option is to do so and as such 'reasonable'. However, as discussed in previous weapon threat defences, some demands are 'unreasonable'. These are demands that put you in an even more dangerous scenario. For example, demanding you to get into their vehicle or to be bound etc.

Generally speaking – don't fight for property, but do fight for your physical well-being.

Sometimes, you will not be able to control the weapon the subject has and as such a good course of action is to run. However, if you run in a straight line, then consider how the gun man needs to react if they choose to shoot at you:

Their target – you – is not moving side to side. Once they have aligned their sights on the target, it is simply getting smaller and thus easy to hit. Their target is also your back – a large target which includes most vital organs.

So if we choose not to comply with the demands the subject is making, we need to make it very difficult for the subject to take accurate aim at us as we run away.

How to execute the technique:
Your first consideration should be if you are with a loved one. If so, running away will leave them to fend for themselves which is not an option for us.

We can consider zigzag running if there is no nearby cover or running at a 90 degree angle to the subject if cover is within 2 seconds distance.

Remember, a person armed with a handgun, normally takes around 2 seconds to aim and shoot and that an average person with a handgun becomes fairly inaccurate when the target is over 15 feet.

Consider how the average subject with a handgun will have probably practiced (if they have practiced at all).

It may be a target nailed to a tree, or a tin can on a bench. This means that it is unlikely they will have practiced shooting at a moving target and most likely won't expect it.

As with all gun threats, you should take immediate action unless you are sure the subject is only threatening you and will not shoot immediately.

If this is the case, they are most likely to want your wallet. To use this to our advantage, we pretend to comply and slowly take out our wallet. We can then ask an OODA question and around half a second to a second later, throw the wallet upwards towards the subject's face.

This will also force them into an OODA loop. However, the wallet must be close enough to the face that it makes the subject flinch. At that moment, turn sideways and run at a right angle to the subject. Of course, keys, your phone, coins etc can all be used in the same way.

Whilst you are running laterally, you will be sideways onto the subject, giving them a smaller target and one which may well be protected by your arm for a large portion of the incident.

So now they have been distracted and have to deal with a smaller, moving target, which is protected to some degree by the arm.

This doesn't mean that they can't shoot you, but the chances are lower and more likely to hit a less vital part of your body.

Once you are behind cover, it's possible that they cut their losses and run off as they do not want to get caught. However, don't bank on it and be prepared to fight or move to more cover etc.

Essentials:
- Take immediate action unless you are sure the subject will not shoot immediately
- If you are sure that they won't shoot immediately, use a distraction – a question and/or throwing your wallet at their face
- Then turn 90 degrees towards your cover and run
- Remember, you must be able to reach cover within 2 seconds

Technique specific exercises:
A realistic drill for this is to use an airsoft BB gun. Your training partner should carry out a gun point robbery. You should have a wallet and throw it towards your training partner's face, then execute the technique. Your training partner must try and shoot at you as soon as they sense you are not complying. PLEASE REFER TO SECTION ON BB GUN TRAINING BEFORE CARRYING OUT THIS DRILL.

Defence against a garrotte

What is it?
This is an escape method in case someone tries to strangle you from behind with some kind of flexible weapon – e.g. wire or rope.

Why do it?
Flexible weapons can be improvised from all sorts of places. If you look around wherever you are now, you'll most likely see something that could serve as an improvised flexible weapon.

Examples include:

Phone charger cables, shoe laces, dog lead, rope, garden wire, string, a belt, even a rolled t-shirt could be used.

As such, it's quite possible that a 'garrotte' improvised or otherwise could be used against you in this way.

How to execute the technique:
If you have had any sort of warning that the attack is coming, then tuck your chin to your chest, put your hands palm out next to your throat and duck. This should prevent the garrotte from being placed properly and/or give you a chance to remove it if it does go on.

However, in the worst case scenario, the garrotte is placed around your throat and pulled tight.

As soon as you sense the garrotte you must immediately and aggressively turn towards the subject and attack their face – ideally a thumb thrust to the eyes which will disorientate them as well as afford you some space.

Carry on attacking until the threat is neutralised or until you are able to safely escape.

Turning whilst a garrotte is tightly wrapped around your throat could potentially be dangerous – perhaps the subject is using a weapon that could slice your throat – for example, a survival saw or cheese wire. However, if you do nothing, you will be in an even worse position, as the subject could slice at your throat anyway and/or choke you to unconsciousness/death. This is why speed is of the essence when making your counter attack.

Essentials:
- Prevent the garrotte from going on in the first place if at all possible – tuck your chin to your chest, hands up by your throat and duck.
- As soon as you sense the garrotte, turn and attack the subject's face

Technique specific exercises:
Making sure you and your training partner are fully aware of the tap out rule and that any strangle hold in training should be carried out slowly, use a traditional martial arts belt as the garrotte – these are wide which helps to dissipate the force against the throat and they are reasonably soft so that you are less likely to cause grazes etc.

Flexible object use - grip

What is it?
A safe and effective method for holding an improvised weapon which has flexible characteristics. For example:

- Phone charger cables
- Shoe laces
- Dog leads
- Rope
- Garden wire
- String
- A belt
- A rolled t-shirt

(For training, we generally use traditional martial arts belts).

You should make it a habit to spot these types of objects when you are out and about. For example, in your place of work is there an extension cable you could pick up and use?

Each object should be considered for it's individual characteristics. For example, a shoe lace could be used as a restraint but they are light so striking would not be effective. However, a leather belt is heavy and a good length to wield as a striking weapon. That is not to say that you should look for the perfect object for the specific situation as time is of course, of the essence. But you should have some idea of the differences in characteristics and a good way to do this is to handle these various objects as part of your training. This will help weed out objects you think would be effective, but actually may be of little use to you in a conflict.

Please also consider the law when using an improvised weapon and how it fits into the 'Conflict resolution model' described in Level 1.

Remember, in the UK it is illegal to carry a weapon away from where you live. A weapon is defined as something made, intended or adapted to injure. Make sure you know the relevant weapon laws in your own part of the world and adhere to them.

However, if you pick up any of these sorts of objects at the time of an incident as a weapon of opportunity, then you will not have committed the offence of possession of an offensive weapon. However, it's use could still be considered unreasonable depending on the circumstances.

A fairly simple example of what might be classed as reasonable use of an improvised weapon would be:

An subject is charging at you with a knife and you are unable to make an escape, so you pick up a brick and throw it at the subject.

Why do it?
A flexible weapon can greatly improve your chances of surviving an attack as it gives you advantages of distance, force, posturing type defences as well as use as a restraint. Flexible weapons of opportunity are plentiful and are generally very easy and simple to use to good effect.

How to execute the technique:
The grip of the flexible weapon depends on its use and it's characteristics.

If you are intending to use it to restrain someone, then you are likely to hold it loosely in both hands to begin with. However, if you are using it to strike at a subject, then one handed is, of course, more effective.

When holding one handed, you generally need around one and a half feet of flexible weapon hanging from the grip. Of course, the weapon needs to be longer than this so that you have something to grip.

Ideally, you should grip the tail of the flexible weapon and wrap it around your hand a couple of times, leaving around one and a half feet protruding to use for striking.

This ensures weapon retention in case the subject attempts to disarm you. Contrary to popular belief, if the flexible weapon you are using has a heavy end – for example the buckle of a belt – you should NOT have this at the end of the striking part of your flexible weapon. This is because the follow through of a strike with a flexible weapon, often causes the end of it to whip back from the subject and into the defender.

Instead, hold the buckle in your hand and wrap the belt around your hand a couple of times leaving around one and a half foot protruding.

Essentials:
- Consider the use and characteristics of the object
- For striking, grip in your strong hand and wrap the object around your hand a couple of times leaving one and a half foot protruding
- Do NOT have the heavy end of the object at the end of the 'tail' of the weapon

Technique specific exercises:
Whenever you pick up a flexible object in your daily life, grip it as described. This will then become a habit and you'll get used to the different characteristics of a range of suitable objects.

Flexible object use - 10 Angles

What is it?
Strikes using an improvised flexible weapon.

Why do it?
The use of an improvised weapon is a force multiplier, meaning that smaller weaker defenders will have a greater chance of neutralising larger and stronger subjects. Flexible objects are readily available in everyday life, whether it's a phone charger lead, a belt, a dog lead or a towel.

How to execute the technique:
In all but the forwards angle strikes, try to strike the target with the end third of the weapon. The end of the weapon will always be moving the fastest, but to strike a target with such a small area takes accuracy which will likely not be present in the heat of the moment. As such, using the end third is sufficient to keep distance from the subject, allows a powerful strike and most importantly gives a greater margin for error.

Targets need to be considered when striking them, particularly with a weapon. Please refer back to the impact weapon trauma chart.

Forwards angle – this is commonly known as the 'towel flick'. You should be holding the flexible weapon in your dominant hand and have your dominant side forwards – i.e. your weapon hand is your lead hand for this strike.

Pull your dominant hand back and across your chest to your opposite shoulder.

Quickly flick your wrist and drive your strong hand forwards. Just before the flexible weapon makes contact, quickly snap your strong wrist back towards you. It is this motion that should cause the tail of the flexible weapon to whip and make a cracking noise against the subject.

The flick goes towards the subject's face in order to distract them and cause pain. This can be used to keep a subject at a distance from you. However, just repeating the same technique won't work for long.

Backwards angle - Hold the weapon in one hand and look over your shoulder on the side you're holding it (remember that by looking over your shoulder, you will lose depth perception as you will effectively have only one eye on the target). If you are in a passive stance, take a step backwards and swing the weapon backwards along the horizontal plane and strike the target. Pivot on your lead foot as you do so.

Horizontal plane, both angles - holding the weapon in one hand, swing it from right to left and left to right on the horizontal plane in a similar motion to a forehand and backhand swing in squash. Pivot on the balls of your feet as you would for hook punches.

Vertical upward angle – this is the weapon being swung upwards on the vertical plane with a one handed grip. However, it is awkward and not usually very effective unless the weapon is heavy – for example, metal chain.

Vertical downward angle – hold the weapon in one hand and raise it up and back. Swing the weapon straight down the centre line on the vertical plane. This may be to target the head in a serious attack or perhaps a limb in a less dangerous incident. Drop your weight as you make contact with the target and pivot on your rear foot.

Diagonal angles – all of the diagonal angles use the same technique as the horizontal plane angles. The only difference is the path of the striking area of the end of the weapon which moves along an imaginary 'X' on the subject's body. Downward diagonal strikes are particularly useful for targeting areas of the subject's leg for a lower level of force. The paths of the striking area of the weapon are described below:

Diagonal down, right to left

Diagonal down, left to right

Diagonal up, right to left

Diagonal up, left to right

Technique specific exercises:
To gain power and skill, a Karate belt used against a punch bag is very useful.

Use of a realistic training mannequin is good too as it assists with target acquisition.

Use of a Karate belts to spar against a padded training partner makes for a more dynamic training scenario. Be sure to wear eye protection though as even the Karate belts can cause serious eye injuries.

Flexible object use, keep away swing

What is it?
A method of posturing with a flexible weapon to deter a subject.

Why do it?
It's always better to keep a subject at a safe distance from you wherever possible. A flexible weapon being swung around violently can provide a good barrier between you and them, as they will not want to be struck with such a weapon.

How to execute the technique:
This technique is no different to the 'Keep away swing' with a stick. It is all about displaying aggression. The weapon should be held in one hand and swung violently and repeatedly from side to side but most importantly, at head height.

This will help deter the subject as they will automatically think they are likely to get struck in the eyes with it, which can cause great pain/blindness, whereas a body shot could be an acceptable risk for them.

It also shows that you are willing and ready to do them serious damage, whereas a low swing may demonstrate a half-hearted and more passive approach.

At the same time, you should be posturing with your body – standing tall, contorted face, shouting, swearing, making violent threats and appearing almost feral and out of control.

This may look aggressive from other's perspectives, but the aim is to deter a physical confrontation and as such is lower down on the response options within the 'Conflict Resolution Model' than getting 'hands on'. You just need to remember to articulate your intentions should you be required to justify your actions.

Essentials:
- Swing the weapon violently and repeatedly from side to side
- Swing at head height
- Use other forms of posturing

Technique specific exercises:
You have a traditional martial arts belt and your training partner has a rubber knife and eye protection. They begin to move towards you and you carry out the technique. See how long you can hold them off for – even with a traditional martial arts belt and eye protection, your partner will still be put off by the technique.

Flexible object use as a restraint

What is it?
Using an improvised flexible weapon to restrain a subject.

Why do it?
There may well be times that you wish to restrain a subject. This is most likely to be when you have detained someone and are awaiting the arrival of the Police.

Perhaps you have disturbed a burglar and managed to pin them on the floor but need to tie their wrists so that they cannot escape or cause you any harm. To tie someone effectively when under the pressure of a real life incident like this is difficult and if you get it wrong, the subject will easily slip the restraints.

As such, this method is simple and effective.

How to execute the technique:
In order to restrain a subject with a flexible weapon, they must either be compliant or under control. You will need both hands to tie them and as such, you will more than likely need a second person to help you.

Once your helper has control of the subject, take the flexible weapon and wrap it once around their wrists so that the tails of the flexible weapon cross.

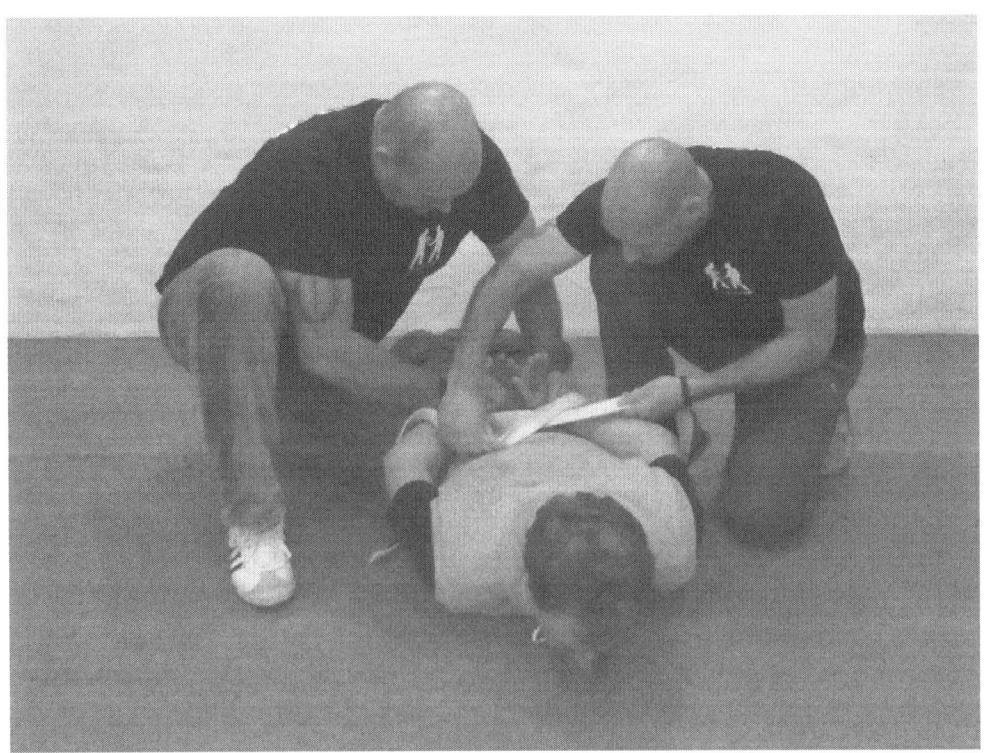

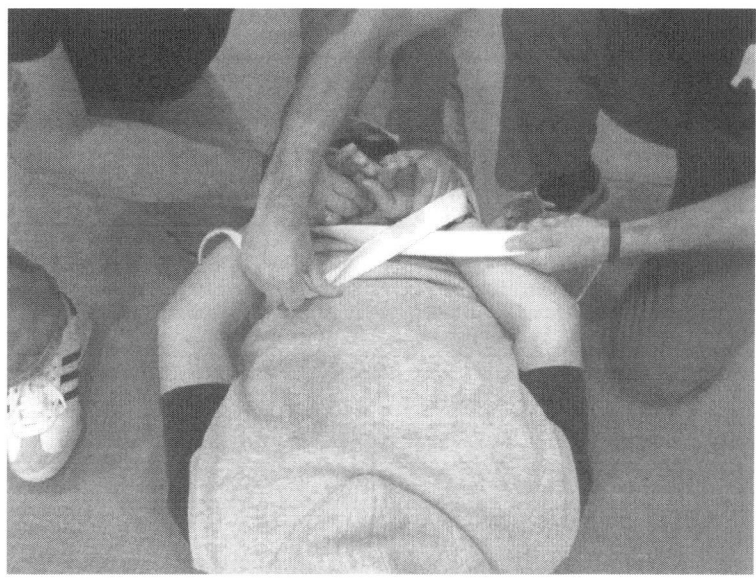

You will notice that if you tie this off now, the subject has a space between their wrists which may allow them to wriggle free.

Therefore, once the tails are crossed over, take one of the tails and wrap it once around the restraint already in place. Once pulled tight, this will reduce the space between the wrists and turn the restraint effectively into two bracelets, like handcuffs, rather than just a loop around the wrists.

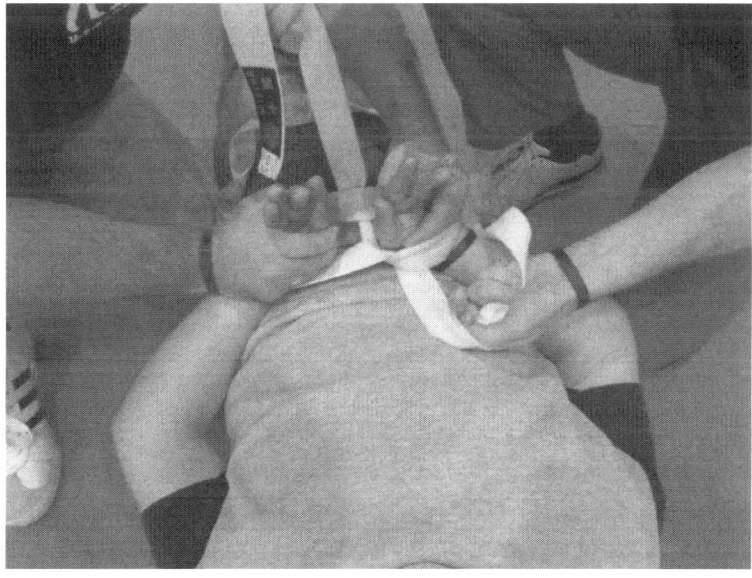

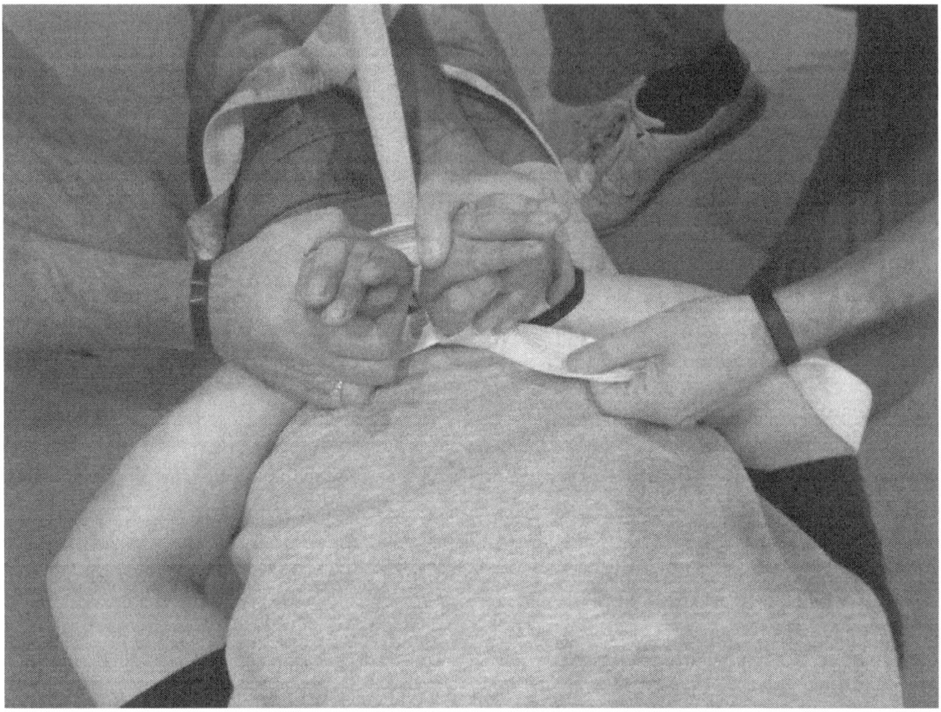

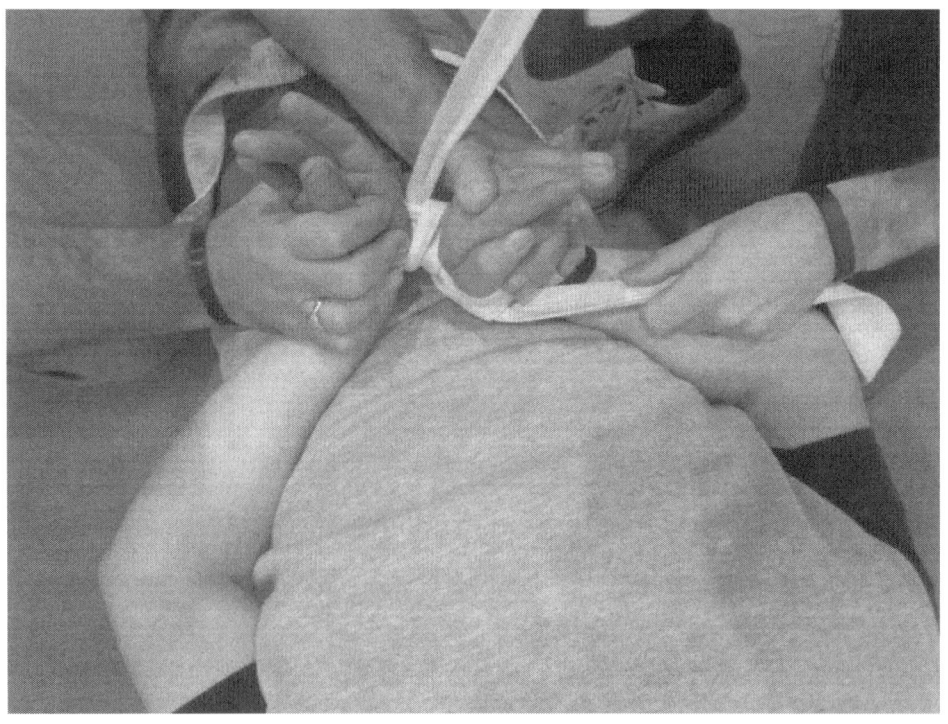

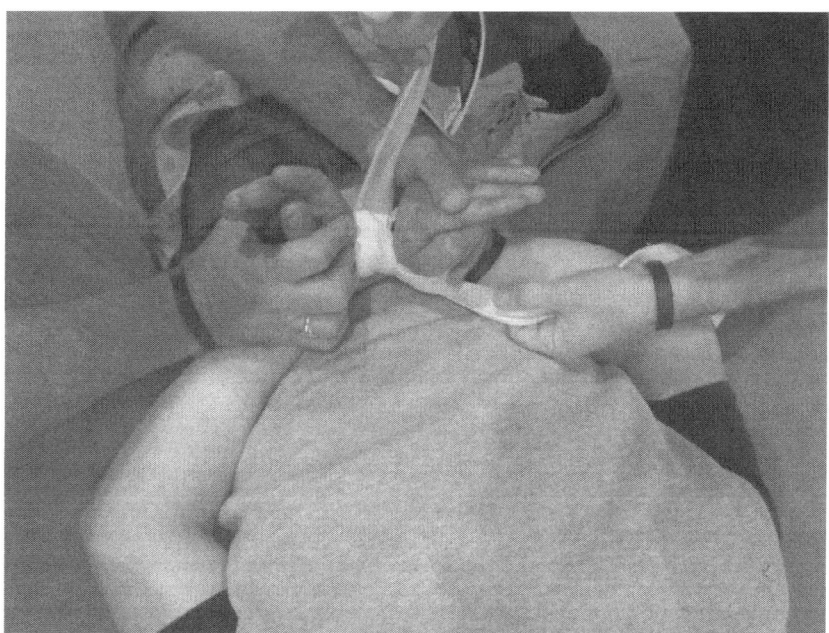

Now take the two tails and tie them off.

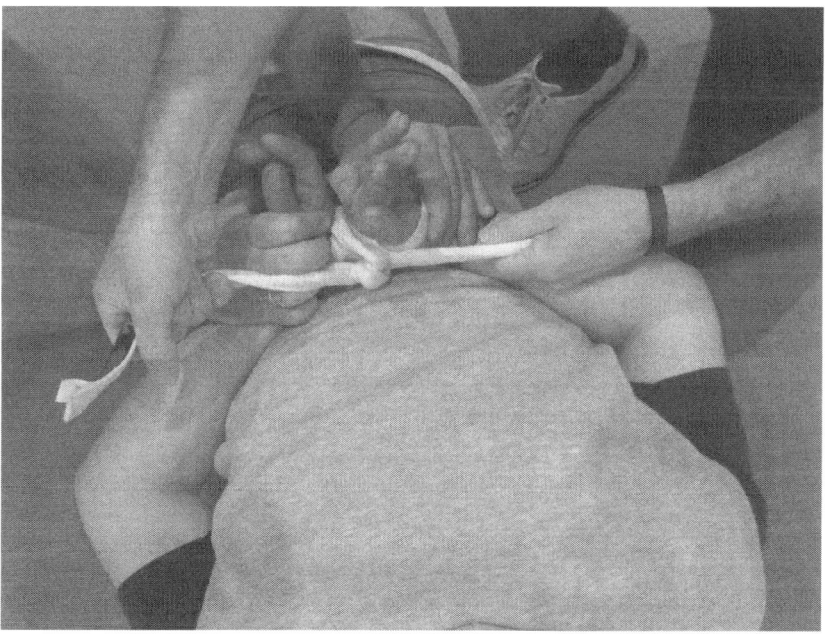

If you left the subject like this for any period of time, they would likely be able to wriggle free eventually. As such, this restraint is designed for you to stay with the subject and hold the tails of the restraint. This will however, free up one of your hands and give you much greater control of the subject. It also allows you to safely change the position of the subject. This may be useful when you have the subject in a ground pin position as changing their position to sitting or standing will reduce the risk of positional asphyxiation.

Ideally, the restraint should be behind the subject's back as when in front, they can still run/grab/strike you.

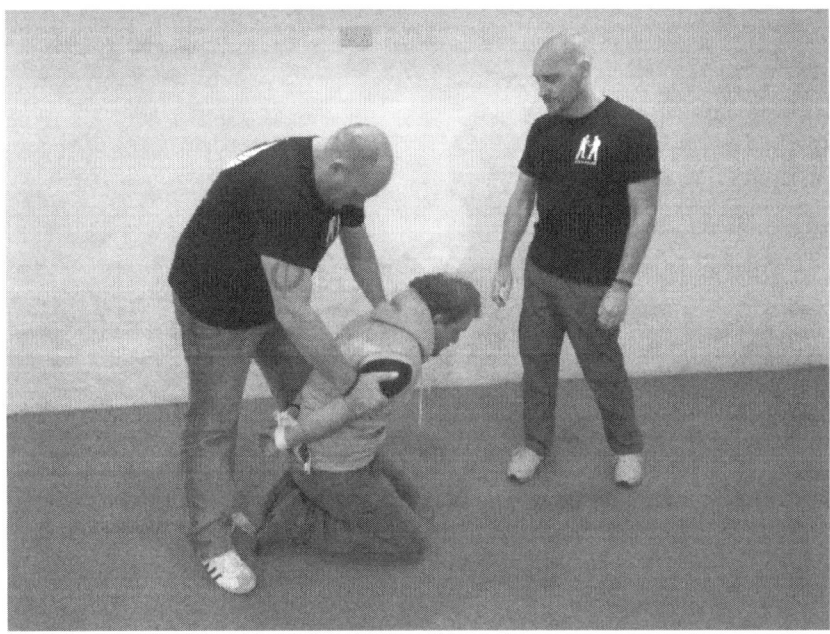

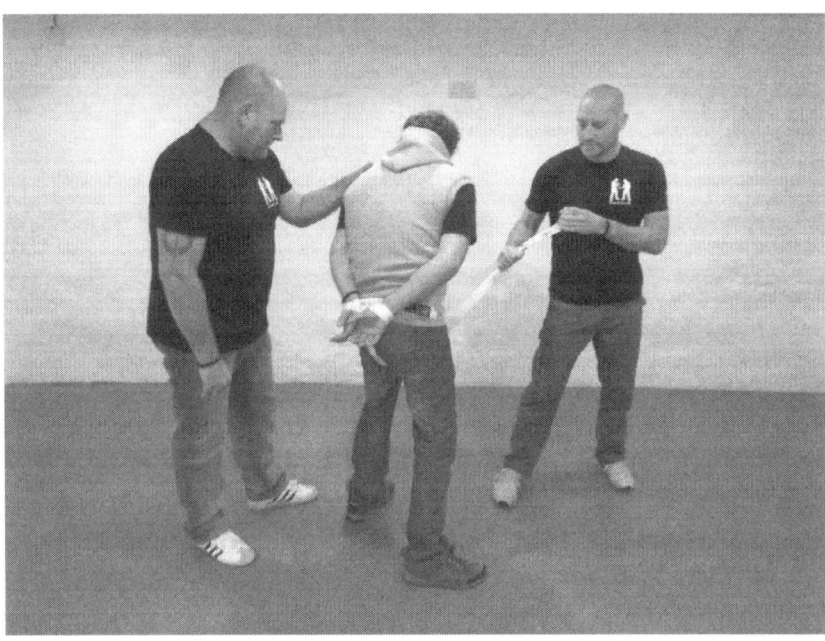

If the subject must be moved or stood, you can gain greater control by putting the tails between their legs and pulling up on them from the other side. (This works whether they are restrained at the front or the back). This will keep the restraint tight and put the subject in an awkward position giving you greater control.

Consider the characteristics of your improvised weapon. If it is thin and non-elasticised like wire, then you may cause injuries to the subject's wrists. You may also cut off the blood supply to their hands which can cause further serious injuries/conditions. Remember, your actions must be reasonable in the circumstances and you must be prepared to justify them.

Essentials:
- Subject must be compliant or under control
- Wrap the flexible weapon around both wrists until the tails cross over
- Wrap one tail around the restraint that is already in place
- Pull tight and tie off
- For further control when standing, pull tails between the legs of the subject and pull upwards

Technique specific exercises:
Using a traditional martial arts belt, practice this on your training partner. Experiment by allowing them to try and wriggle free and see how long it takes them. Remember in reality, you would keep hold of the restraint at all times.

Be sensible in training – do not cut off the blood supply to your training partner's hands when practicing using a restraint like this.

Flexible object use as a garrotte

What is it?
Using an improvised flexible weapon to restrain or strangle a subject.

Why do it?
The word 'garrotte' conjures up an image of a rather nasty and violent act where we might strangle a subject to death with a piece of piano wire.

However, this is not the only way the technique can be used. The same technique can be used to restrain, control and move a subject or render them unconscious. Circumstances will dictate at what level you use this technique.

You must also remember that the characteristics of the object you are using will also have a bearing on how injurious the technique is – something flexible and wide like a rolled up t-shirt will of course be less injurious than a thin and inflexible piece of garden wire.

How to execute the technique:
Approach the subject from behind with the flexible weapon in both hands (palms down) with around a foot of the weapon between them.

Quickly throw the weapon over the subject's head and pull it into their throat.

Drop your strong hand under your weak hand effectively crossing the weapon over.

As you do so, turn towards your weak side 180 degrees so that your back is against the back of the subject.

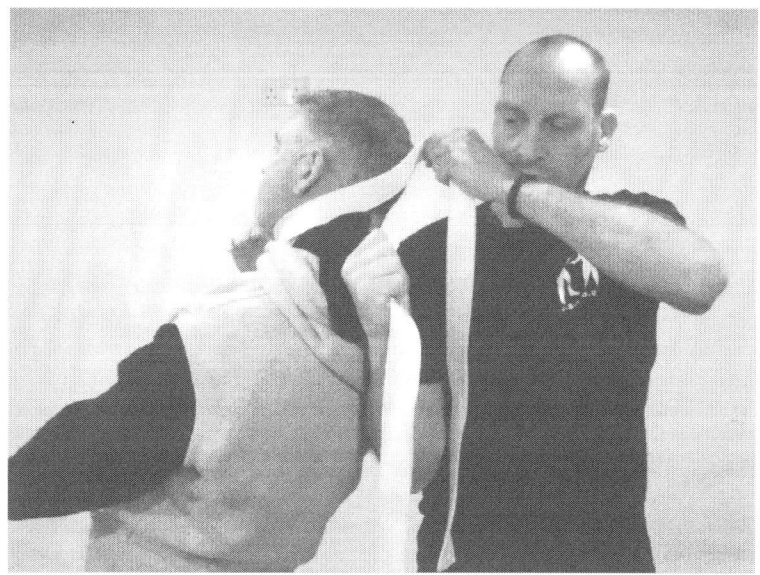

You will now have both of your hands next to just one of your shoulders as if you are carrying a sack of potatoes on your back.

This is the point at which you must decide what level of force you are using.

You could pull everything in tight in order to cut off the subject's airway/carotid arteries to render them unconscious.

You could pull tightly and bend forwards, lifting them from the ground so their entire body weight is pushing their throat against the garrotte. Or you could simply hold them in this position without stopping their breathing or even walk them to another area.

An example of when this could be used:

You see a person being held at knife point, so you take your belt off and approach the subject, execute the technique and lift them off their feet shouting "DROP THE KNIFE". If they do, then provided it's safe, you could release them (securing their knife of course).

If they don't then perhaps you could justify maintaining the grip until they are rendered unconscious. Hopefully they won't think to do so because of the panic you will be subjecting them to, but bear in mind they could still lash out at you with the knife - unfortunately when rescuing people, you often have to take risks to your own safety.

Essentials:
- One foot of flexible weapon between both hands
- Approach from the rear
- Quickly throw the weapon over the subject's head and pull into their throat
- Cross your hands over and turn 180 degrees

Technique specific exercises:
Using a traditional martial arts belt, practice this on your training partner, making sure you are both using the tap out rule and putting the technique on slowly. Never lift your training partner off the ground in training.

Be sensible in training – do not cut off the airway or blood supply to your training partner's brain when practicing. To practice using more force and speed, use a realistic training mannequin.

FIRST AID

Dealing with head injuries

What is it?
This is information so that you can recognise a head injury and know how to respond appropriately.

Why do it?
Head injuries are a very common result of an assault. They can also be very serious. As such it is important to be able to recognise a head injury and to be able to respond appropriately.

How to execute the technique:

Types of head injury:

- Contusion (bruising)
- Concussion (the brain having been knocked about inside the skull)
- Compression (the brain swelling against the skull)
- Fracture (damage to the skull)
- Wound (a laceration to the skin around the head)

Be aware that spinal injury is common alongside head injuries.

What to look for:

- Brief / complete loss of consciousness
- Scalp wound
- Dizziness or nausea
- Loss of memory of events before or during the injury
- Headache
- Confusion
- Reduced level of response
- Leakage of blood or watery fluid from the ear or nose
- Unequal pupil size

How to respond:

- Sit them down and place something cold on the injury
- Treat any scalp wounds like a bleed by applying direct pressure to the wound (do not tie anything tight around their head)
- If they are alert and responsive, wait with them until they recover and encourage them to seek medical help
- If they are not alert or responsive, then call an ambulance
- If they lose consciousness, treat them using the 'DRSABC' procedure

Essentials:
- Sit the casualty down
- Apply something cold to the injury
- Treat wounds as a bleed (do not tie anything tight around their head)
- If they are alert and responsive – wait with them and encourage them to seek medical help
- If they are not alert or responsive call an ambulance
- If they lose consciousness, use DRSABC

Technique specific exercises:
As already stated, it is advisable to train with the St John's Ambulance or similar organisation every year to keep up to date and refresh your skills.

CONFLICT KNOWLEDGE

The five likely reactions of a person who has been hit

Knowing how someone is likely to respond when you hit them, goes hand in hand with the principle of 'Knowing your enemy'. This information also relates to how YOU are likely to respond when you get hit. Knowing what is likely to happen in either case will reduce the shock and surprise during a violent incident. It also allows you to tailor your training to the most likely scenarios.

The five likely responses of the person who has been hit are:

- They create distance
- They clinch, or grab the person hitting them in a vertical grapple
- They counter strike
- They drop semi/un conscious
- They take the shot and stare at the person who has hit them

Remember, these are guide lines and not the only responses, but they are the most likely.

Essentials:
- Distance
- Clinch
- Counter strike
- Drops
- Takes the shot

Technique specific exercises:
Include these reactions in your training – for example, when sparring, your training partner could sometimes try to clinch or create distance. Perhaps when you carry out counter attacks in any of the self-defence techniques, your training partner could drop pretending to be semi-conscious.

Post Traumatic Stress Disorder

PTSD is mentioned in this book, as it is often survivors of a traumatic assault that come looking for training. It is important to be able to recognise PTSD and deal with it as it can be a serious and life changing condition.

This book is certainly not a self-help manual, but the information here will help those who suffer from PTSD recognise the signs and symptoms and seek support if they have not already been diagnosed. It will also prepare those who may be attacked in the future to understand their emotions post conflict. Lastly it may allow you to recognise the signs and symptoms in friend or loved one and be able to offer support.

Post-traumatic stress disorder is a normal reaction to an abnormal event.

Post-traumatic stress disorder is a psychological and physical condition that can be caused by extremely frightening or distressing events.

PTSD can occur after experiencing or witnessing traumatic events including:

- Military combat
- Natural disasters
- Serious accidents
- Terrorist attacks
- Violent deaths
- Personal assaults such as rape, or other situations in which the person felt extreme fear, horror, or helplessness

Signs and symptoms can include:

- Flashbacks, nightmares or frightening thoughts, especially when exposed to anything reminiscent of the traumatic event
- Sweating and shaking
- Avoidance of reminders of the event and a refusal to discuss the experience
- Numbness and feelings of estrangement or detachment from others
- Inability to remember aspects of the traumatic event
- Decreased interest in life
- Increased consciousness of one's own mortality
- Flight/fight syndrome
- Problems with concentration
- Problems with sleeping
- Irritability or outbursts of anger
- Hyper-vigilance and alertness to possible danger
- Re-experiencing the traumatic event
- Feelings of guilt
- Long-term behavioural effects
- Alcohol abuse

- Drug dependency
- Failed relationships/divorce
- Severe depression, anxiety disorders or phobias
- Chronic illness headaches, stomach upsets, dizziness, chest pain and general aches and pains, together with a weakened immune system
- Employment problems

Treatment

Your GP may feel that you would benefit from seeing a counsellor, a community psychiatric nurse, a psychologist or a psychiatrist.

For treatment to be effective, it is important that you and your family understand that PTSD is a medically recognised anxiety disorder that happens to some people after an extremely traumatic experience.

PTSD is often treated with psychotherapy, medication, or a combination of the two.

Therapies can include:

- Cognitive-behavioural therapy (CBT)
- Eye movement desensitisation and reprocessing (EMDR)

In terms of what you can do for yourself or a loved one who is suffering from PTSD the following is a guide:

- Visit the GP
- Keep a normal routine
- Plenty of exercise/activities
- If helping a loved one – don't just say 'I'm here if you need anything'. Be pro-active and knock on their door, take them shopping, ask them questions.

Distance and it's effect on PTSD.

Hatred and aggression causes us far more trauma than the threat of danger itself.

For example:

During World War 2, survivors of concentration camps suffered a great deal more with PTSD than the survivors of aerial bombings.

The victims of concentration camps had to look their sadistic captors in the face knowing that another human being denied their humanity and hated them enough to personally slaughter them and their families as though they were nothing more than animals.

Civilian bombing victims were put at just as much threat of danger as the camp victims, but, the distance allowed them to deny that anyone was personally trying to kill them.

PTSD has a large spectrum and even if you are involved in a relatively minor incident such as a road rage argument, you may well find that you experience some or minor versions of the signs and symptoms described above. It is less likely to cause long term problems, however, the treatment and self-help should always be considered.

Realistic training and/or regular exposure to personal aggression – perhaps working as a Police Officer for example – can condition someone to be less susceptible to PTSD in similar circumstances, although this is not guaranteed of course.

Group Think

Group think is a little bit like having blinkers on.

When you train in a specific group in a specific way, it is likely that you will all begin to think that the way you do things is the only way.

For example, training in a specific martial arts system with a group of people who all enjoy it, will likely lead to all members of the group 'attacking' each other in the same (often proscribed) way. This can lead to the belief that this is how ALL people attack, when of course this is not the case.

For example, when training in Karate, it may be that you 'attack' your partner with a reverse punch. Your partner will then learn how to defend against a Karate reverse punch, but nothing else.

This 'Group think' can be prevented by:

- Mixing up your training partners
- Pressure testing techniques you have been taught
- Talk and train with people who have real world experience of violence
- Train in other systems
- Don't ask someone to attack you in a certain way when trying to test yourself or a technique

A good instructor will use new students to attack in demonstrations. This way, the new student has no idea of how they are expected to behave and as such will behave naturally and not in a 'set manner' which is easy to predict. There is no merit or value in defending against a pre-determined movement, aside from learning basics.

Essentials:
- 'Group think' is a bad habit as a result of insular training and breeds a false sense of confidence

To prevent this:
- Mix up your training partners
- Pressure test techniques you have been taught
- Talk and train with people who have real world experience of violence
- Train in other systems
- Don't ask someone to attack you in a certain way when trying to test yourself or a technique

Technique specific exercises:
Scenario training is particularly good as there will be no proscribed or pre-determined movements.

'Conflict immersion' is also a great drill which essentially is a mini scenario and cuts out thinking time. The student has a blindfold put on and music is played so they are unaware of where the 'subject' is approaching from. The student has no idea what the attack will be. As soon as the blindfold is removed, the 'subject' carries out the attack. This means the student is immediately 'in' the scenario and has no option but to carry out an immediate defence.

Cross training in other systems is really beneficial. However, it is important to have a good foundation in your main style or system and THEN cross train to develop certain areas of your own self defence arsenal and/or find alternatives that suit you better. For example, you may train in a self-defence system that covers a wide spectrum of defensive tactics and fighting skill, but you don't feel your punching is very strong. As such, you may decide to take some boxing classes to develop this area.

LEVEL 6: COMBATIVES

Superman punch

What is it?
A long distance hand strike.

Why do it?
This strike is effective at kicking distance so can come as a surprise to the subject. It can also allow you to gain superior power.

How to execute the technique:
From fighting stance, drive your rear knee forwards propelling you forwards.

Your lead foot should leave the floor slightly to aide this propulsion and land back down as the base leg. Your lead leg is effectively hopping forwards.

As you jump forwards with this movement, your rear arm should be pulled backwards slightly.

As you land, your rear arm carries out a cross punch. However, your upper body leans forwards as your rear leg gets sent back behind you to balance this additional leaning forwards of your upper body. This movement and the propulsion forwards is what gives you the additional distance and power.

This movement, whilst simple, requires good coordination and full commitment – hence why it is taught in Level 6.

If you struggle with this strike, try to think of the technique as a 'jumping punch'. Then refine it.

Essentials:
- Drive your rear knee forwards and jump a little – hopping forwards with your lead leg
- Your rear arm pulls back slightly
- As you land, your rear leg drives backwards as you execute a rear cross variation by leaning your upper body forwards

Open hand to the back of the head

What is it?
A palm of the hand strike to the back of the subject's head.

Why do it?
The strike causes a great deal of pain and concussive force. It is excellent for distraction. It also adheres to the old saying (mentioned when discussing open hand vs. closed fist strikes) 'soft to hard and hard to soft' meaning that one should strike a hard surface such as the skull with a soft body weapon such as an open palm and a soft surface such as the solar plexus with a hard body weapon such as a closed fist.

Lastly, the body weapon fits the target area well.

How to execute the technique:
Bear in mind the danger of striking such a vulnerable target – this area effectively houses the brain stem. That said, different levels of power put into the strike will, of course, cause different levels of injury.

The strike tends to be more effective when carried out in multiple short rapid strikes rather than a full extension power strike.

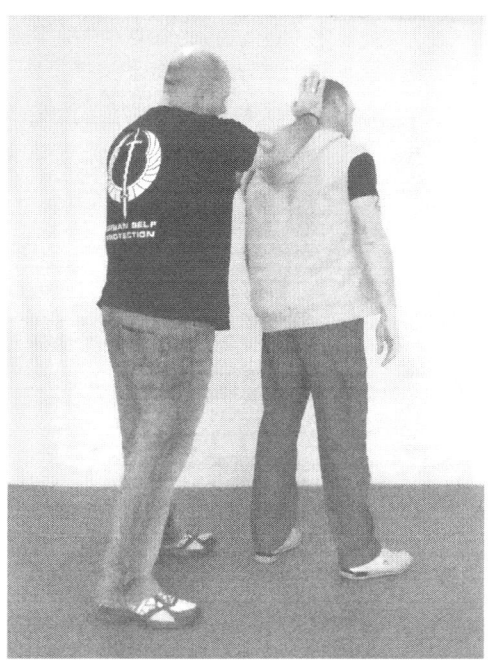 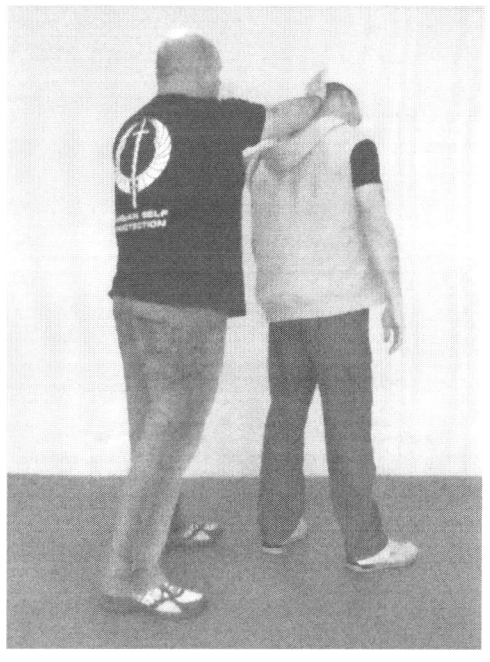

The strike is simply a matter of carrying out short sharp strikes with the palm of your hand to the lower part of the rear of the subject's head, from an appropriate position during a confrontation. This could be standing, on the ground, as part of a counter attack when moving outside the subject's fighting arc, or during a breakaway technique.

Essentials:
- Heel of the palm
- Repeated short sharp strikes
- Target the lower part of the back of the subject's head

Technique specific exercises:
A realistic training dummy is a fantastic way to practice this. If practicing on a training partner, reduce the power by 'pulling' the strike to just a light touch.

Chin jab

What is it?
A palm of the hand pushing strike to the subject's chin in order to control and move them.

Why do it?
This technique is most likely to be used when you want to quickly take control of a subject who is displaying 'Warning' and/or 'Danger signs'.

It's quick, simple and puts the subject off balance at the same time as disrupting their vision.

How to execute the technique:
When you make the decision to execute this technique, distract the subject with a question if appropriate, then lunge quickly forwards, reaching your lead hand around their waist (under their arm) and into the small of their back, whilst simultaneously thrusting the palm heel of your rear hand under their chin, fingers vertical.

Push their chin up and back and use your arm around their waist to control how far back they lean.

Hold them at the balance tipping point and either walk them backwards out of harm's way, or continue to push the chin back and take them to the floor.

Essentials:
- Ask a distraction question if appropriate
- Lunge forwards quickly
- Thrust the palm of your hand under the subject's chin
- Simultaneously reach around the subject's waist
- Get them to their balance tipping point
- Then control them or take them down

Technique specific exercises:
A scenario where the 'subject' is arguing with the student's 'friend' begins to get heated. The student steps in when the subject displays 'Warning/Danger' signs and controls the subject.

Be mindful of your training partner's teeth, tongue and neck when executing this technique in training.

Testi tap

What is it?
A groin strike using the back of the hand.

Why do it?
This technique can drop the subject to their knees as it is a whipping like strike to the groin. It can also be used quite covertly and without telegraphing.

How to execute the technique:
When you make the decision to execute this technique, distract the subject with a question if appropriate, then, with your fingertips pointing downwards and the back of your hand towards the subject's groin, flick your hand quickly in a whipping motion, with the fingernails being the end of the 'whip'.

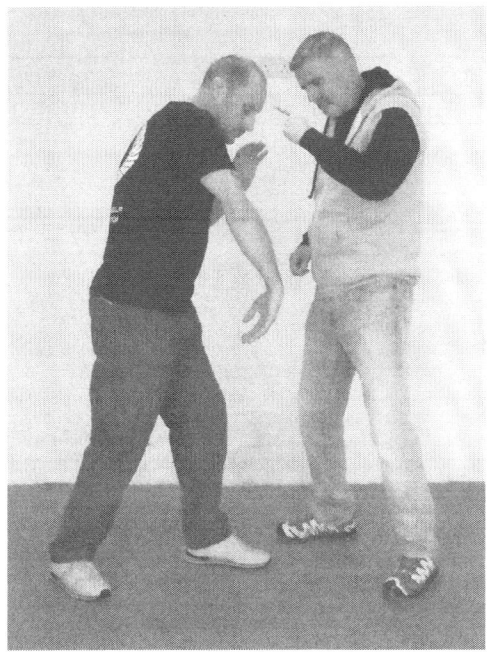 

Aim in and slightly upwards. Recoil quickly.

Essentials:
- Ask a distraction question if appropriate
- Fingers pointing down
- Back of hand towards subject
- Flick in a whipping motion
- Fingernails are the striking surface

Technique specific exercises:
Obviously practice on a pad. However, you can practice follow ups from this pre-emptive strike such as sleeper holds, double arm restraint or throat control for example by simply striking your training partner's thigh to simulate striking the groin, then execute the follow up move. Example overleaf.

Reverse wrist lock

What is it?
A control and restraint technique using the subject's wrist.

Why do it?
This technique can be used to control a subject using pain compliance. It is a low level use of force. This method relies on turning the wrist in one direction, however, USP also teaches the 'Cavalier lock', which requires the wrist to be turned in the other direction – as such, there is a contingency plan should the technique be applied incorrectly.

However, remember that trying to apply any control or restraint technique on a combative subject is incredibly difficult. This is for someone who is either compliant, weaker than you (even if that's by way of intoxication) or after softening them up with other techniques and is usually only successful when used as a surprise tactic without hesitation. Hesitation usually ends up with resistance from the subject.

How to execute the technique:
The technique can be applied from various positions, but most commonly a lapel grab or when the subject simply has their hand at their side.

Imagine the subject has grabbed your left lapel with their right hand. Their knuckles are facing upwards.

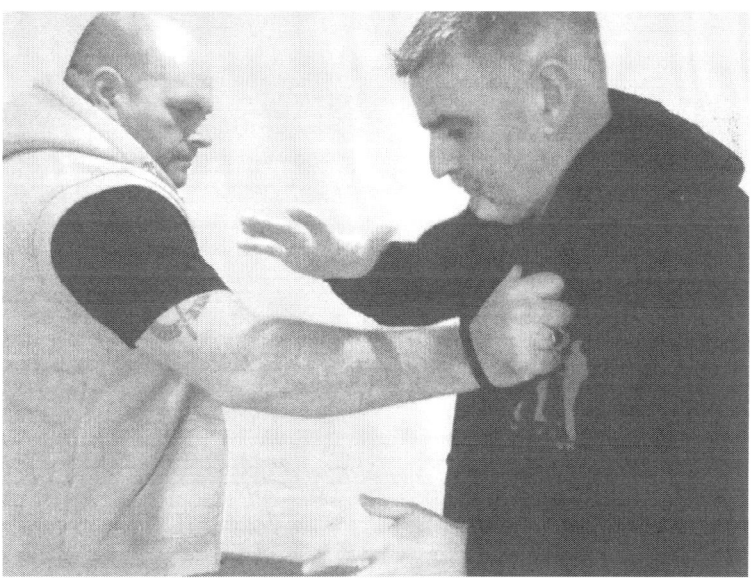

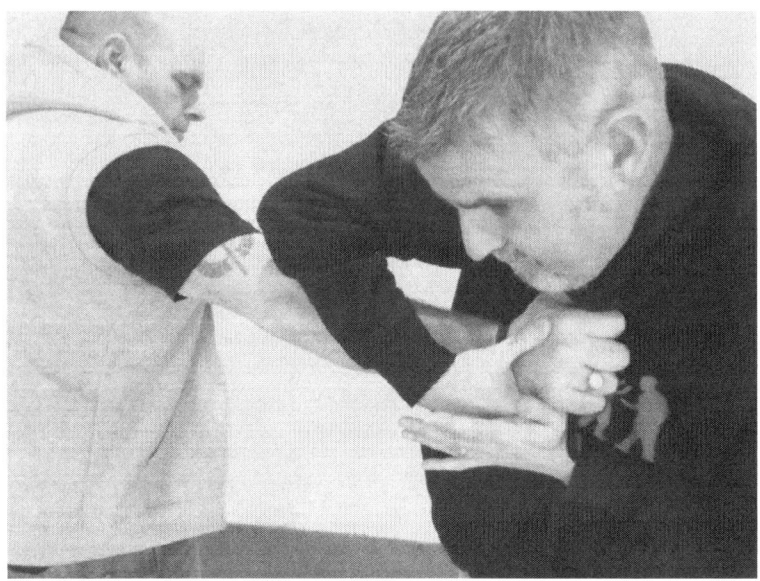

With your right hand, reach over the top of their right hand, placing the web of your right thumb across the back of their wrist, whilst hooking the little finger side of their right hand with your fingers.

Pull your right hand back slightly to roll the subject's little finger upwards (in this case clockwise).

Place the web of your left thumb also against the back of the subject's wrist and hook around the thumb side of their hand with your fingers.

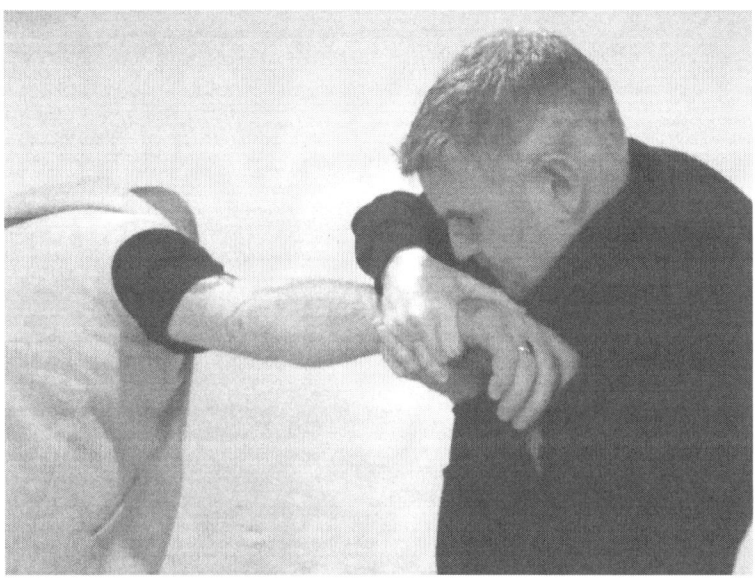

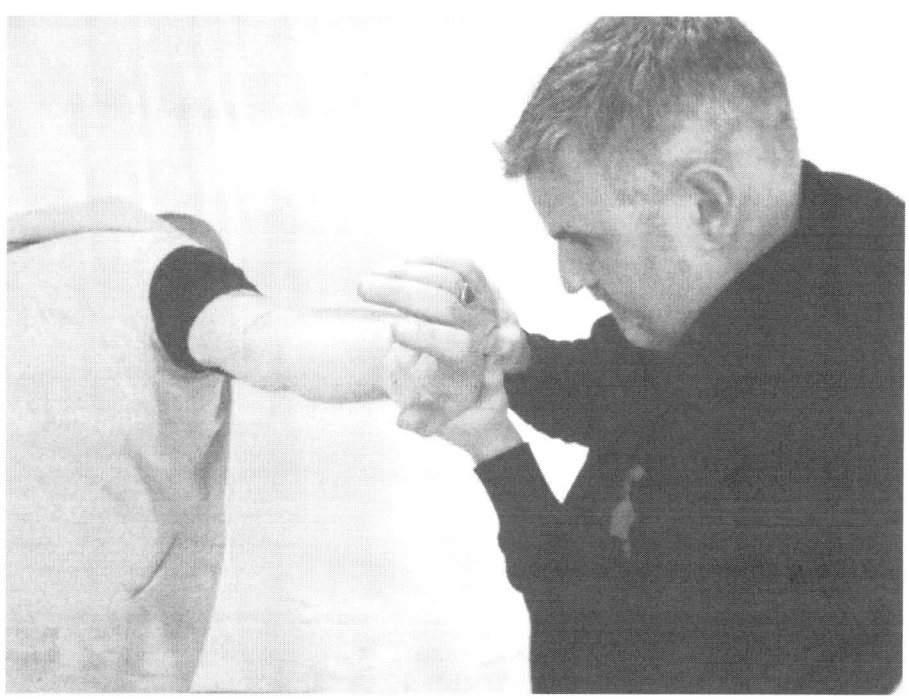

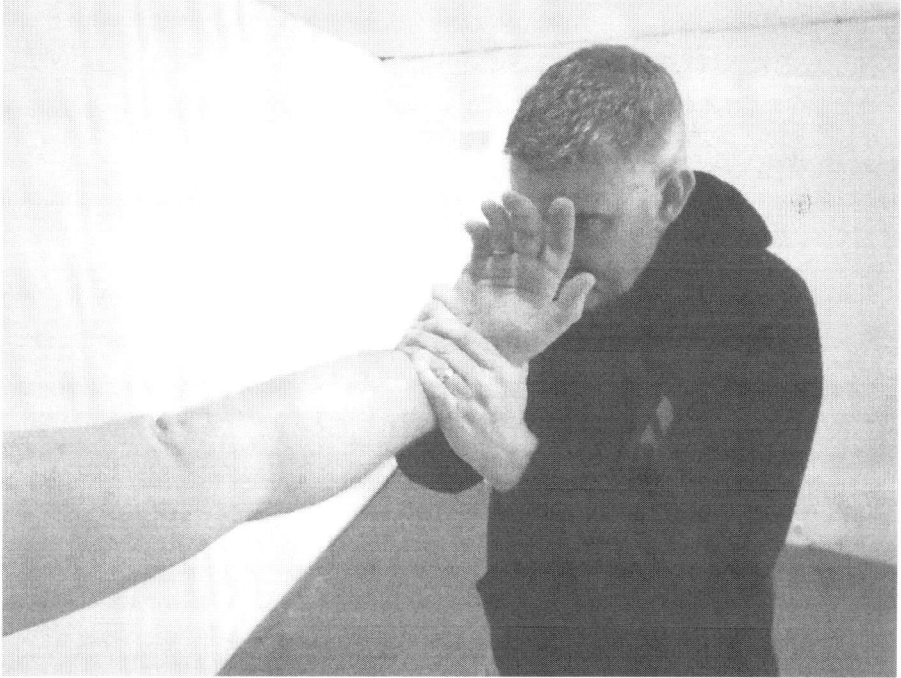

You will look as though you are 'choking' the subject's wrist. It is important that you do not simply turn their wrist using your fingertips and thumbs. You must maintain pressure with the full area of your hands, i.e. your palms must be in contact with the subject.

Grip tightly and continue turning in the same direction until the subject's right hand is palm uppermost.

Bend their wrist with your thumbs and thumb joint until you obtain pain compliance.

Hold them in this restraint or continue to bend the wrist to take the subject to the floor.

Remember this important note on pain compliance:

When you use a technique to cause pain to force the subject to comply, remember to give them verbal commands at the same time if possible.

When you cause pain, remember only to do so for a few seconds. If you leave the pain compliance technique on for too long, this can cause the subject to have an adrenaline rush (if they haven't already had one). This will dull the pain you are applying and give them the benefits of adrenaline such as additional strength etc.

So apply the technique for maximum of five seconds, then release it and apply again if required.

Essentials:
- Reach over the back of the subject's hand
- 'Choke' their wrist with both hands
- Turn it so their little finger moves upwards
- Continue turning until their palm faces upwards
- Bend their wrist to obtain pain compliance

Technique specific exercises:
Practice obtaining this wrist control from various positions.

Thumb lock

What is it?
A control and restraint technique using the subject's thumb and wrist.

Why do it?
This technique can be used to control a subject using pain compliance. It is a low level use of force. Once the technique is applied, it can be held with one hand, allowing the other hand to protect against head butting or to make an emergency phone call for example.

This is a complex motor skill hence why it is found in Level 6.

How to execute the technique:
The technique is applied from a 'Reverse wrist lock' or from 'Ground pin' position to transition them to standing whilst still under control.

Once you are in the correct position, you should grab the subject's thumb and thumb joint with your hand that is closest to the subject. Grab it as though it were a joy stick.

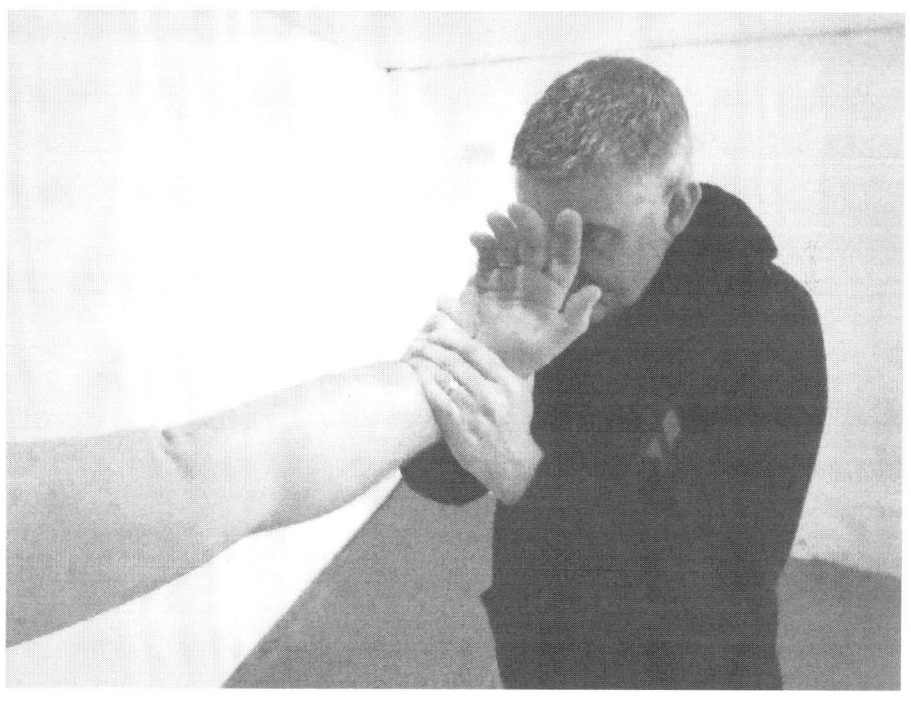

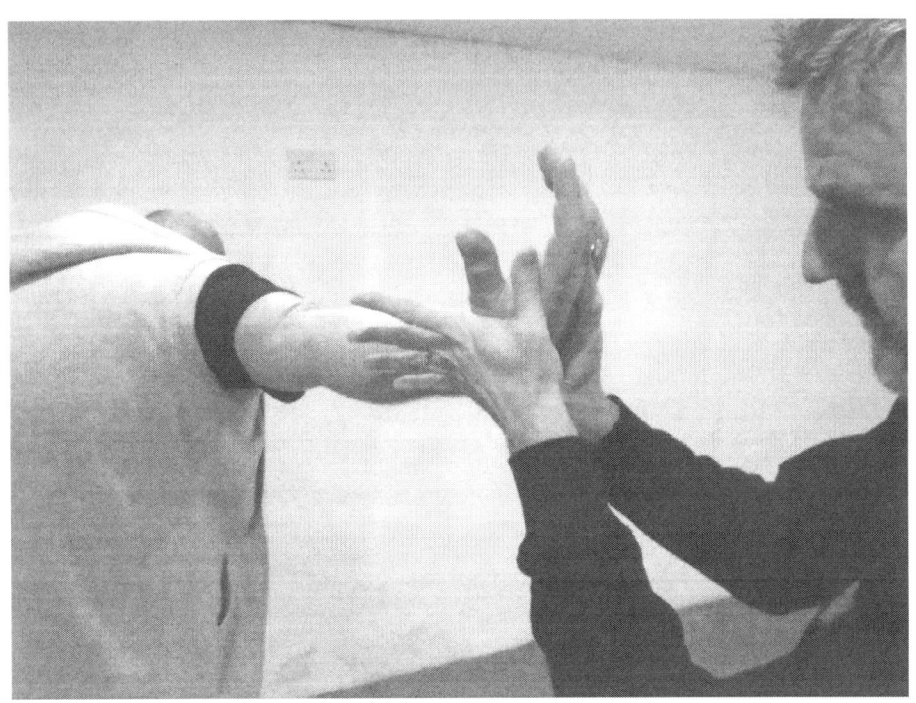

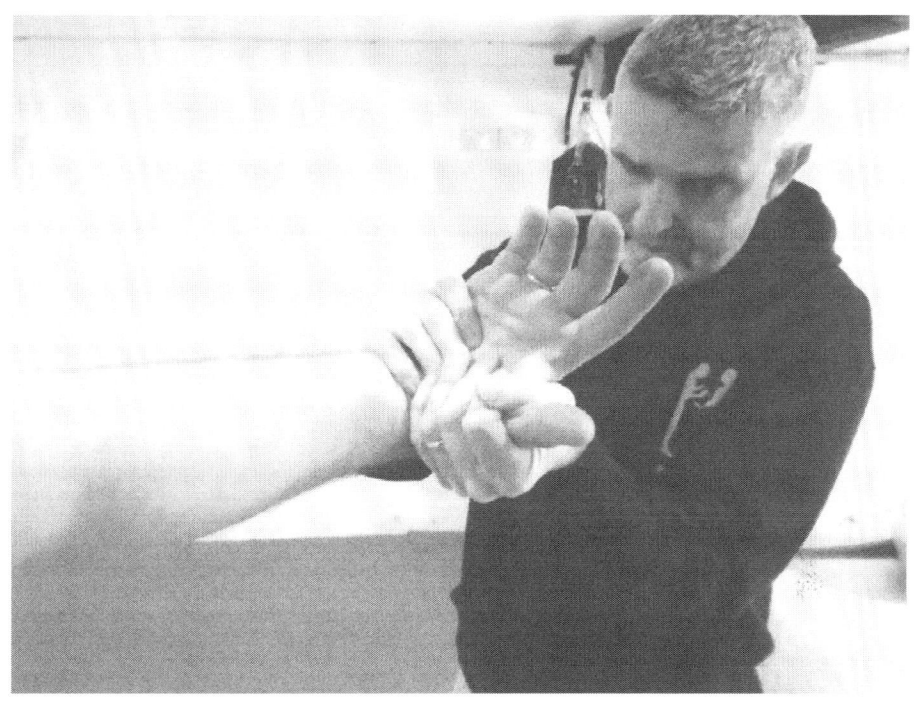

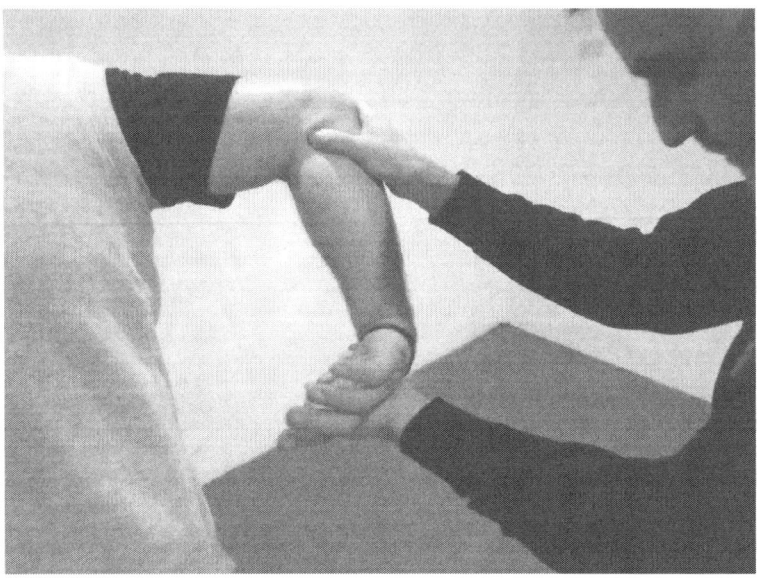

With this hand, turn their fingertips towards their body.

With your non-gripping hand, push against the inside of the subject's elbow so the arm bends.

At the same time, drive your gripping hand forwards, so the subject's arm folds underneath their armpit.

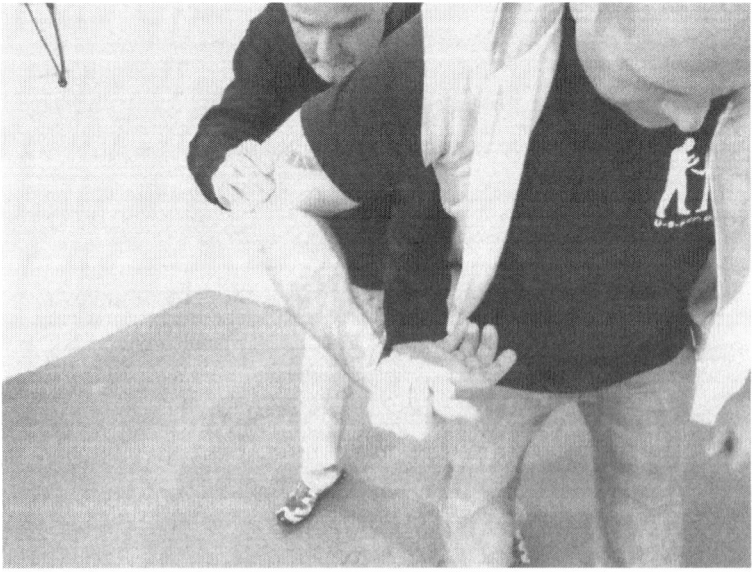

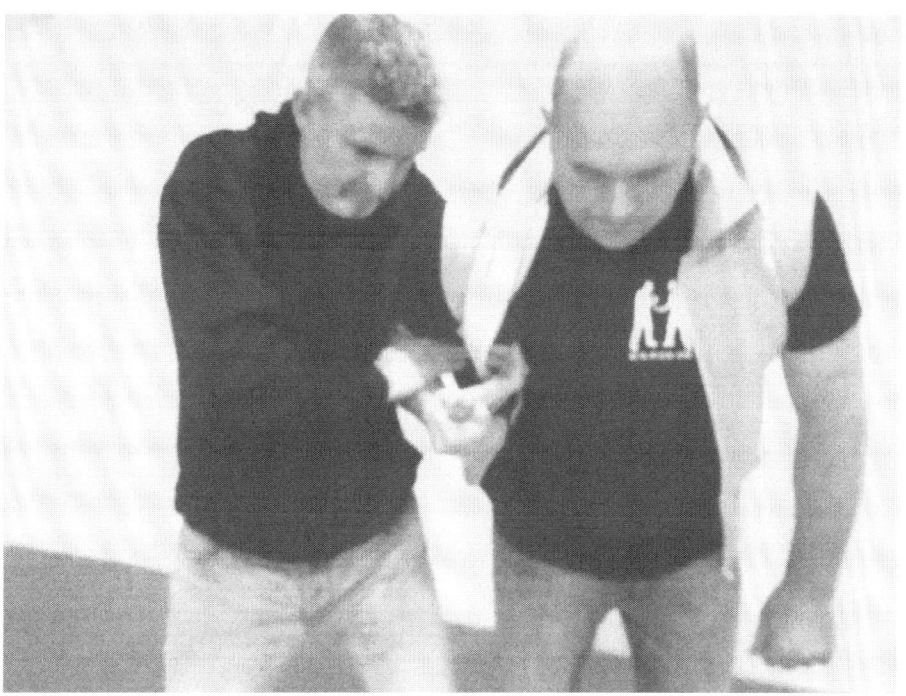

Tuck their elbow under your arm pit.

Pull your gripping hand backwards – it should still have hold of the thumb. The subject's fingertips should be pointed upwards.

Simply pull back on the subject's wrist to apply pain. Should this not work, use your free hand to grab the four fingers of the subject and turn them towards you.

Essentials:
- Begin from 'Reverse wrist lock' or 'Ground pin position'
- Grab the thumb and turn the subject's fingertips towards them
- Bend their elbow and fold their arm underneath their armpit
- Tuck their elbow under your armpit

Technique specific exercises:
Practice obtaining this wrist control from various positions.

Use of a guillotine choke

What is it?
A method of applying a neck lock with the subject bent forwards facing you – perhaps whilst they attempt to carry out a tackle.

Why do it?
The position the subject begins in is normally as a result of a very common attack – the tackle. It is natural to grab around a subject's head to try and control them. This technique is simply a method of refining this natural movement and making it as effective as possible.

How to execute the technique:
The subject is bent over, facing you, with their head close to the side of your hip.

Reach over their neck with your nearest arm.

Fold this arm so that your forearm is placed across the front of the subject's throat, with your thumb uppermost.

With your free hand, grab the little finger side of your hand.

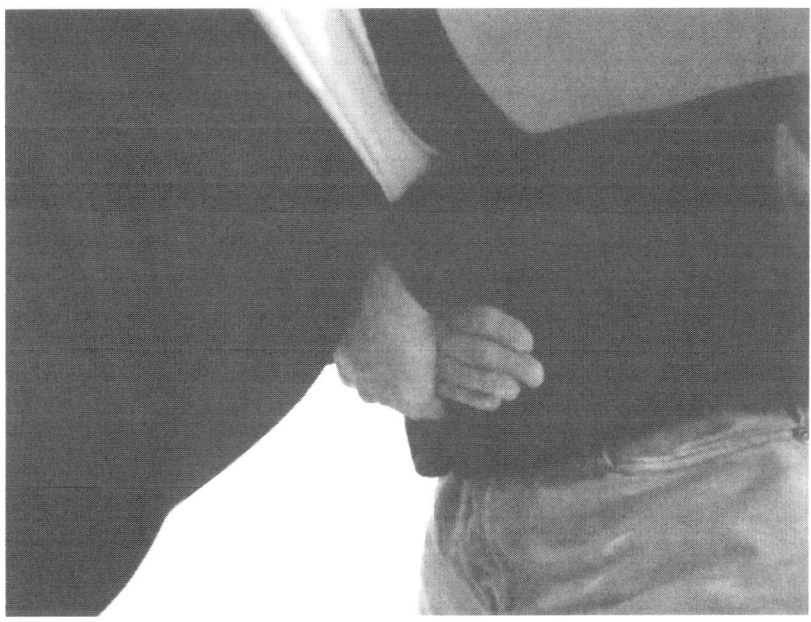

It is tempting to lean backwards to crank the subject's neck – whilst uncomfortable, this will not necessarily neutralise them. Instead, pull your forearm straight upwards against the subject's throat. This will depress their windpipe cutting off oxygen to the brain, rendering them unconscious within seconds if you have the hold on in the right position.

Essentials:
- Reach over the subject's neck
- Place your forearm, thumb uppermost, against the windpipe
- Pull your forearm upwards

Use of an 'air' headlock

What is it?
This is a method of applying a choke hold to the subject when you are behind them. It can be applied for control/restraint, pain compliance or to render them unconscious.

Why do it?
In a physical confrontation, it's a very natural act to grab someone around their head and neck. This gives a good deal of control of the body as most Martial Arts systems will tell you – "where the head goes, the body will follow".

With any physical defence technique, there is potential for injury to varying degrees and these, of course, need to be considered. However, potential injuries from neck holds are worthy of special mention.

There are, of course significant dangers to the subject when applying this technique. It is possible to damage their windpipe and/or prevent them from breathing which can lead to unconsciousness, brain damage or death. 'Blood headlocks' can also dislodge blood clots and cause various other serious conditions including pulmonary embolisms. The more serious injuries tend to be caused when applied with speed, maximum force and for longer periods of time.

That said, the body is quite robust and can take a certain amount of abuse without significant permanent injury. It must also be mentioned that the injuries described being caused, can be completely reasonable under the right circumstances.

The technique is simple to apply, but to make it effective there are some nuances.

How to execute the technique:
Slide your dominant hand under the chin of the subject, so their windpipe is in the middle of your forearm.

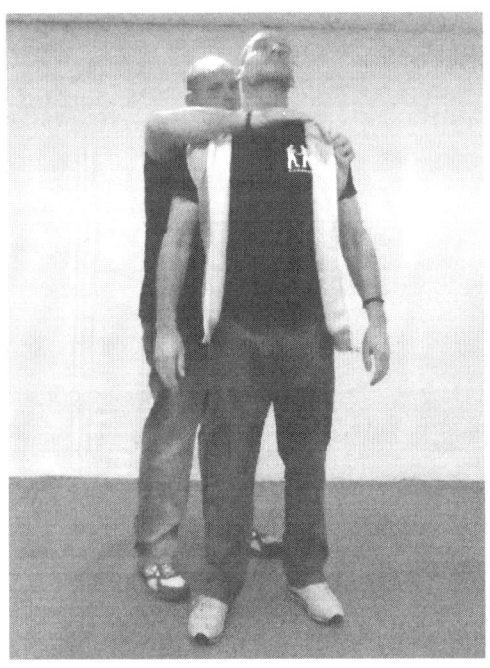 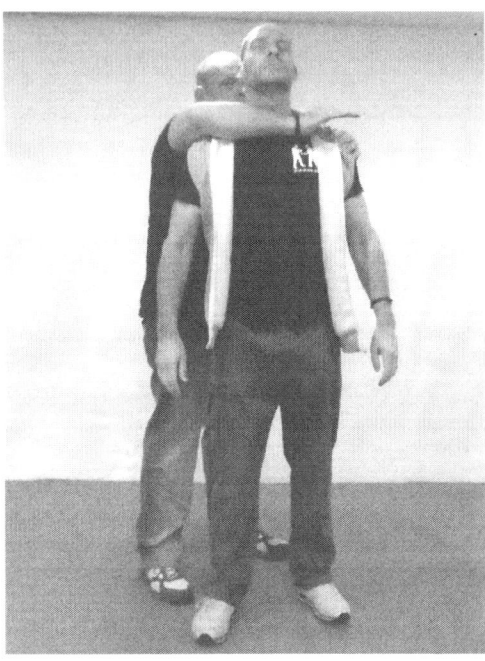

Your knuckles should be facing the sky and thumb towards you, so the bony part of your forearm is against the throat.

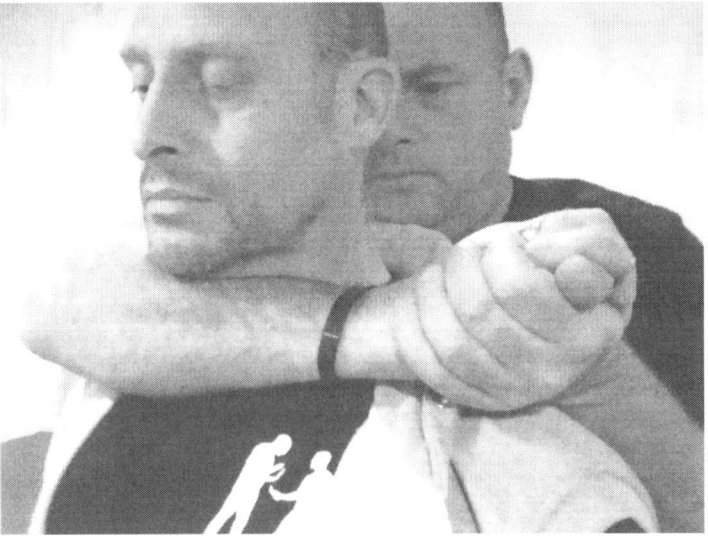

Place your non-dominant hand palm to palm with the other making a 'Gable grip' described previously.

The fingers of your dominant hand should wrap over the top of your other hand's thumb.

The fingers of the non-dominant hand should wrap over the little finger side of the dominant hand.

Your non-dominant hand should pull your other hand back towards you, whilst your dominant elbow should be pulled back towards you with the shoulder. This essentially puts a 'bar' (your forearm) across the subject's windpipe and both ends of the 'bar' are drawn backwards at the same time in order to maintain the pressure on the windpipe.

Inflate your chest in order to prevent any gaps for movement.

If you are using for control/restraint, then the pressure applied doesn't have to squeeze the windpipe – just applying light pressure should suffice.

If you are using it for pain compliance, then slow application until compliance is gained should be used.

If you are using this to render the subject unconscious, then the hold will need to be maintained for a period of time until they become unconscious. There are various estimates to how long this would take, but with the hold in the right place, it would be around the 10 second mark until consciousness is lost. The general rule is, the longer it's on, the longer they're out. Of course, the longer the hold is in place, the higher the risk of serious injury/death is to the subject too.

In most situations, the subject being rendered unconscious should be your cue to escape immediately. (If safe for you to do so, lay the subject down carefully in recovery position to prevent them from hitting the floor too hard or choking to death on their own vomit). However, they will likely regain consciousness in a few seconds, so there are some circumstances that may require you to maintain the hold, even until brain damage or death is caused. For example, perhaps the subject is suffering from drug induced psychosis and will immediately go on a rampage hurting or killing people when they come round. Or perhaps you have been injured and cannot escape.

Essentials:
- Slide your primary hand under the subject's chin, placing the bony part of the forearm across their throat
- Grab your own hands in a 'Gable grip'
- Pull backwards
- Inflate the chest
- Recovery position if safe to do so

Technique specific exercises:
This is best practiced on a realistic training dummy.

If used in sparring or any other training with a partner, the hold should ALWAYS be applied slowly, giving your partner the opportunity to tap out.

Use of a 'blood' headlock

What is it?
As with an 'Air headlock', this is a method of applying a choke hold to the subject when you are behind them. It can be applied for control/restraint, pain compliance or to render them unconscious.

Why do it?
As mentioned before, in a physical confrontation, it's a very natural act to grab someone around their head and neck.

With any physical defence technique, there is potential for injury to varying degrees and these, of course, need to be considered. However, potential injuries from neck holds are worthy of special mention.

There are, of course significant dangers to the subject when applying this technique. It is possible to damage their windpipe, prevent them from breathing which can lead to unconsciousness, brain damage or death. 'Blood headlocks' can also dislodge blood clots and cause various other serious conditions including pulmonary embolisms. The more serious injuries tend to be caused when applied with speed, maximum force and for longer periods of time.

That said, the body is quite robust and can take a certain amount of abuse without permanent injury. It must also be mentioned that the injuries described being caused, can be completely reasonable under the right circumstances.

The technique is simple to apply but, as with the 'Air headlock' to make it effective, there are some nuances.

How to execute the technique:
Slide your dominant hand under the chin of the subject until the crease of your elbow is in front of the subject's windpipe.

This will mean your bicep and forearm are placed against each of the two main carotid arteries on the side of the neck. The objective of this technique is to compress the arteries at the side of the neck.

As mentioned before, the mechanics of how a blood headlock renders someone unconscious are disputed:

Some say restricting the oxygenated blood to the brain is what causes unconsciousness. Others say that compressing the baroreceptors of the carotid artery, confuses the body into thinking it's blood pressure has risen. This causes a reflex which widens the brain's blood vessels with the intention of relieving high blood pressure. However, since no blood pressure increase has occurred, the reflex causes a dramatic decrease in the blood pressure to the brain, causing loss of consciousness.

Either way, it can cause unconsciousness in seconds.
Your knuckles should be facing the sky and thumb towards you.

Place your dominant hand on top of the bicep of your free arm.

Then place your free hand on the back of the subject's head, palm facing them. Keep your hand low on the back of their head so your fingers are less accessible.

 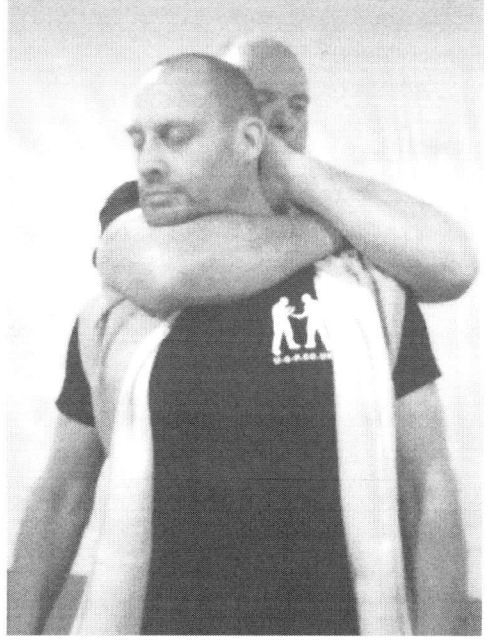

Constrict the muscles in your arms and inflate your chest in order to prevent any gaps for movement.

If you are using for control/restraint, then the pressure applied doesn't have to squeeze the neck – just applying light pressure should suffice.

If you are using it for pain compliance, then slow application until compliance is gained should be used.

If you are using this to render the subject unconscious, then the hold will need to be maintained for a period of time until they become unconscious. There are various estimates to how long this would take, but with the hold in the right place, it would be around the 10 second mark until consciousness is lost. The general rule is, the longer it's on, the longer they're out. Of course, the longer the hold is in place, the higher the risk of serious injury/death is to the subject too.

In most situations, the subject being rendered unconscious should be your cue to escape immediately. (If safe for you to do so, lay the subject down carefully in recovery position to prevent them from hitting the floor too hard or choking to death on their own vomit). However, they will likely regain consciousness in a few seconds, so there are some circumstances that may require you to maintain the hold, even until brain damage or death. For example, perhaps the subject is suffering from drug induced psychosis and will immediately go on a rampage hurting or killing people when they come round. Or perhaps you have been injured and cannot escape.

Releasing the hold slowly and steadily may reduce the risk of dislodging a blood clot – it allows the blood flow to gradually increase. Releasing quickly can cause a high pressure flow of blood which may be enough to dislodge a clot.

Essentials:
- Slide your dominant hand under the subject's chin, placing the crease of your elbow in front of the windpipe
- Grab the bicep of your free arm
- Place your free hand on the back of the subject's head
- Constrict the muscles in your arms
- Inflate the chest
- Recovery position if safe to do so

Technique specific exercises:
This is best practiced on a realistic training dummy.

If used in sparring or any other training with a partner, the hold should ALWAYS be applied slowly, giving your partner the opportunity to tap out.

Biting

What is it?
Using your teeth to bite the subject.

Why do it?
Biting someone is incredibly simple as the movement is something practiced daily when eating. It also causes a great deal of pain and can cause a subject to release you. If drawing blood, it can also have a psychological as well as physical effect on the subject. However, there are of course dangers with biting a subject. They include the risk of contracting blood borne illnesses. A second risk is that the subject will copy what you are doing. It is often the case when something is effective, the subject will retaliate in kind.

How to execute the technique:
To reduce the risk of contracting illness, do not bite fully and only bite on the subject's clothing which may act as a barrier should blood be drawn.

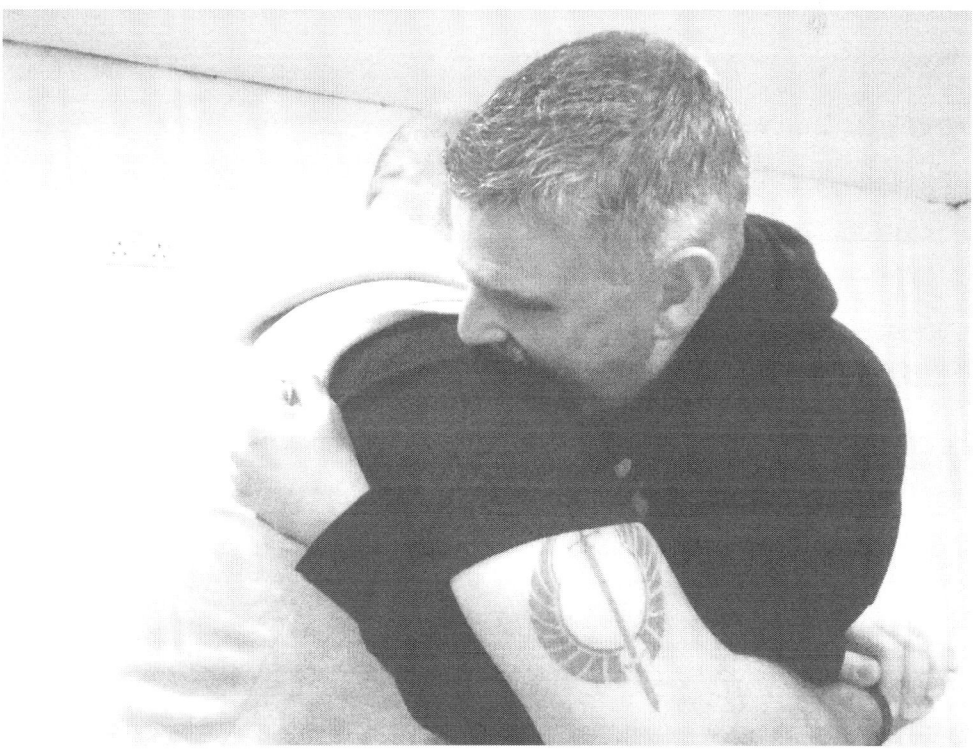

However, biting fully and drawing blood is valid if you are in danger of dying anyway.

If you do get blood or other body fluids in your mouth, spit it out and rinse your mouth out with water – obviously do not swallow the water or the body fluids.

Remember, blood may lead to identifying your subject through DNA analysis. As such consider safely retaining blood stained clothing for the Police. However, never take risks with your health by retaining the blood in your mouth or on your skin in order to help identify a subject. Your safety must come first.

Essentials:
- Do not bite fully
- Bite on clothing
- Spit any blood out immediately
- Rinse mouth out with water
- Go straight to hospital

Technique specific exercises:
If used in sparring or any other training with a partner, making a short, sharp 'barking' noise, can represent a bite – this allows them to react realistically and allows you to train the technique safely.

Spitting

What is it?
Spitting saliva into the subject's face.

Why do it?
Spitting is a disgusting act and can quickly escalate a confrontation. However, it can be used as an effective distraction technique.

How to execute the technique:
Make sure you spit quickly without telegraphing.

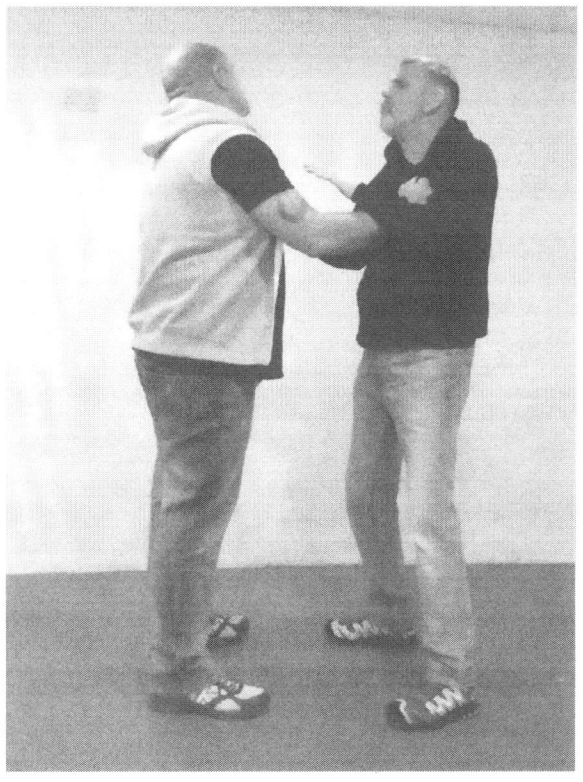

Spit towards the subject's face only. Spitting anywhere else will unlikely have any distraction effect at all.

Essentials:
- Do not telegraph
- Spit only at the face

Technique specific exercises:
If used in sparring or any other training with a partner, making a spitting noise can represent the act itself – this allows them to react realistically and allows you to train the technique safely and without actually spitting at your training partner.

Throat control and twist

What is it?
This is a higher level of force variation on the throat control, which attempts to damage the windpipe.

Why do it?
Grabbing someone's throat is quite a natural action and is very easy. It can cause the subject to panic as it is an aggressive act and the throat is a very sensitive area. By causing damage to the windpipe, the subject is likely to stop their attack.

How to execute the technique:
Grab the subject around the wind pipe with your thumb on one side and your fingers on the other.

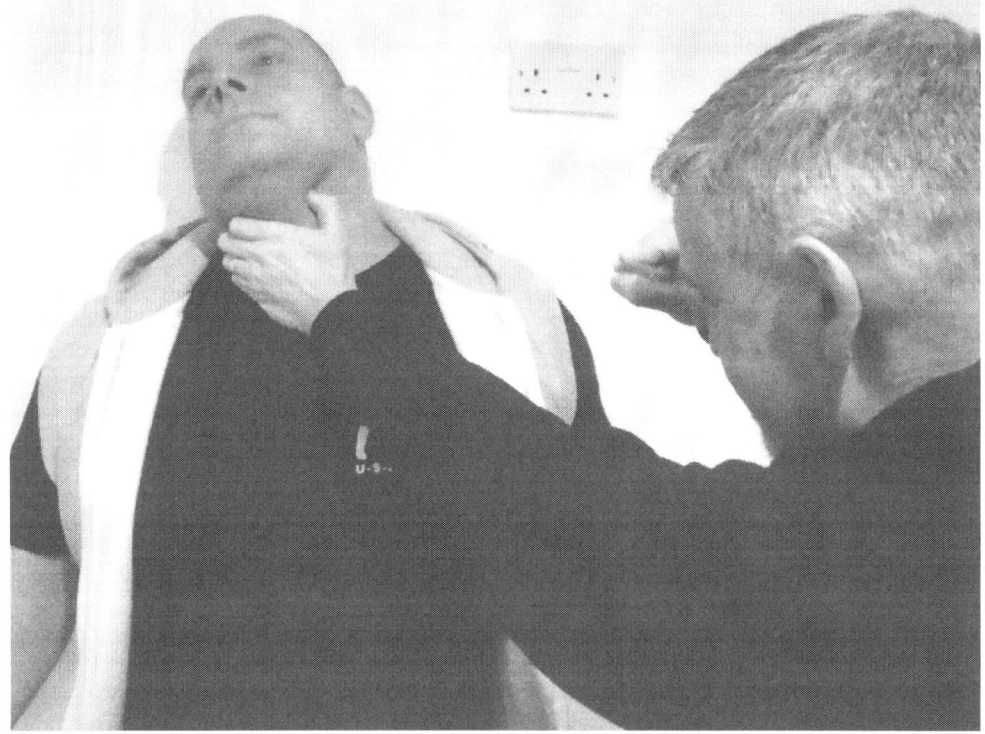

Squeeze the wind pipe tightly and yank it side to side violently.

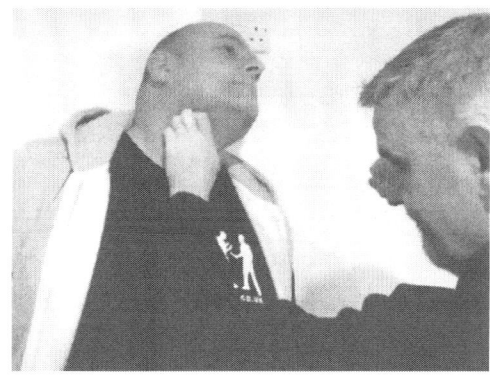 

Essentials:
- Grab the windpipe with one hand, thumb one side, fingers the other
- Squeeze the windpipe
- Yank side to side

Technique specific exercises:
The side of a focus pad can be used to grab and practice with, as it is similar in size and shape to a windpipe. It goes without saying that this should not be practiced on a live training partner.

Blitzing

What is it?
This is a high level force tactic whereby the subject is overwhelmed with rapid, aggressive multiple attacks.

Why do it?
This technique is a force multiplier as it can be executed effectively in various positions by people of all shapes and sizes. It overwhelms the subject's senses with multiple short, sharp, aggressive attacks aimed at the subject's face and neck to cause maximum distraction.

How to execute the technique:
This tactic can employ many different attacks. However, the most common and effective attacks to the face and neck are:

- Thumb thrust
- Eye poke
- Claw
- Throat twist
- Head twist
- Reverse head twist
- Ear grab
- Lip grab
- Biting
- Spitting
- Elbow strikes
- Hammer fists
- Open hand strikes
- 'Barking' (shouting) directly into the subject's ear

Essentially, the attacks should instantly follow each other without a pause, maintaining the pressure and aggression on the subject. It will require experimentation to ascertain what attacks follow each other well.

You should move from one attack to the next without chambering the body weapon. For example, a forward hammer fist with the right hand, could fold straight into a right forward elbow followed immediately by a claw strike with the right hand.

You should 'lock on' to the subject and keep them close to you whilst moving out of their fighting arc.

You must be as aggressive as possible to overwhelm the subject and ensure there is no pause in conflict.

The following is an example:

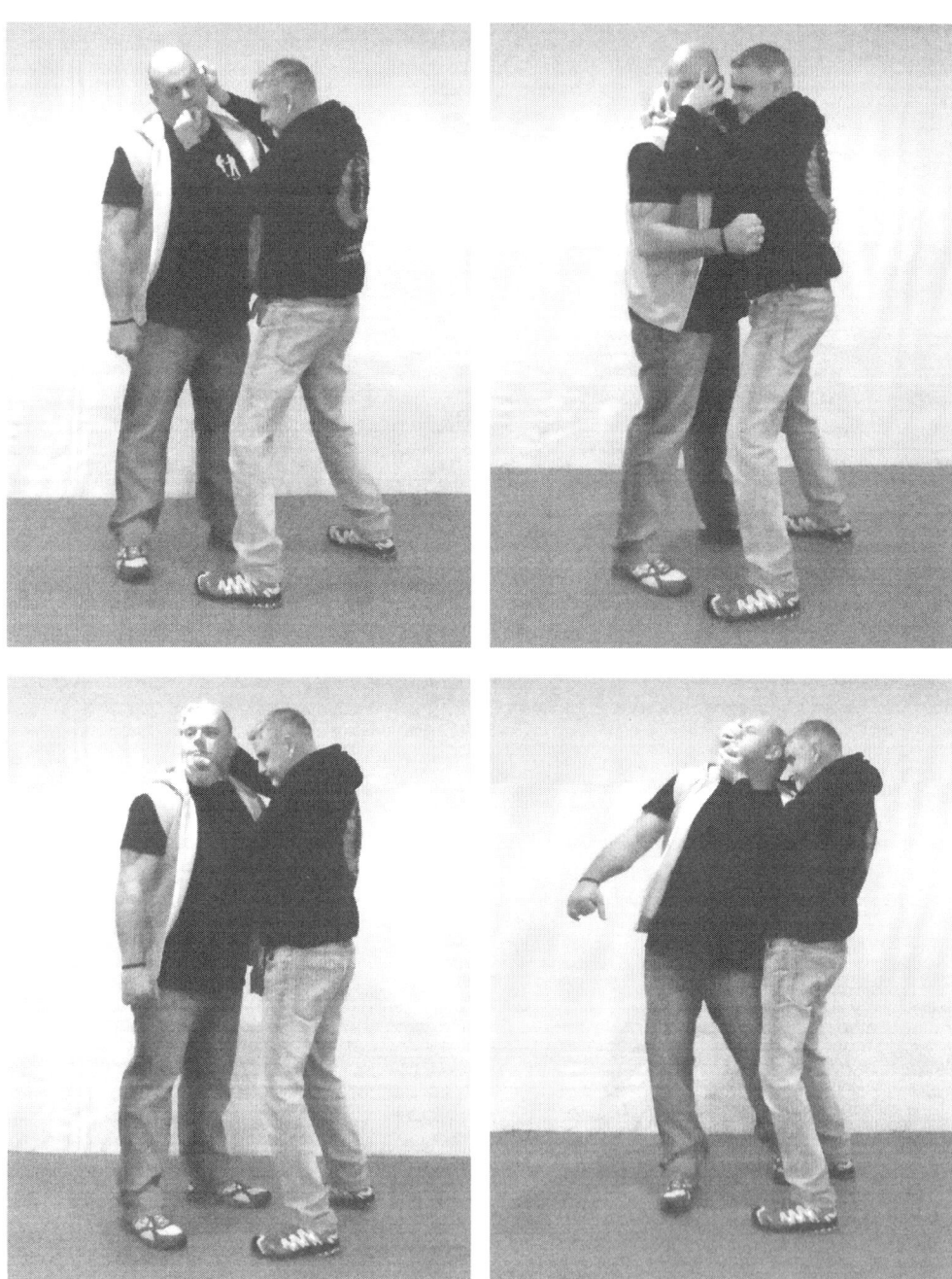

This technique should keep the subject stuck in the OO area of the OODA loop as the rapid attacks prevent them from making a decision and acting.

Essentials:
- Lock on
- Keep the subject close
- Move outside their fighting arc
- Do not chamber
- Move straight from one short sharp attack to the next
- Focus attacks on the face and neck

Technique specific exercises:
This can be practiced with a slow light touch on a training partner and at full speed on a realistic training mannequin.

COMBINATIONS

Triple rear roundhouse kick

What is it?
This is a rapid repetition of the rear roundhouse kick.

Why do it?
This combination simply teaches how to carry out the same strike multiple times with power and speed.

How to execute the technique:
Execute a rear roundhouse kick as per normal.

Retract the foot to the floor before executing the next. However, it is not necessary to bring the foot all the way back to fighting stance. You may retract to a square on position. The reason this is viable is because of the speed of the attack – the subject should not have time to attack your groin, so a bladed stance is not necessary and will slow down your combination.

As your foot touches the floor upon retraction, it should 'bounce' off the floor to carry out the second kick. Of course this is repeated for the third kick with the exception that the final retraction should return you to a fighting stance.

The combination should be fast and aggressive.

Essentials:
- 3 rear roundhouse kicks
- Fast and aggressive
- Retract the foot each time, but not to a bladed fighting stance, with the exception of the final kick where you DO return to fighting stance

Multiple skip knees

What is it?
This is a method of changing positions in order to carry out multiple rear knee strikes.

Why do it?
It allows you to control and move the subject off balance and repeat powerful knee strikes with a degree of randomness that prevents the subject having the opportunity to ascertain a pattern of attack making it harder for them to counter attack. It keeps them in the OODA loop in a similar way that 'Blitzing' does.

How to execute the technique:
From a clinch position, quickly switch into the opposite stance.

As soon as you land in the switched stance, execute a rear knee strike.

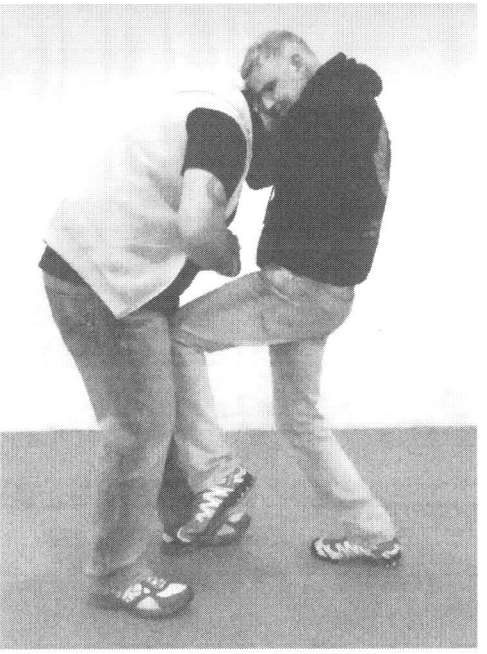

It maybe that you carry out two knee strikes, then skip and carry out another two with the opposite leg and so on.

You may also consider moving the subject between sets of knee strikes. Whilst you have the subject in a tight gripped 'Proper clinch', step back with your lead leg and use the momentum to twist your hips and upper body to follow. This will allow you to yank the head of the subject to a different position. Then carry out another set of knee strikes and/or skip knees. This will disorientate the subject and make it much harder to defend against your strikes.

328

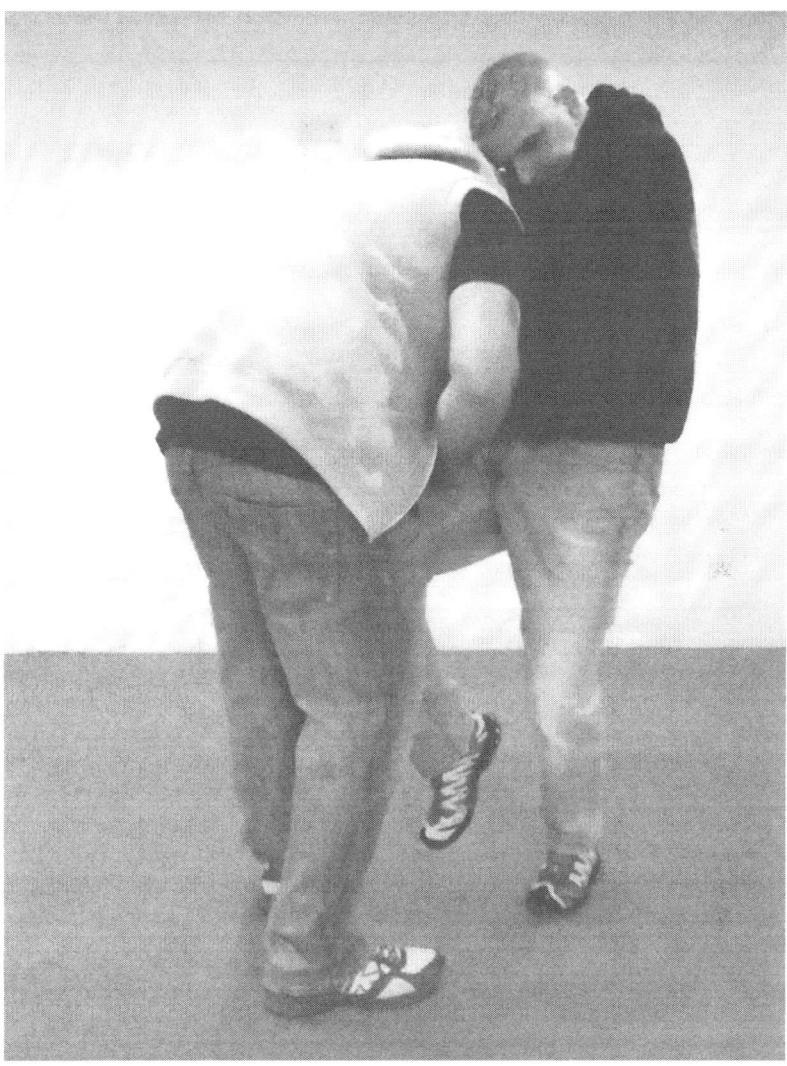

Essentials:
- Switch quickly to opposite stance and execute a rear knee strike from the new position
- Keep the subject guessing rather than too many repetitions of the same strike
- Move the subject by swinging your lead leg back and yanking them around in the same direction between sets of knee strikes/skip knees

Lead roundhouse kick, cross

What is it?
This is a kick, punch, combination.

Why do it?
This combination uses several fighting principles –

- Using a weaker, but quick strike to distract as a set up for a more powerful blow.

- Attacking low to draw the subject's mind to this area and then following up with a high attack to keep them guessing.

It also teaches range changes and the 'marriage of gravity' principle.

How to execute the technique:
Execute a lead roundhouse kick.

As your kicking foot lands, execute a cross punch.

Essentials:
- Execute the cross punch at the same time that your kicking foot lands

Cross, lead hook, rear roundhouse kick

What is it?
This is a punching and kicking combination.

Why do it?
This combination teaches broken rhythm and awkward range changing.

How to execute the technique:
Execute a cross punch.

'Step n drag' forwards and execute a lead hook punch.

Execute a rear roundhouse kick, modifying it to the position of your subject. Often stepping out further to the side, or even slightly backwards will help modify the kick enough to be able to strike the correct target area even if the subject is too close for a normal rear roundhouse kick.

Essentials:
- 'Step n drag' to close the range for the hook punch
- Modify your kick to allow you to execute it even if the subject is in an awkward position

Skip roundhouse kick, roundhouse knee

What is it?
This is a kick/knee combination.

Why do it?
This combination allows you to adjust your position to use a more powerful strike and then close the distance and follow up quickly with a second powerful strike. It also teaches you to make quick decisions and adapt to the subject's various positions/movement.

How to execute the technique:
Execute a skip roundhouse kick.

If the subject is beginning to move backwards when you kick, then you should land forwards and execute a roundhouse knee with the opposite leg.

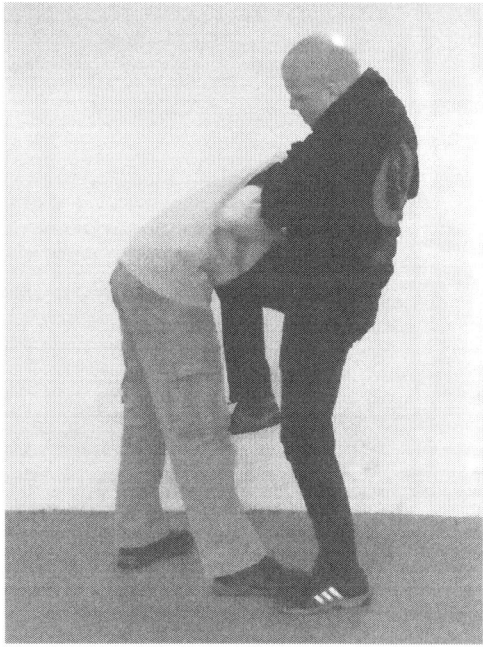

However, if the subject isn't moving backwards when you kick, then you should retract the kicking foot and allow it to 'bounce' off the ground straight into a rear roundhouse knee with the same leg.

Essentials:
- If the subject is moving backwards, land forwards and use opposite leg for the knee strike
- If the subject isn't moving backwards, retract the kicking leg and use it again to execute the roundhouse knee

Technique specific exercises:
Your training partner should hold a kick shield for the initial kick and either move backwards for the knee strike or stay put. They should not tell you if they are going to stay put or move backwards, you will need to quickly ascertain this and adjust the combination to suit.

Rear knee, rear roundhouse kick

What is it?
This is a knee/kick combination following the subject as they move backwards.

Why do it?
It is quite possible that when you execute a rear forward knee strike, the subject is forced backwards. If this happens, the range of course changes and this combination allows you to 'chase' the subject with a further powerful strike.

How to execute the technique:
Execute a rear forward knee strike and retract the leg back to a fighting stance.

As the subject moves backwards, execute a rear roundhouse kick.

Essentials:
- After the knee strike, retract the leg
- Use the same leg to carry out the rear roundhouse kick

Technique specific exercises:
Your training partner should hold a kick shield for the initial strike and move backwards for the second strike.

Demonstration of your own combinations 5-10 strikes, with defender and subject at various distances and in various positions

What is it?
This is a combination of your own creation where you start in various positions and at various distances from the subject, who is also in various positions.

Why do it?
Creating your own combinations, allows you to fit the system together around your strengths and natural reactions. It allows you to experiment with what works and doesn't work. It improves coordination adaptability and aggression and turns set combinations into realistic dynamic counter attacks.

With various positions and distances, you will be able to develop your adaptability for counter striking in a wider spectrum of possible scenarios.

How to execute the technique:
As before, these combinations are of your own creation and can be different every time.

However, you will find certain combinations or parts thereof, being used repeatedly. This is fine as you are working with your natural reactions and strengths.

You may also find that you use the same strike several times in succession – e.g. a rear forward hammer fist three times. This is fine too. Just remember that too frequent repetitions of the same strike will allow the subject to predict your next move.

It is still important to experiment though.

Each combination should be:

- Aggressive
- Flow together well
- Be moving to the dead side of the fighting arc
- Attempt to use high and low attacks to create confusion in your subject
- Try to keep the combination constant and without any pauses or hesitations
- Remember the overall guiding principles and incorporate them:

(Danger)
Attack
Move
Scan
Breathe

Refer to the principles of striking/combinations set out at the start of the book to make sure that you maintain effectiveness.

You might start lying on the ground and the subject kneeling next to you at a distance of a foot away.

You might start facing away from the subject on your knees who is stood facing your back at a distance of 4 feet away.

Or you are both stood by a wall and the subject is stood to your side.

The variables to change during experimentation are:

- Your starting position
- The distance between you and the subject
- The position of the subject

The following is an example:

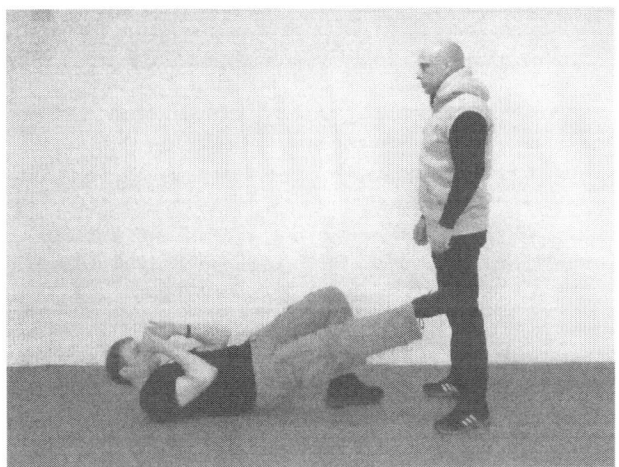
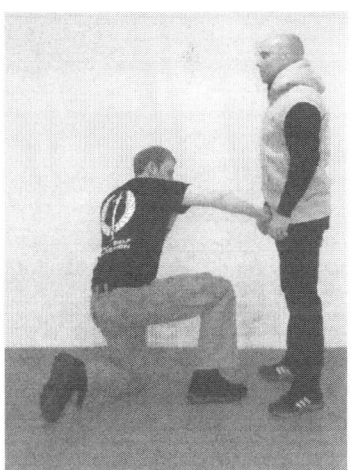

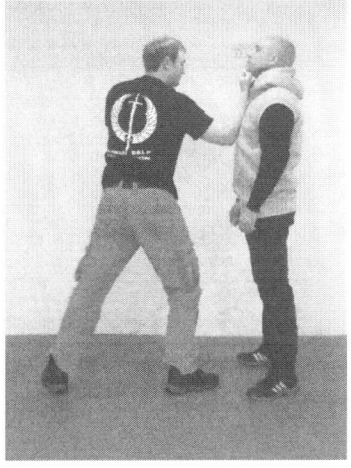

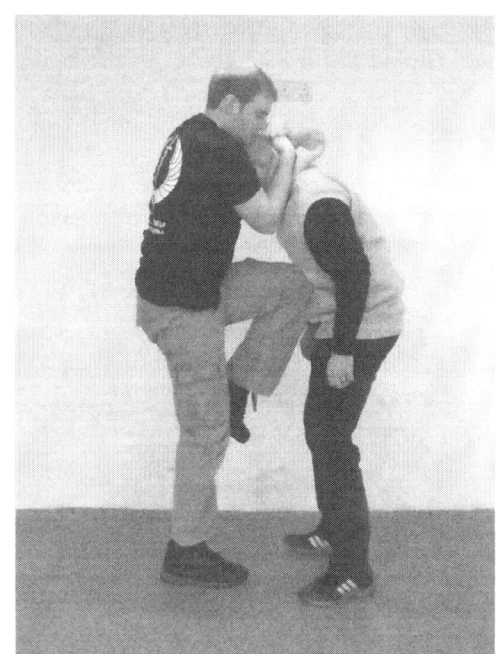

Essentials:
- Experiment
- Minimum of 5 strikes varying distance and starting positions
- Don't repeat strikes too frequently
- Be aggressive
- Move away and to the dead side of their fighting arc, keeping them inside yours
- Try to create combinations that naturally flow well together
- Avoid pauses
- Mix high and low attacks where possible
- Use DAMSB mnemonic

Technique specific exercises:
Creating good combinations for counter attacking is arguably one of the most important parts of USP. The reason we counter attack is so that once we have escaped a dangerous situation, we prevent it from happening again.

There are lots of different methods of practicing these combinations:

On a punch bag or realistic training mannequin, using a 'Marking drill', or 'Puppeting' drill.

Carrying out combinations in the air is another method – just make sure you are using your mind's eye as to where the targets on the subject are so you're not just throwing out wild strikes.

GROUND

Defence against a mounted headlock

What is it?
This is a breakaway technique against a subject who is in the mount position and has their arm around your neck in a headlock. You are face to face with the subject.

Why do it?
This is a very dangerous position as the subject has a positional advantage and it's likely you won't be able to see what's happening. Secondly, as the subject has their arm around your neck they may be able to choke you.

How to execute the technique:
You must use the table principle taught in Level 3.

Firstly, place your hand against the outside of the subject's elbow that has you in the head lock, to prevent the arm from being able to brace out when you execute your hip buck and roll. Tuck your elbow into your ribs.

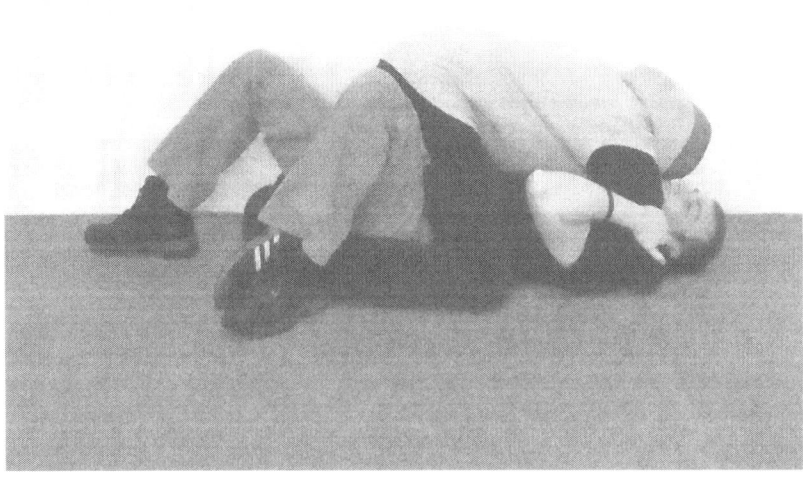

You must also hook the subject's foot on the same side as the elbow that you have blocked to prevent their leg from being able to brace out when you execute your hip buck and roll.

Keep your knees bent and feet planted on the floor.

Raise your hips violently off the ground and turn to the side you have already blocked.

The hip buck is to raise the subject's centre of gravity and undo the foundation of their knees holding them in position, thus making it easier to off balance them.

Once they have rolled over, you will likely roll with them.

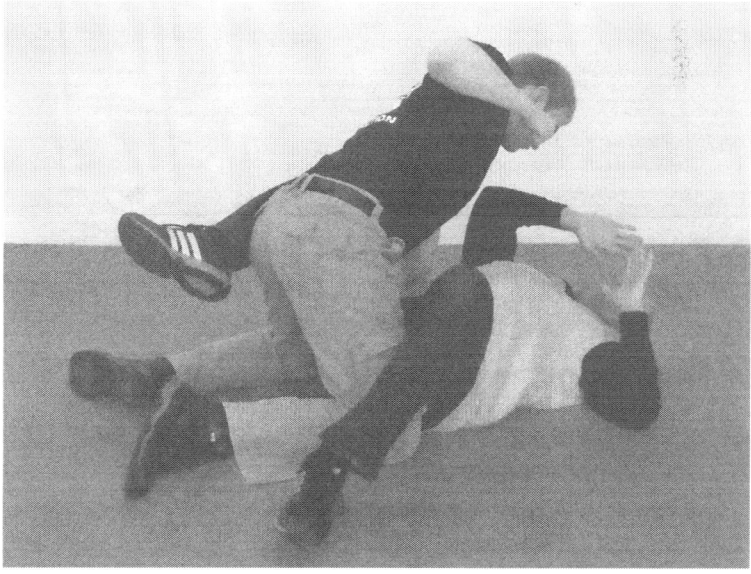

Attack their face to aide in releasing you.

With your hand, under hook the pit of their knee. Swing your arm up so their leg swings over your head. This will land them in a position where they are lying on their side facing away from you which is a bad position for them and a good position for you. This also prevents them from locking their legs around your waist.

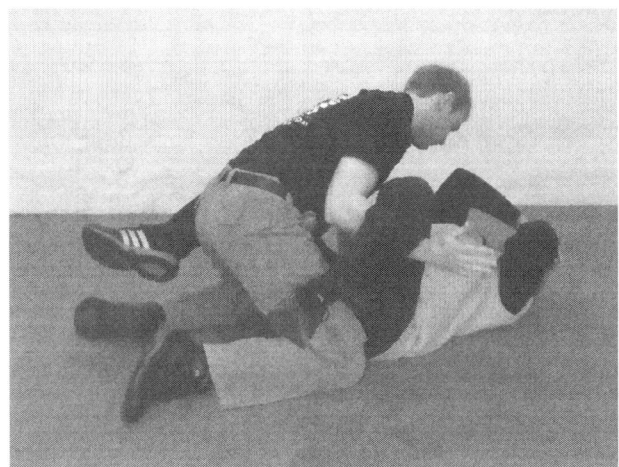

Push onto the subject's body to help you stand up. This will keep them in position as you do so.

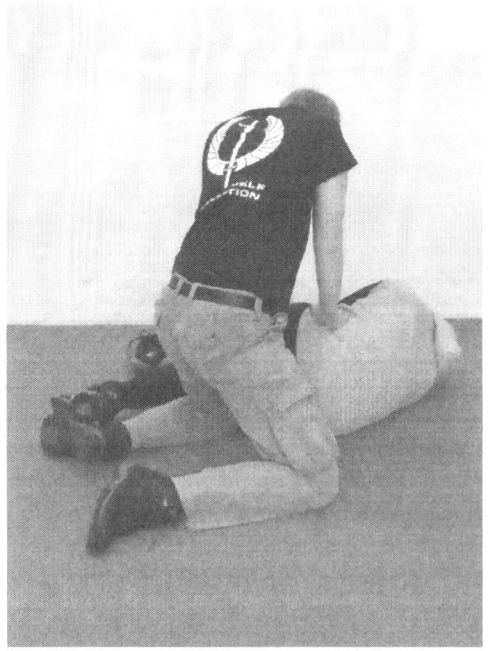

Essentials:
- Block the elbow
- Hook the foot on the same side
- Hip buck and roll
- Attack the face
- Hook the leg over your head
- Get up

Technique specific exercises:
Try to use the technique when ground sparring if you end up in the same position.

Defence against prone headlock

What is it?
This is a breakaway method for when you are lying face down and the subject is on your back and has you in a rear headlock.

Why do it?
Whilst you should never allow yourself to end up in this position, physical confrontation is fast and dynamic and can't always be controlled. As such, this technique should be practiced as the subject has a huge advantage over you and could render you unconscious and/or kill you in this position quite easily.

How to execute the technique:
Block the subject's elbow on the side of the attacking arm with your hand and tuck your elbow into your ribs. This is to prevent it from being able to brace out when you attempt to roll the subject.

Try to tuck your chin in at the same time using your opposite hand to assist. This may prevent your air way from being depressed by the subject's arm.

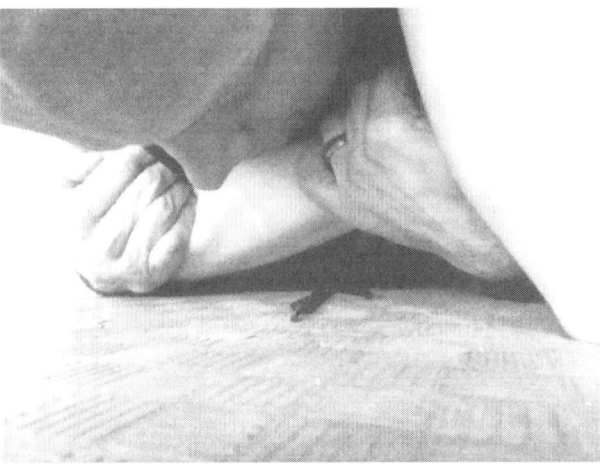

Begin to roll to the side you are blocking.

At the same time, try to bend your opposite knee and drag it in line with your hips.

With your upper body twisting, push down with your left knee against the floor to aid in the twist.

As the subject loses their balance, roll quickly in the opposite direction.

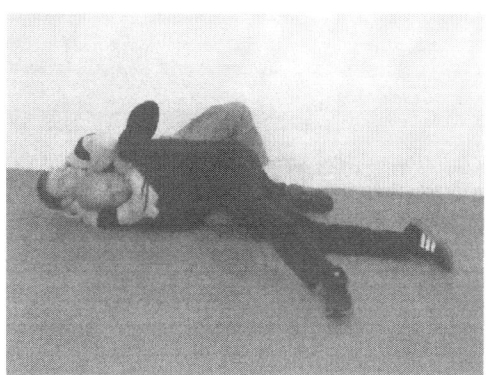 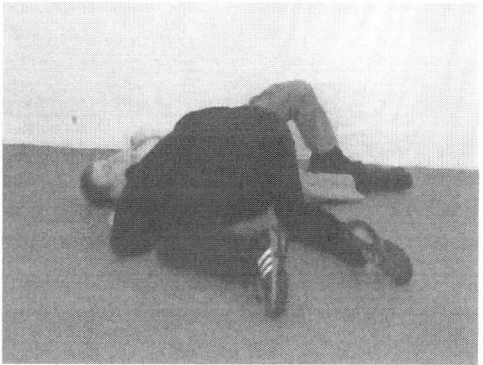

If this doesn't release the hold, 'walk' on the floor so that you move away from the subject. Even this may not work, so be prepared to attack the subject's eyes and fingers to aid the release.

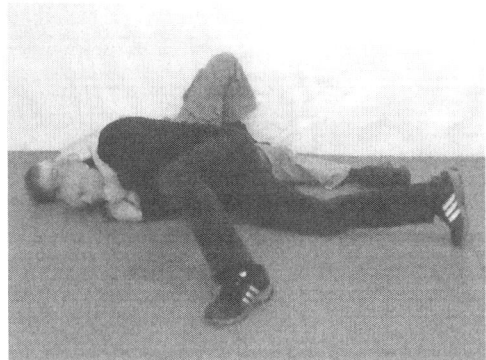

Stand up and escape.

Essentials:
- Tuck your chin in
- Block the elbow
- Use your opposite leg to help initiate the roll
- As the subject loses balance, turn in the opposite direction
- 'Walk' along the floor away from the subject
- Be prepared to attack the eyes and fingers of the subject to aid the release
- Stand and escape

Defence against a side headlock on the ground (scarf hold)

What is it?
This is a breakaway method for when you are lying on your back and the subject is at your side with you in a side headlock. They will be facing away from your legs.

Why do it?
This is a very common hold for various Martial Arts and as such, there are lots of people who are trained in how to do it effectively. As well as this, it is natural for a subject to try and put you into a headlock during a physical confrontation. The subject has the positional advantage and good control over you.

How to execute the technique:
Your arm closest to the subject may be behind them or in front of them. It is easier to execute the technique with your arm in front of the subject, however, the technique will work in both positions.

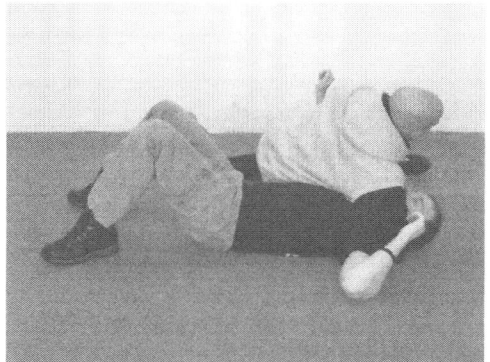 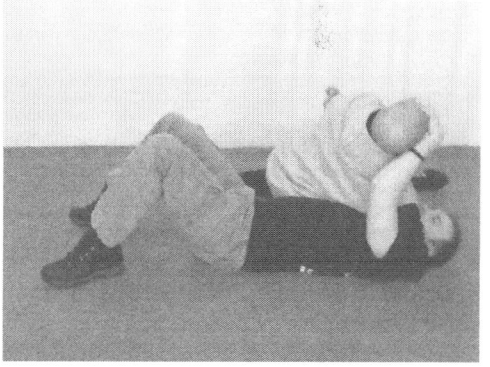

With your arm furthest from the subject, reach over their shoulder nearest to you and hook your hand onto their face in the same way as you do for a standing 'Side headlock'. Place your thumb under their nose and finger(s) in their eye(s).

Pull their head back as far as you can towards your groin.

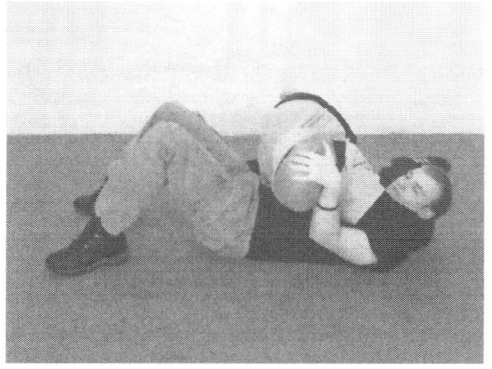 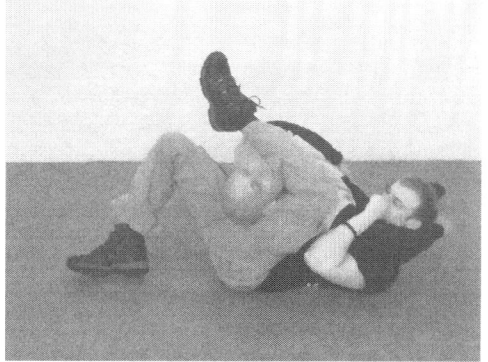

Shrimp away from the subject and hook your top leg over the subject's head. You need to have the subject's windpipe in the crease of your knee. Hook your top foot into the crease of your lower leg.

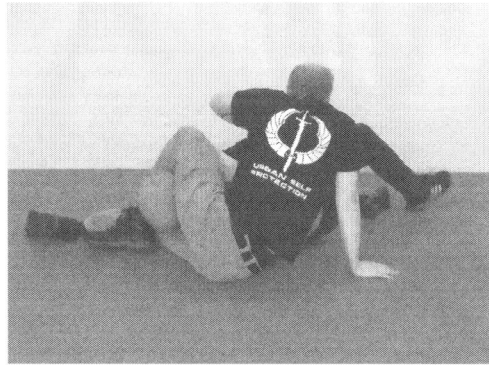

Pull your top knee downwards and the subject will roll to prone position and you will end up kneeling either side of their head. Unhook your legs and push down on the subject's back to aide you standing up and to keep them in this position.

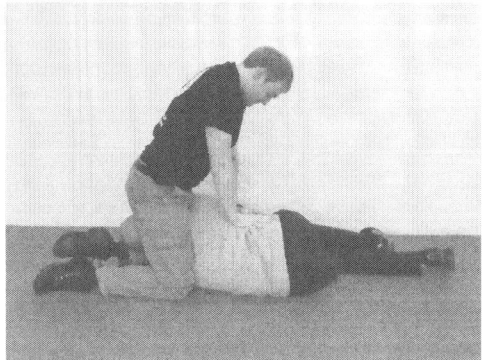
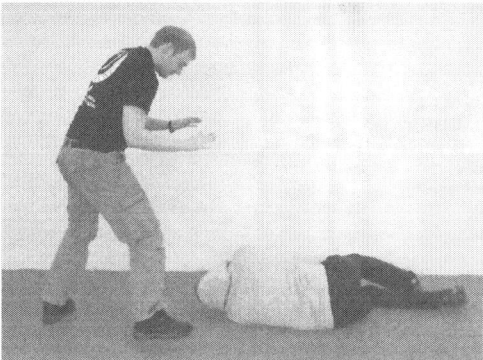

If your arm is behind the subject to start with, the technique is the same. However, it is harder to get the subject's windpipe into the crease of your top knee. Practice will allow you to experiment with various ways to work around this problem. It may require the use of your other hand to force the subject's head into the correct position, an extended shrimp or something else. It is important to work on this position and develop a strategy that works for you.

Essentials:
- With your hand furthest from the subject, grab their face and pull their head back
- Shrimp out and hook under the subject's jaw with your top leg
- Hook your top leg into the crease of your bottom knee and roll the subject onto their front

Technique specific exercises:
As suggested above, you need to practice the two starting positions and experiment until you have an effective strategy.

Defence against a rear naked choke

What is it?
An escape method from being held around the neck by the subject's arm from behind, whilst you are both on the floor.

Why do it?
If you do not escape quickly and decisively from this position, you can lose consciousness. You are also being controlled on the ground and other subjects, if present, could easily stomp on you.

How to execute the technique:
To start, reach up and hook the subject's arm with your fingers.

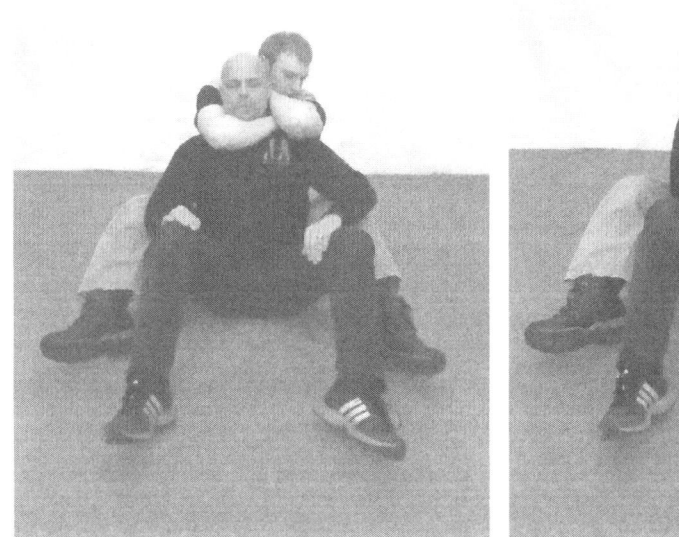

Pull it sharply down if possible to release a little pressure from your neck and throat. Keep hold tightly of this arm and pin it to your chest.

Tuck your chin in if possible, to prevent the lock from being reapplied.

Execute an aggressive hip buck and thrust your upper body backwards into the subject, putting all your weight onto their chest.

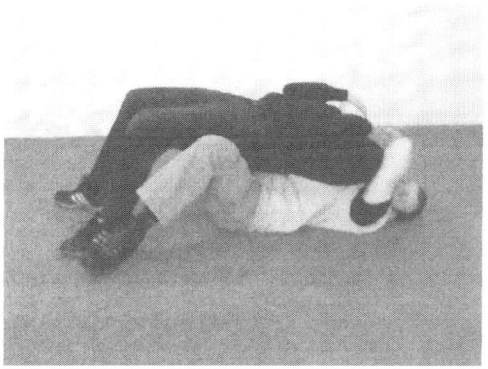
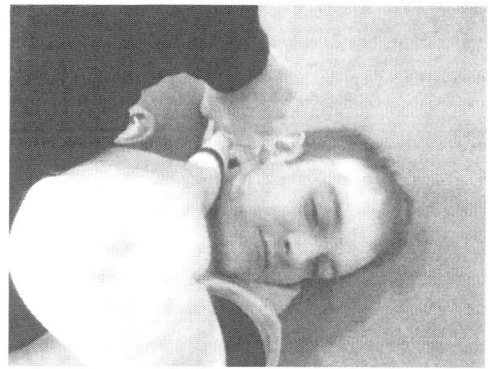

Reach back with both hands with your fingers splayed. Hopefully you will poke the subject in the eye, but all you should be trying to do, is feel along their arm or hand until your reach their fingers.

Once you reach their fingers, perform a 'Finger manipulation'. If they don't let go immediately, they should be distracted enough for you to turn towards the side of the attacking arm and roll out of the hold.

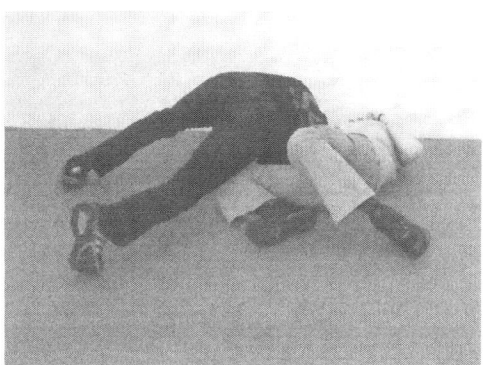
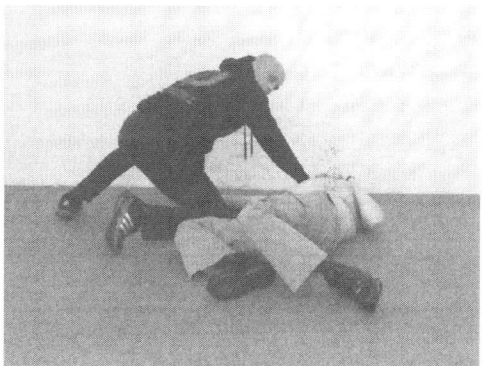

Some fighting systems are teaching these headlocks but using balled fists to avoid finger break defences and/or to tighten up the lock. If this is the case, 'crush' their fingertips into their fists – this is no doubt difficult, but will cause pain.

Essentials:
- Hook the attacking arm and pull down
- Pin the arm to your chest
- Tuck your chin in
- Violently hip buck and thrust your upper body backwards onto the subject
- Reach for the subject's fingers and execute a finger manipulation
- Turn to the side of the attacking arm

SELF DEFENCE

Defence against a full nelson

What is it?
This is a breakaway method against a full nelson hold. This is when the subject is behind you and reaches under your armpits, then behind your head to control you. They may also try to bend your head forwards.

Why do it?
This is a common hold and has the potential to seriously damage your neck and/or hold you whilst a second subject attacks you.

How to execute the technique:
If the subject is bending your head forwards, place the palm of your hand against your forehead and your elbow against your thigh. This will brace your head and prevent the subject from forcing it any further, thus reducing the chances of neck injury.

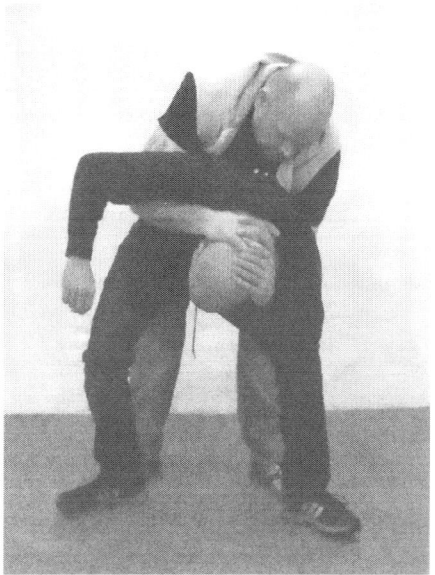

With the non-bracing hand, reach behind you and take hold of one of the subject's fingers or thumb and execute a 'Finger manipulation'.

If the subject is NOT trying to bend your head forwards, then immediately reach back and execute a finger break.

Essentials:
- Brace your head if required
- Finger manipulation

Defence against Dirty Fighters

What is it?
The reality of a street confrontation is that there are no rules. The subject will most likely not adhere to 'gentleman's' rules and use any tactic that might give them an advantage. The following gives examples of common tactics employed and how to deal with them.

Why do it?
Dirty fighters tend to be very good at using their chosen tactic, are likely experienced with violence and the tactics and techniques they use, are often very dangerous.

USP teaches most of these tactics and techniques as well. The difference is, USP teaches when it is reasonable and lawful to use them. Dirty fighters may employ these at any time, reasonable and lawful or not.

How to execute the technique:

Biting:
Drive your fingers into the face (ideally the eyes) of the subject to push their head backwards. If you have to continue fighting with the subject for whatever reason, attempt to put them into a rear headlock. Obviously as you apply the headlock, you are vulnerable to being bitten on the arm so be careful. However, once the lock is on, they will not be able to bite you again.

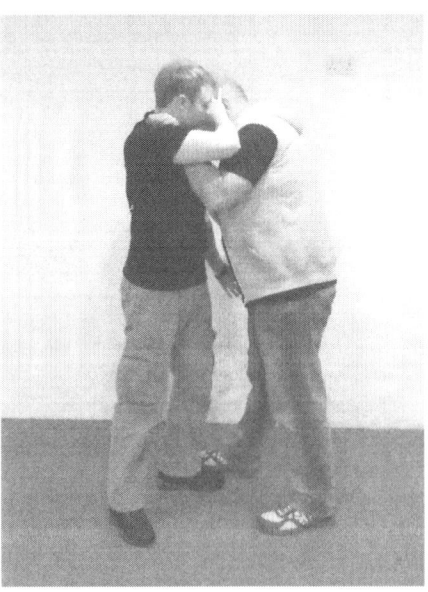 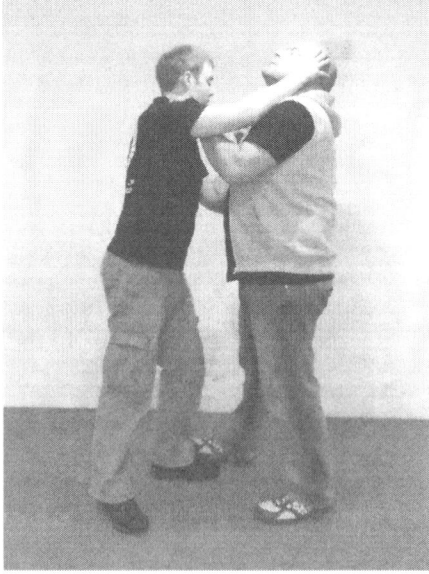

If you do get bitten, arrest any bleeding if necessary and wash the wound out as soon after the confrontation as you can. Attend casualty as soon as possible.

Eye gouges:
Thrash your head away from the subject's fingers.

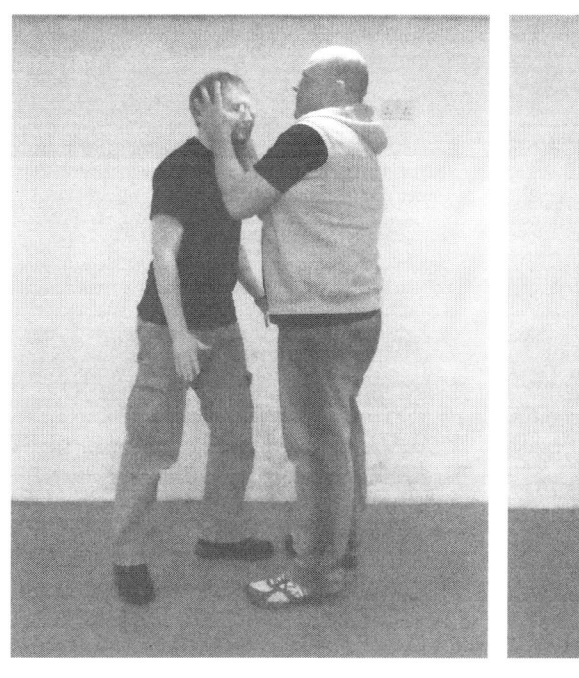
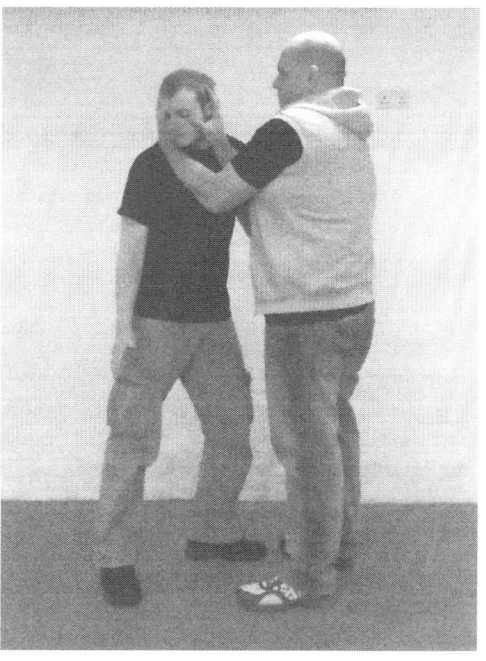
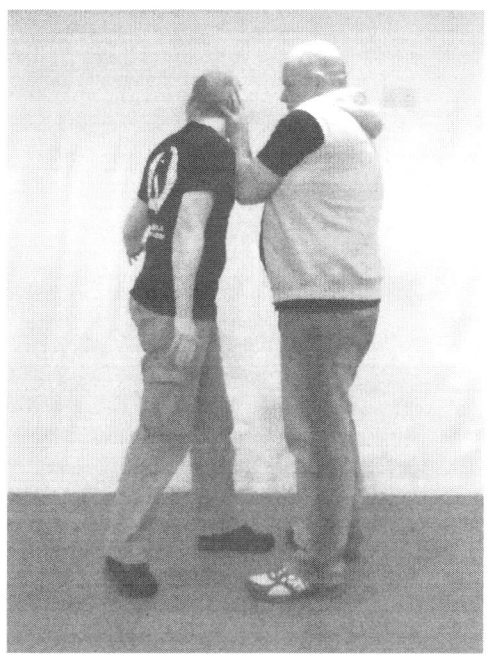

If they are still locked on, execute a 'Finger manipulation' on the attacking hand(s).

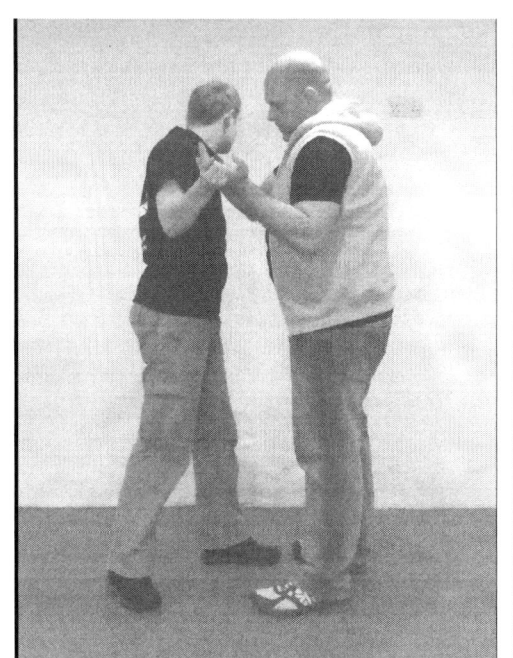 

Head butting:
A lapel grab is the likely starting position for a subject to head butt you in the face. If the subject grabs you in this way, or, for any other reason, you think that the subject is about to head butt you, the basic defence it to drop your chin to your chest. This moves your face out of the line of attack and replaces it with the top of your head which is harder and less vulnerable. USP has a full defence against clothing grabs which incorporates this basic defence.

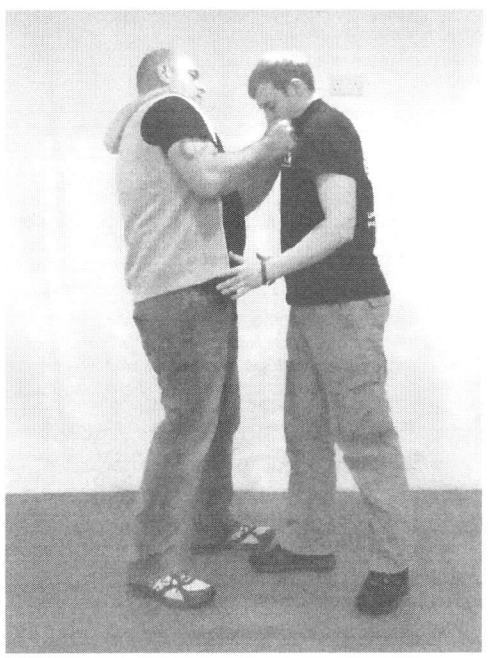 

Distractions:
Be aware that subjects may use distraction to gain an advantage before they attack you. For example, the subject may ask you directions. As you turn to point the way for them, they carry out the attack. Or, a subject may approach and ask you for the time. As you look at your watch, they carry out the attack.

There endless ways to distract people, so always treat an unknown person as a potential threat – don't be suckered into taking your eyes off the subject/their hands.

Tactile subjects:
Subjects often use innocent appearing touch as a way of positioning you/them to get a guaranteed first shot. This could be putting an arm around you after an argument and apologising to you. However, the arm then suddenly pulls you into a side headlock. Perhaps they offer a handshake after an argument but as you shake hands, the subject grips tightly and head butts you.

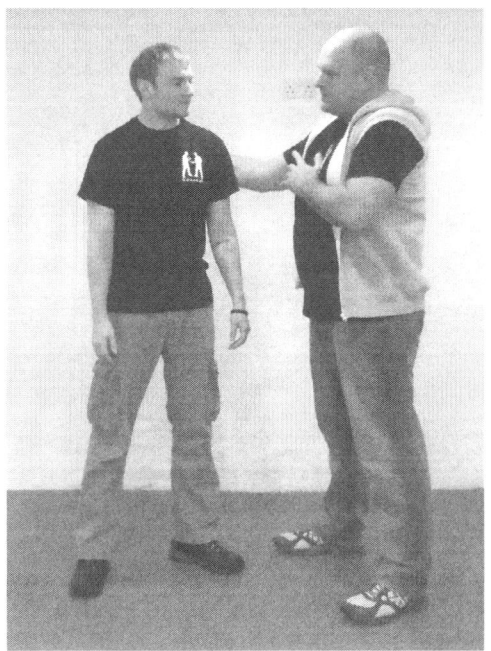 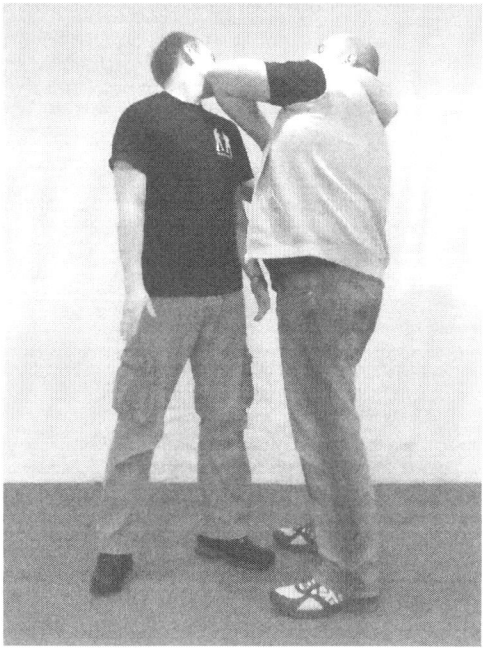

Using acting and touch, is a way of sneaking into your personal space and gaining a good position to attack you.

Lying:
If you have control of the subject – perhaps in a ground pin or headlock – they may realise they cannot fight their way out of the position. As such, they may pretend to give up or make promises to persuade you to release them. However, as soon as you do, they may attack you again.

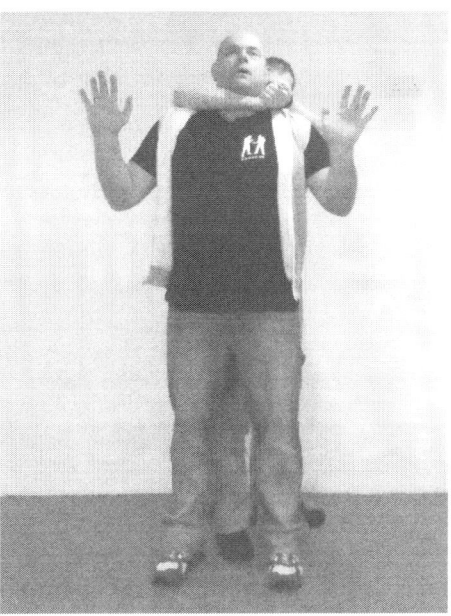 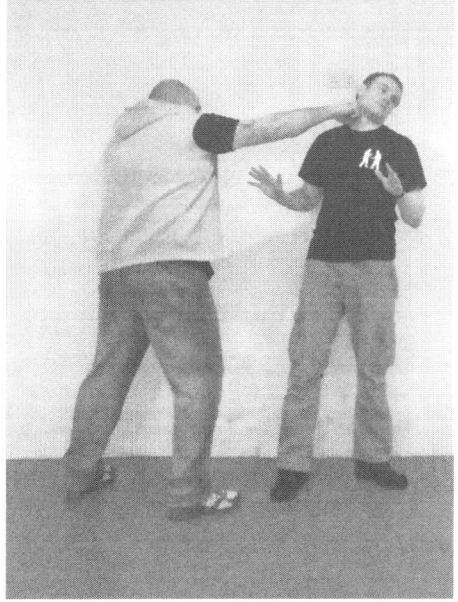

To deal with this, when the subject says they give up, maintain the control you have and position yourself so you can move away from them quickly. Then shove them (to put them into an OODA loop), release and gain space as quickly as you can. Be prepared to carry on fighting again if necessary.

Stamina:
Generally speaking, dirty fighters are naturally good at fighting and as such do not tend to train much. Therefore, their stamina is likely to be fairly low, so trying to outlast them may be all that's required. Don't count on this though!

Essentials:
- Biting: eye gouge, headlock
- Eye gouges: shake head, 'Finger manipulation'
- Head butting: drop your chin to your chest
- Distractions: don't be caught out, keep your eyes on the subject
- Tactile subjects: be aware and maintain your personal space
- Lying: gain a good escape position, shove, gain space
- Stamina: try to outlast the subject

Technique specific exercises:
All of these tactics can be practiced in various areas of training be it 'Operant conditioning', pressure testing or scenario training.

Defending yourself whilst on a push bike – subject straddles the front wheel and grabs handlebars

What is it?
A method of protecting yourself when on a push bike and a subject grabs your handlebars and straddles your front wheel.

Why do it?
Many people ride push bikes. Push bikes are desirable items for theft and in many ways immobilise you or at least make defending yourself difficult.

This method is to deal with a subject grabbing the handlebars - perhaps they intend to steal your bicycle or attack you.

How to execute the technique:
Ask the subject a question to distract them using the OODA loop.

Execute a 'Power slap' and get off the bicycle.

As soon as you have gotten off of the bicycle, place it between you and the subject sideways on (if they have let go of the handlebars). This helps you maintain your personal space as discussed in 'Protecting personal space'.

Use the same principles discussed in 'Protecting personal space' – broken record technique for someone pestering you, assertive body language and voice for 'Warning signs' and act quickly (escape or fight) when 'Danger signs' are displayed.

If the subject displays 'Danger signs', topple the bicycle towards them and either escape on foot or execute a pre-emptive attack.

If they still have hold of the handlebars, you at least have better mobility to fight or escape.

Essentials:
- Ask a question
- Power slap the subject
- Get off the bike
- Place the bicycle sideways on between you and the subject if possible
- Use the 'Protecting personal space' principles
- If 'Danger signs' are displayed, topple the bicycle towards the subject and escape on foot or execute a pre-emptive attack

Technique specific exercises:
Obviously using a real push bike is the best way to train this, but remember the additional dangers of a hard training surface, any members of the public nearby (on foot or in vehicles) and the various metal parts that could strike you or your training partner.

Ideally, use an open space such as a park in a quiet spot.

Defence against being attacked by a dog

What is it?
These are tactics to use when a dog (be it stray or otherwise) is biting you.

Why do it?
Regardless of breed, almost any size dog when it attacks a human is incredibly dangerous and very difficult to deal with.

How to execute the technique:
Adopt the following defensive position:

- Drop your chin – this helps to protect your throat as some attack dogs are trained to attack this area.

- Put your weak arm out in front of you between your throat and groin height. This is to 'offer' the dog should it attack you – it is less likely to go for your throat or groin if you do and a bitten arm is more survivable than a bitten throat or groin.

- Make your hands into fists to prevent your fingers from getting bitten off too easily.

- Stand bladed – this helps to protect your groin too.

- Don't make eye contact with the dog as this it may see this as a threatening gesture.

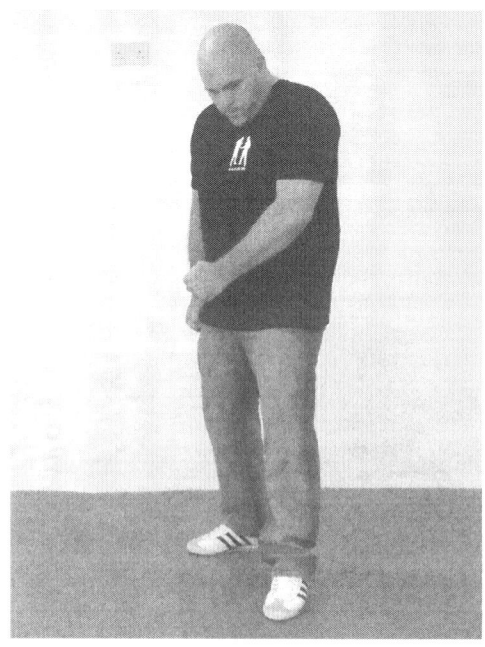

Take the attack on your weak arm if possible.

Do not thrash around – this will make your injuries worse and excite the dog further. If you simply try to stay still, the dog MAY lose interest and release you as it does with a toy.

However, if this doesn't work quickly, then grab the dog's collar / scruff / ear and drag it towards somewhere that has a closing door to aid separation – for example a car, or a shop.

As you drag the dog, try to kick it in the ribs as you move (be careful not to lose your balance though).

Position yourself inside the doorway and the dog outside. Close the door as much as you can and when the dog releases you, shut the door fully.

Certain dogs once locked onto you are incredibly difficult to remove.

You can consider attacking the dog's eyes with a sharp object or perhaps get a passer by to obtain a fire extinguisher or an aerosol can to discharge at it's face. Most dog's skulls are very strong so hitting it in the head with something is not likely to help. Dog handlers often carry 'bite break sticks' - a piece of strong flat plastic around 10 inches long and 3 inches wide. This is inserted into the dog's mouth sideways and twisted to force the jaws open. You could consider using an improvised object to do the same.

Essentials:
- Adopt the defensive position – drop chin, stand bladed, offer your weak arm, make fists, don't make eye contact with the dog
- Take the attack on your weak arm if possible
- Don't thrash around
- Stay still momentarily as this may cause the dog to release
- Grab the dog's collar / scruff / ear and drag it towards somewhere that has a door
- Kick the dog in the ribs as you move
- Close the door separating you and the dog
- Use sharp objects or sprays to attack the dog's eyes to aid release if locked on

Technique specific exercises:
This is very difficult to practice realistically. The author is lucky enough to have a friend who is a dog handler and has been able to carry out training drills with his dog. However, with just a training partner and some pads it isn't going to be very realistic.

But, you can drill the scenario using a punch bag and a Martial Arts belt:

- Tie the middle of the martial arts belt to the top of the punch bag.

- Make a small knotted loop that cannot close.
- Place your weak wrist into the loop – this simulates the dog's jaws locked onto your arm.
- Two training partners will take hold of an end of belt each.
- They then yank the belt back and fourth – this simulates the dog's head movement.
- The punch bag simulates the weight of the dog.
- Stay still for a moment in case the 'dog' decides to release you.
- When it doesn't, grab the punch bag as you would the dog's collar.
- Drag the punch bag to a doorway whilst kicking it.

You could also add dog barking sound effects on a CD or MP3.

USP has it's own YouTube channel, on which is a video made with the help of the author's dog handler friend. It is filmed from the perspective of the defender being attacked by a dog and should be watched to help give you a flavour of the reality of such an incident.

Third party protection - bag piping

What is it?
This is a third party protection technique.

Why do it?
Defending a friend or loved one is often MORE important to someone than being able to defend themselves. The third party may be less able/skilled than yourself and be targeted by a subject. Perhaps the subject has an issue with your loved one and begins to argue with them. When the subject shows 'Warning' or 'Danger' signs, you may wish to step in to protect your loved one from a likely attack.

How to execute the technique:
Step in front of the third party.

Use your hand to grab the wrist of the third party on the same side (i.e. right to right/left to left).

Pull their arm under yours and pin it against your body with your forearm and elbow.

Step into a bladed stance with your hand out stretched.

Which hand to grab with?

If you use your dominant hand to grab the third party's wrist, you will be in your usual comfortable fighting stance, but will have lost its use for striking/defending.

If you use your non-dominant hand to grab the third party's wrist, you will be in your less natural fighting stance, but you will have the use of your dominant arm for striking/defending.

Either way is valid. Practice both, find which is best for you and stick with that one and discard the other to prevent confusion.

If the subject tries to attack you, kick them or use your free hand to grab/push/strike them.

If they try to move around you to get to the third party, turn so you are still facing the subject and kick out/push etc if required.

The third party should stay behind you and move with the turn, whether you turn clockwise or anti-clockwise, as you have a good grip on their arm. This movement, prevents the subject from being able to 'track' the third party.

For a short child, you can use a similar technique albeit not very pleasant for the child: grab the child's hair instead of their wrist and pull them into the small of your back. This gives you the same degree of control over the third party and keeps you between them and the subject. Obviously this can be painful for the child, so should only be used when necessary. Do not grab their collar as doing so could potentially choke the child.

There are times when it is appropriate to disengage from the third party and push them backwards out of harm's way and deal with the subject head on. These are close range edged weapon attacks where two hands are required to control the weapon hand or where the subject is moving in rapidly and you cannot back up quickly enough because of the third party being there. If you do disengage with the third party, try to use conflict communication to tell them to escape. Move and position yourself so that you stay between the subject and the third party until they can escape.

Essentials:
- Step in front of the third party
- Grab the third party's wrist
- Pin their arm against your body
- Blade your stance and put your free hand out
- Use kicks/free hand to defend
- Turn to face the subject if they move, keeping the third party behind you

Technique specific exercises:
Have two training partners. The first plays the role of the third party. They should act as though they are shocked and unable to defend themselves.

The second training partner plays the role of the subject. They should verbally abuse the third party and when they display warning/danger signs, you should execute the technique.

The subject should then try to tap the third party on the head, which simulates an attack getting through your defence.

You should move accordingly and feign kicks etc.

Do this for twenty seconds and see how many taps on the head your third party receives, the goal of course, is to receive none.

Third party protection - evacuation

What is it?
This is a third party protection technique to remove a friend or loved one from a dangerous situation such as a riot, pub brawl, shooting etc, where missiles (stones, glasses, bullets etc) are flying in their direction.

Why do it?
As per 'Bag piping', defending a friend or loved one is often MORE important to someone than being able to defend themselves. The third party may be less able/skilled than yourself and unsure how to react. This technique allows you to protect the third party using your body as a shield for them and escort them quickly and effectively to safety.

This technique also uses the same movement as the 'Chin jab', so your muscle memory should already be present.

How to execute the technique:
Quickly scan to decide your escape route and where the threat is coming from.

Turn the third party to face away from the threat and stand behind them putting your arm under theirs, around their waist and against their stomach.

Use your hand to grip the back of the subject's neck as high up as you can, splaying your fingers to provide as much protection to their head as you can.

Line your forearm along the protectee's neck and spine, again shielding the most vulnerable areas.

Use your torso to shield the protectee's back.

Fold the protectee forwards so they bend at the waist. This should make their upper body a smaller target. Do not bend them over too far or they will lose their mobility.

Move forwards quickly, but don't run as you will both be likely to trip over.

Give clear loud commands to the protectee as you evacuate them.

Essentials:
- Turn protectee away from the threat
- One hand on protectee's stomach, the other on their neck, fingers splayed
- Forearm on neck and spine
- Your torso protects their back
- Bend them forwards
- Give loud verbal commands
- Move quickly, but don't run

Technique specific exercises:
Walk with your training partner along the length of your training location.

Other training partners should be placed in a line at either side of you and your 'protectee'. These other training partners should have tennis balls and/or focus pads to hand to throw at you and your 'protectee' to simulate rocks, glasses etc.

These other training partners should have decided ahead of the drill who will throw missiles.

Whenever the chosen person chooses, they begin to throw 'missiles' at you both. Your training partner should act as though they are shocked and unable to defend themselves.

You must then carry out the technique and decide which direction is the best escape route (behind cover or an exit) and position yourself to shield the protectee.

Provided everyone is wearing safety goggles, you could do a similar drill using airsoft guns to fire bb's instead of throwing tennis balls etc. PLEASE REFER TO SECTION ON BB GUN TRAINING BEFORE CARRYING OUT THIS DRILL.

You could also practice pushing your protectee to the ground instead of running in the case of a grenade attack or shooting.

WEAPONS

Defence against close in knife threat (additional problem)

What is it?
This is a set of principles to adhere to when held at knife point. On this occasion, there is an additional problem for example, the subject is also holding you in a headlock or by your hair, or perhaps they have covered the knife blade with their other hand making it harder to defend against.

Why do it?
As per 'Close in knife threat – problem solving', if a subject threatens you with a knife in close quarters, it could be positioned anywhere. The subject may also be causing an additional problem such as a grab or hold. There are countless other possibilities. As such, using a few basic principles and practicing them in all manner of close in knife threats with additional problems, should allow you to adapt to an unusual threat.

For example, the subject may stand in front of you and hold the knife horizontally across your throat with their second hand covering the blade. They may hold it pointing upwards under your chin and grab your hair to control you, or even very close in next to your groin whilst gripping your lapel with their other hand. They could rest the point on your face millimetres from your eye ball and have you backed against a wall or perhaps under your arm pit next to your artery with their other hand over your mouth.

How to execute the technique:
The overriding principle is to deal with the biggest danger first (most often the knife) or both at the same time if possible. This means that you should ignore the grab or other additional problem and deal with the knife as per 'Close in knife threat – problem solving'. Once the knife is controlled, you can then consider the secondary problem if it is still an issue.

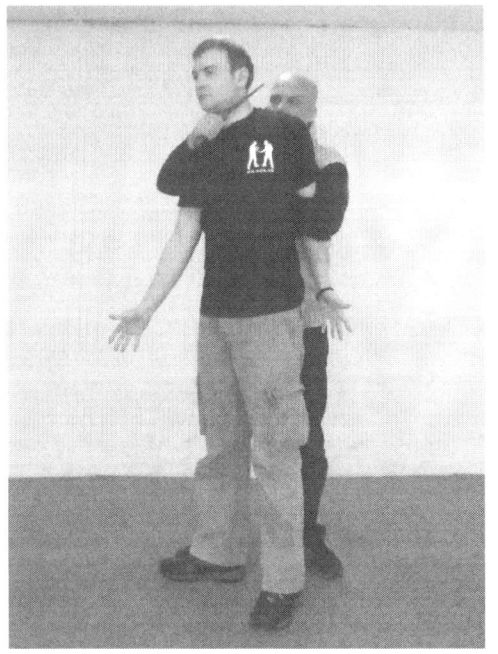
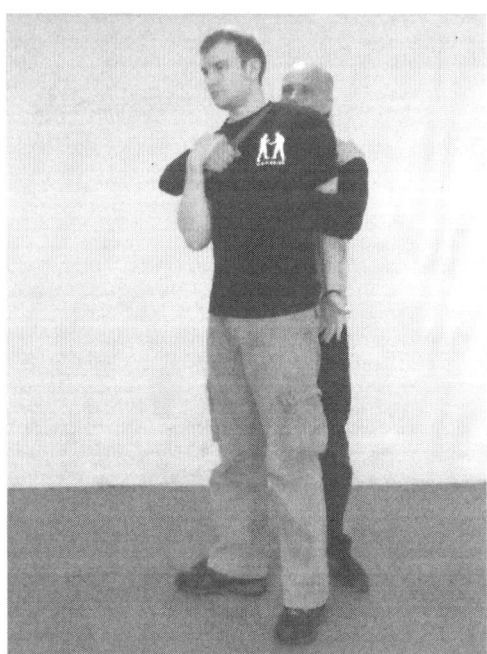

Remember, there may be positions that are incredibly difficult / impossible to defend yourself against. In these cases, you should ACT your way into a better position. For example, you could act as though you are begging for your life and turn slightly in order to do so. This turn may give you a much better position to defend yourself in.

Essentials:
- Deal with the biggest danger first
- Consider the potential method of injury when you move – stab or slash
- Execute a body defence
- Execute a hand defence (deflect or control)

- Follow up with kick and run for a deflection or 'Frenzied knife defence' principles for control
- Consider humanising yourself and/or distracting the subject
- If you are in a particularly difficult position, consider acting your way into a better position

Technique specific exercises:
This is something that needs to be approached in a slow, considered and methodical way. Your training partner should hold a safe training knife in various different positions and add in additional problems. Each time, you should go through the principles slowly to solve the problem, always dealing with the biggest danger first. Sometimes there may be more than one way to solve the same problem. As you spend time experimenting with different problems and different methods to solve them using the principles, you will eventually find methods and positions that suit you best. Your thinking time will also reduce enabling you to react more quickly.

After spending sometime experimenting slowly in this way, try carrying out the same drill, but with your training partner acting aggressively and reacting if they spot you beginning a defence. Your defences should be full speed now.

Should a defence not work at full speed, take it back to slow time experimenting and solve the problem before moving back to full speed practice.

Defence against mounted knife attack

What is it?
This is a technique/set of principles used to survive a frenzied knife attack when you are on the ground on your back and the subject is straddled across your stomach in a mount position.

Why do it?
This is an exceedingly dangerous position to be in of course: The subject is armed, they are in a superior position, you have less manoeuvrability and there are other dangers associated with being on the ground.

As such, a defence allowing you to survive the knife attack and allowing you to remove the subject and get up is essential.

This technique is almost exactly the same as the 'Defence against a frenzied knife attack' and as such makes it easier to learn, retain and operationalise under stress – a 'buy one, get one free' technique.

How to execute the technique:
As per the 'Frenzied knife attack defence', the first principle is to grab the wrist of the knife hand with both of yours to control it.

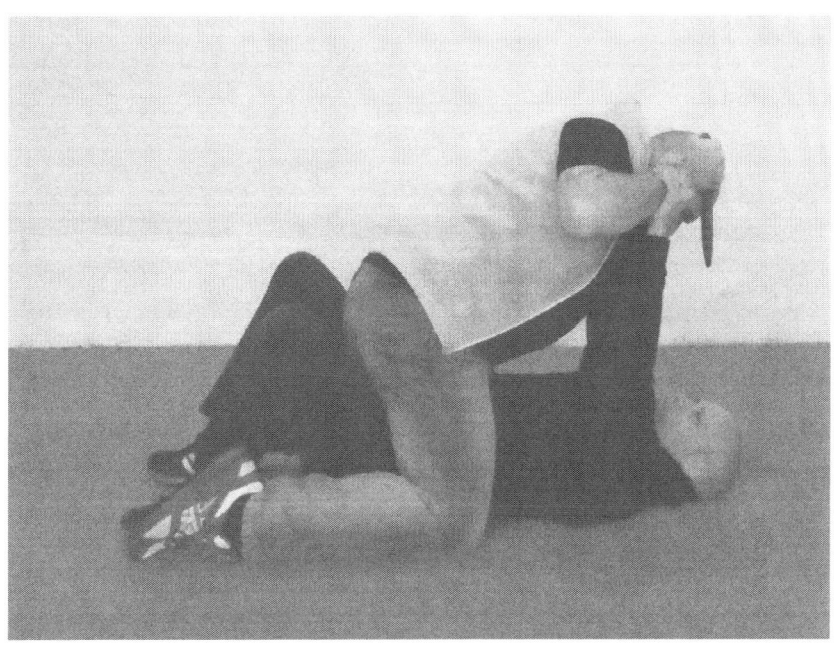

Use hip bucking/wiggling to assist.

As per the frenzied knife attack, we need to close the distance for the same reasons as before. To do this, pull the subject's knife hand towards the ground at the side of you and execute a powerful hip buck to aid you with this.

Once you are in this position, use your foot from the side the knife has landed to wrap the subject's leg as per the table principle. Carry out a further hip buck and roll, maintaining grip on the knife wrist at all times with both hands.

You should end up on top of the subject in their guard. Maintain pressure using your bodyweight to keep the knife wrist pinned to the floor.

Move out of the guard position and around to the head end of the subject. From here, counter attack if possible and escape.

Essentials:
- Grab the wrist of the knife hand with two hands
- Hip buck and pull their hand to one side
- Wrap their foot on the same side
- Carry out a hip buck and roll as per the table principle
- Keep weight over their wrist to maintain control
- Move around to their head
- Counter attack if possible and escape

Technique specific exercises:
Eye protection should be worn when carrying out full speed attacks, even with a rubber knife. Have your training partner alternate grips and hands used for each time you run through the technique.

Build up the resistance levels from your training partner. This may lead to the technique not going as planned and turn into a ground 'fight'. If so, maintain grip on your training partner's wrist and problem solve various positions you end up in.

Third party protection – knife threat

What is it?
This is a technique/tactic to allow you to rescue a friend or loved one, from a subject standing behind them with a knife to their throat.

Why do it?
This is a high risk technique, hence it is in Level 6. However, there is a great deal of knife crime and a threat to the throat is a common method to force the victim to do as the subject commands. As such, it may be that your loved one is in this position and you have come across the incident. Intervening is dangerous even when you are proficient at doing so, which means if you have no training in this rescue method, then you are likely to do something inappropriate or freeze which could be even more dangerous.

How to execute the technique:
As this is a knife threat, it is likely that you have a little time and as such, talking to the subject may be appropriate. Try to do so in a calming manner and humanise the victim by stating things like "He has two young kids who love him".

You need to be fairly close to attempt the technique, so ACT your way forwards if you have to. Keep your hands out stretched and open palmed giving the impression of compliance.

Keep your hands at the same height as the knife so you have less distance to travel when attempting the technique.

Try to position yourself so that the victim's head partially blocks the subject's view of you to gain a tactical advantage.

Ask a question to distract the subject and half a second to a second later execute the following technique:

Carry out an open hand palm strike against the subject's elbow – this will most likely be a similar movement to a small open hand hook or power slap. This slap should push the subject's knife away from the victim's throat for a split second.

With your other hand, over hook the subject's wrist.

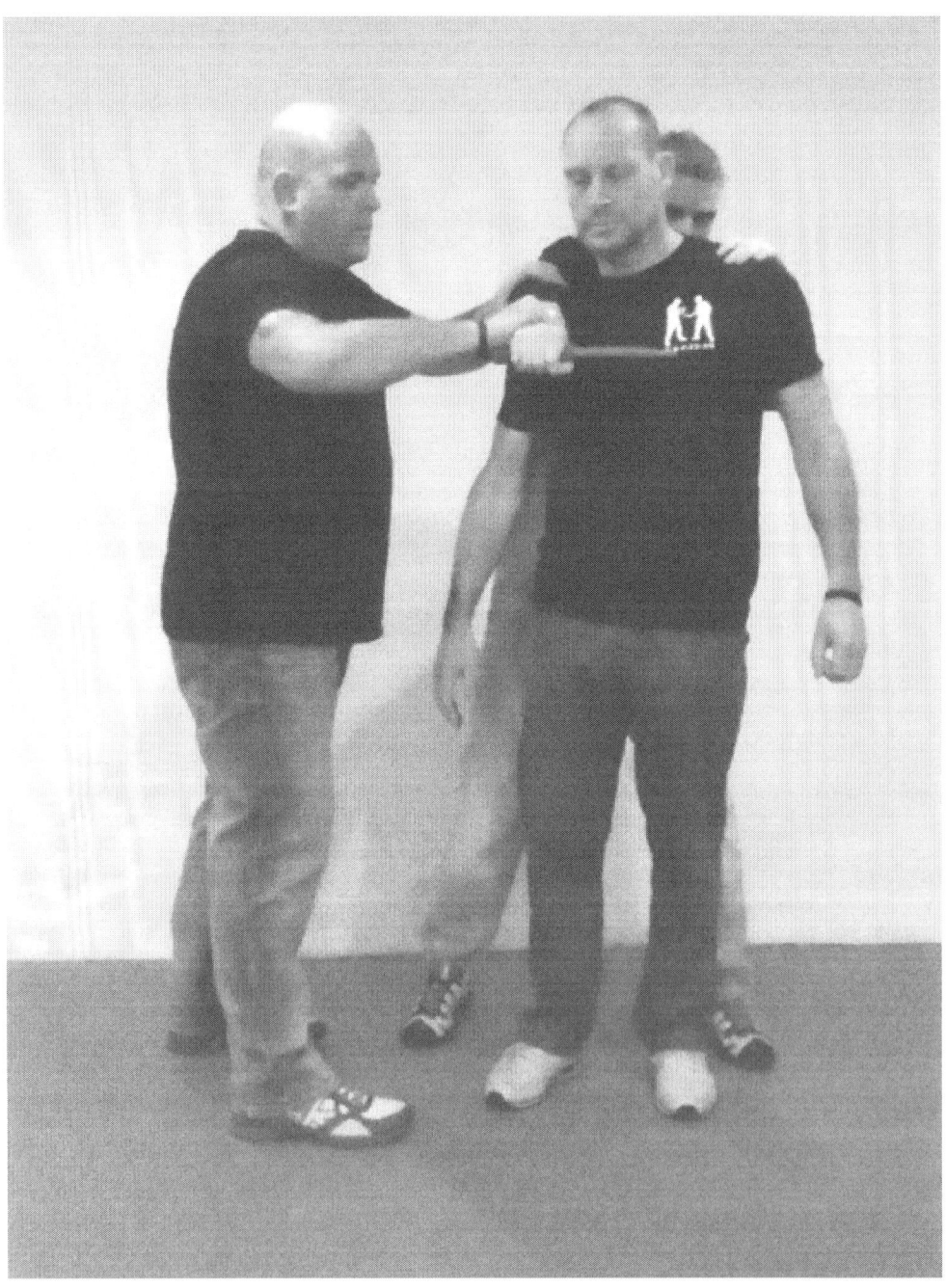

Pull the subject's arm away from the victim and turn your body 180 degrees (pivot on the ball of the foot on the same side as your slapping hand). Straighten their elbow against your body and control the arm.

With your slapping hand, attack the subject's face, pulling them away from the victim.

You should also be shouting to the victim to run.

The situation will dictate what you do next. You may be able to drop the subject backwards onto the floor and then run, or you may have to control the knife with both hands and carry out the 'Defence against a frenzied knife attack'.

However, should you come across this incident from behind the subject and they do not see/hear you, then simply sneak up and execute the physical part of the technique – positioning and talking are unnecessary under these circumstances.

Essentials:
- If approaching from the rear, sneak up and execute the technique
- If not, humanise the victim
- Have you hands outstretched and palms open at the height of the knife
- Position yourself close to the victim and out of the subject's view if possible
- Ask a distraction question
- Slap the subject's elbow
- Hook their wrist
- Pull their arm back and pivot to control it
- 'Reverse head twist'
- Shout to the victim to run

Technique specific exercises:
This attack can be added into scenario or conflict immersion training to add pressure and realism.

Weapon stripping

What is it?
This is a technique to allow you to take a weapon from a subject's hand.

Why do it?
You may not be able to run from an incident as it would leave others vulnerable to attack by the subject. Or perhaps you are trapped as because of the environment you are in. You may work in law enforcement, security or the Military and it is your duty to disarm the subject.

How to execute the technique:
Weapon disarms, particularly disarming knives, are too dangerous to carry out during the melee of a fight. As such, it is only recommended to carry out a disarm, once you have control of the subject. This could be when you have a second person helping you to pin the subject to a wall or the floor and the subject's arm is unable to move. It could also be if you have a particularly good ground pin on the subject on your own.

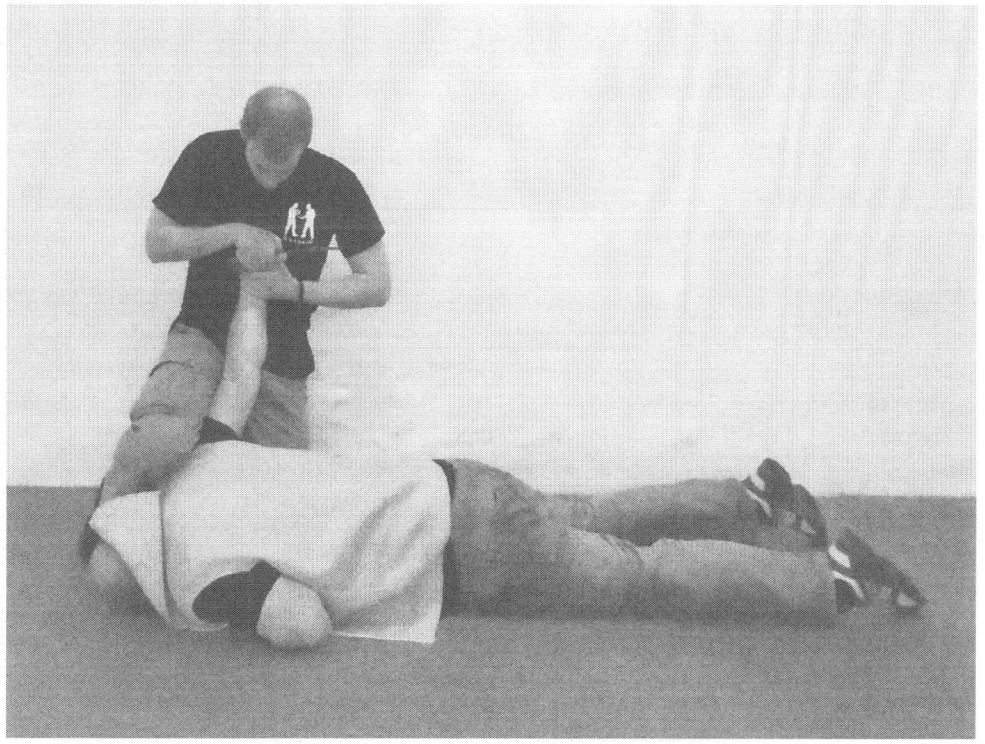

You should control the subject's hand/wrist with one hand. The technique is to use the thumb joint area of the palm of your free hand to apply pressure to the subject's thumb tip, forcing it to bend in half and then forcing the thumb tip towards the lower thumb joint causing both joints in the thumb to bend and have pressure applied to them.

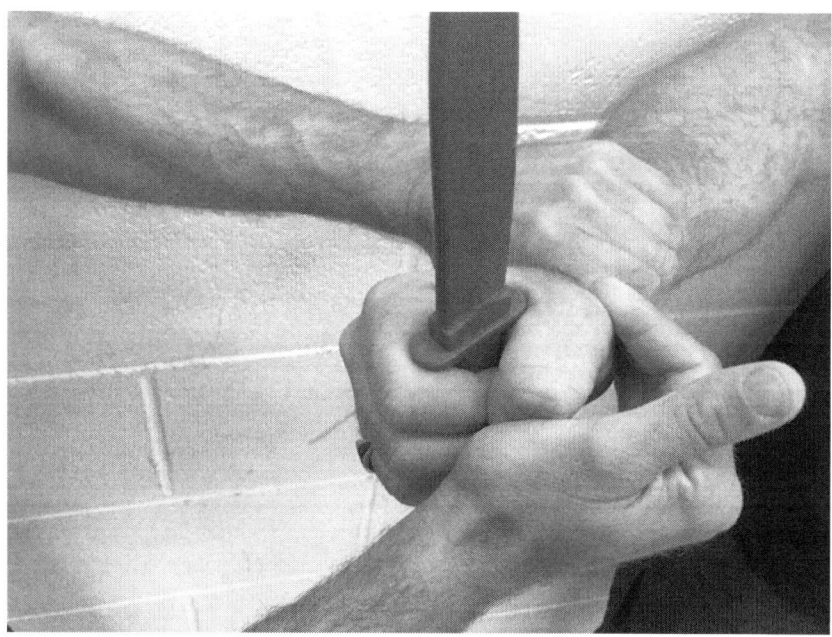

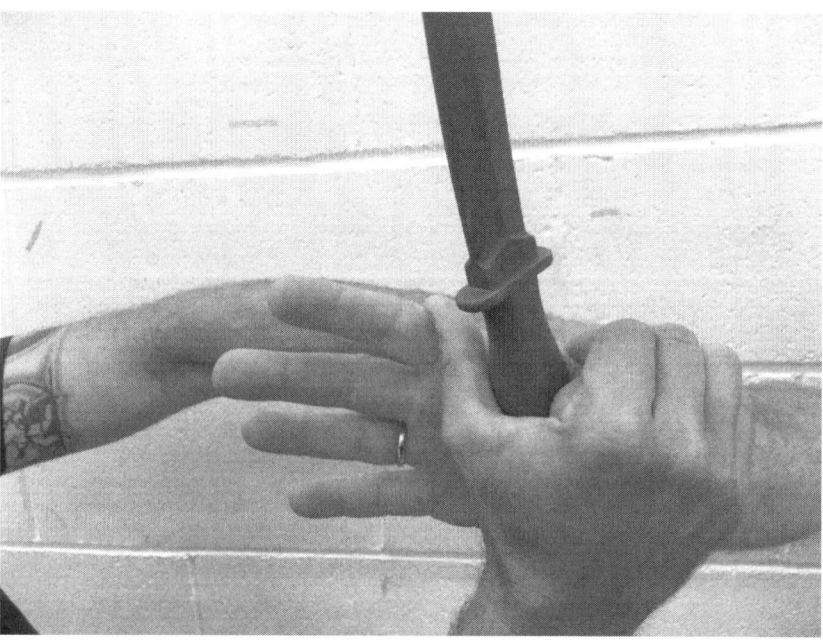

This should cause pain to the subject allowing you to gain their compliance. The subject should release their grip.

Take the weapon away from them and put it in an appropriate place where you control it and the subject cannot reach it. Bear in mind other potential subjects, so don't throw it behind you in case someone else picks it up and attacks you with it.

The technique works in a number of other situations too:

- The subject grabs your lapel but are of a low threat to you (perhaps a drunken family member).
- You may be a Close Protection Operator who's principal has shaken the hand of a subject and the subject refuses to let go.
- You may work in law enforcement, security or Military and the subject has grabbed a fixed object to prevent you from escorting them away.

Essentials:
- You must have control of the subject
- Control their wrist with one hand
- Use the thumb joint area of the palm of your hand to apply pressure to the subject's thumb
- Bend their thumb tip towards the palm of their hand then further bend it towards the thumb joint causing both thumb joints to bend
- Take the weapon and secure it

Technique specific exercises:
As with any technique using force against your digits, care must be taken to apply pressure slowly when training so your training partner can tap out before they get injured.

Long gun disarm side (in front of your arm)

What is it?
This is a method to deflect, control and disarm a long gun such as a shot gun or rifle, when the subject is stood at the side of you and threatening you with it. The gun is positioned in front of your arm.

Why do it?
In many countries, it is far easier to legally obtain a shotgun than any other type of firearm. As such, it is prudent to learn an effective defence in case you are ever threatened with one.

How to execute the technique:
Remember that as with any threat with a weapon, do not fight for property, but do fight for your well-being.

Carry out the deflection and technique as soon as you see the gun.

The exception is if it's slightly out of range and/or it's obvious the subject is not immediately going to shoot. In which case:

Place your hands with palms facing the subject at the same height as the gun in a submissive posture. This is to give the appearance of compliance, but keeps your hands close to the weapon so that as you execute the defence, you do not have to move your hands too far.

The subject may well speak to you to tell you their demands.

If you judge that you have time ask them a question to engage their brain. Use the same question in training every time as trying to think of something on the spot puts you at a disadvantage.

Wait for around half a second to a second and then explosively and without telegraphing, deflect the barrel of the gun with your hand. If you have not been able to reposition your hands to accommodate a deflection with them, then using your forearm to deflect is fine (for example you may decide to deflect immediately and not to carry out positioning and talking to the subject).

The deflection is a momentary parry.

At the same time as the deflection, move your body out of the line of fire.

With your other hand and arm, under hook the barrel of the gun.

Move aggressively forwards and grab the subject in a bear hug, ideally using a 'Gable grip'.

The muzzle should be pointed upwards and the subject should not be able to move it.

Execute knee strikes to the groin, then slide both hands/arms around the gun and yank it violently out of the subject's grip.

Remember, at any point during the struggle it could discharge and shoot you, so you must maintain the deflection of the barrel.

Carry out the post disarm procedure learnt with 'Handgun defence'.

Essentially, this is the 'Long gun defence front' but executed from a slightly different position.

If the subject is larger than you, you would be better bear hugging the subject's arms and the gun as per 'Long gun defence front'.

If the subject is holding the gun at hip height, you would be better bear hugging around their upper arms as per 'Long gun defence front'.

Essentials:
- Deflect immediately unless the weapon is out of reach or you are sure the subject will not fire immediately
- If this is the case, raise your hands to gun height
- Ask an OODA question
- Deflect the muzzle and move out of the line of fire
- Under hook the barrel
- Bear hug the subject
- Execute knee strikes to the groin
- Disarm

Technique specific exercises:
An airsoft rifle can be used with appropriate safety equipment to check the speed of your deflection. PLEASE REFER TO SECTION ON BB GUN TRAINING BEFORE CARRYING OUT THIS DRILL.

The muzzle can be positioned in different areas at the side of the body/head

Long gun disarm at the side (behind arm)

What is it?
This is a method to deflect, control and disarm a long gun such as a shot gun or rifle, when the subject is stood behind you and threatening you with it.

Why do it?
In many countries it is far easier to legally obtain a shotgun than any other type of firearm. As such, it is prudent to learn an effective defence in case you are ever threatened with one.

How to execute the technique:
Remember that as with any threat with a weapon, do not fight for property, but do fight for your well-being.

Firstly, look over your shoulder so you can see what you are dealing with. This is a natural reaction anyway, so should not cause the subject to feel threatened.

Carry out the deflection and technique as soon as you see the gun.

The exception is if it's slightly out of range and/or it's obvious the subject is not immediately going to shoot. In which case:

Place your open hands at the same height as the gun in a submissive posture. This is to give the appearance of compliance, but keeps your hands close to the weapon so that as you execute the defence, you do not have to move your hands too far.

The subject may well speak to you to tell you their demands.

If you judge that you have time ask them a question to engage their brain. Use the same question in training every time as trying to think of something on the spot puts you at a disadvantage.

Wait for around half a second to a second and then explosively and without telegraphing, turn out of the line of fire and in towards the subject. The forwards momentum towards the subject is designed to give you a psychological advantage, it gets you further away from the muzzle of the gun and you may well put the subject off balance too.

At the same time as the turn, your nearest arm should deflect the barrel of the weapon by under hooking it and the subject's arms.

Bear hug the subject from their side, using a 'Gable grip' if possible.

The muzzle should be pointed upwards and the subject should not be able to move it.

 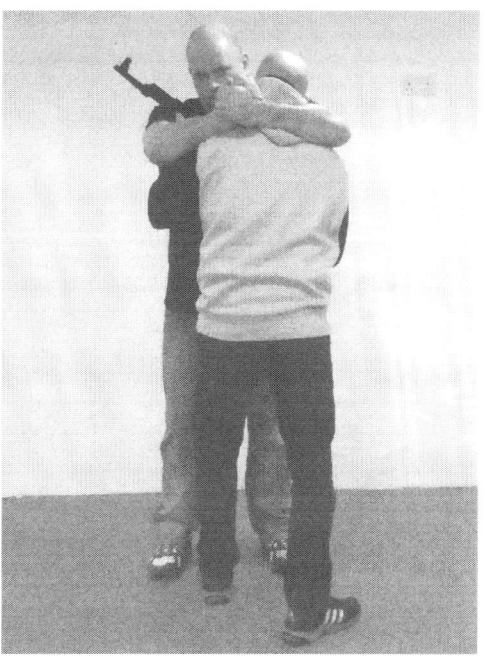

Remember, at any point during the struggle it could discharge and shoot you, so you must maintain the deflection of the barrel.

Attack the subject with knee strikes if you are in a position that allows this, or stomp their instep and/or bite their neck, ear or face. Head butting them may also be viable.

Once the subject is 'softened up' grab the gun with both hands and yank it violently from their grip.

Carry out the post disarm procedure learnt with 'Handgun defence'.

Essentially, this is the 'Long gun defence rear' but executed from a slightly different position.

If the subject is larger than you, you would be better bear hugging the subject's arms and the gun as per 'Long gun defence rear'.

If the subject is holding the gun at hip height, you would be better bear hugging around their upper arms as per 'Long gun defence rear'.

Essentials:
- Look over your shoulder
- Deflect immediately unless the weapon is out of reach or you are sure the subject will not fire immediately
- If this is the case, raise your hands to gun height

- Ask an OODA question
- Turn out of the line of fire and move forwards towards the subject
- Deflect the barrel by under hooking it
- Bear hug the subject from the side
- Attack the subject but maintain control of the gun
- Disarm

Technique specific exercises:
An airsoft rifle can be used with appropriate safety equipment to check the speed of your deflection. PLEASE REFER TO SECTION ON BB GUN TRAINING BEFORE CARRYING OUT THIS DRILL.

The muzzle can be positioned in different areas of the front of the body/head.

Defence against active killer – playing dead

What is it?
There have been numerous incidents of terrorists and criminals using this 'marauder' tactic of shooting or stabbing anyone and everyone.

There are different types of people who carry out these attacks, for various reasons and using variations of the tactic. However, an active killer is someone who is armed, has used deadly force and continues to do so.

According to this definition, this can include someone with a machete instead of a gun for example.

The technique teaches you to pretend that you have been killed in the attack so that the subject(s) leave you alone.

Why do it?
This tactic has been used successfully by many victims of active killer incidents and is easy to practice and operationalise. It can also be used in conjunction with the 'Drop n roll' technique learnt in Level 1 – i.e. once you have dropped to the floor, you can play dead at any point thereafter.

How to execute the technique:
The playing dead technique is there for you to blend in to the background of other dead people and not be checked by the subject(s). However, it is not a fool proof way to survive: subjects may follow up with headshots to those lying on the floor to make sure they are dead. Moreover, this technique is unlikely to work if the attacker is targeting you specifically.

As soon as you realise you and others are being shot at, drop to the floor. If the incident is a stabbing attack, then drop to the floor near to wounded victims.

You must relax all of your muscles. Common mistakes include having heels in the air with toes on the floor – the ankles must be relaxed. Elbows in the air with hands on the floor is also a common mistake.

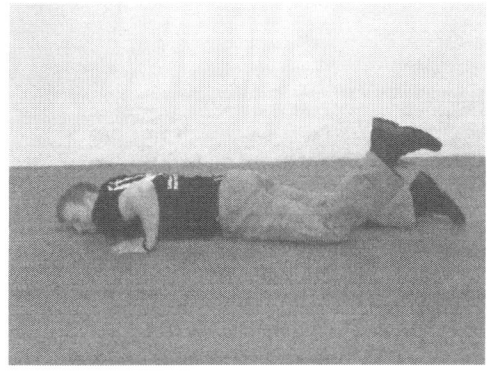
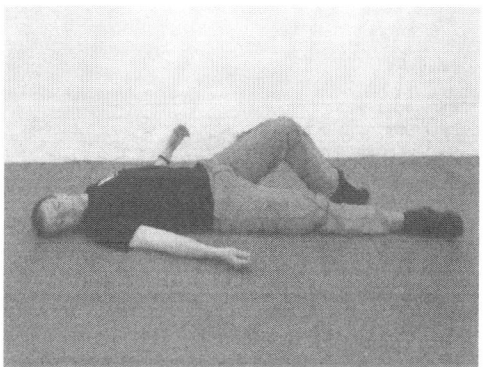

Most people who are shot die with their eyes open. The only people who die with their eyes shut, are those who have been knocked unconscious first or have passed out through blood loss prior to death. As such, you should try to keep your eyes open for a shooting.

The eyes can be almost closed if the attack is a stabbing incident. This also allows you to see what's going on around you.

However, you must be disciplined – If you are playing dead with your eyes open, pick a spot either on the wall, floor or ceiling and look at it. Do not be tempted to move your eyes from that spot if you are even remotely suspicious that the subject(s) are nearby. If you have to blink, do so slowly and when you are not in view of the subjects – quick movements are picked up more easily than slow ones.

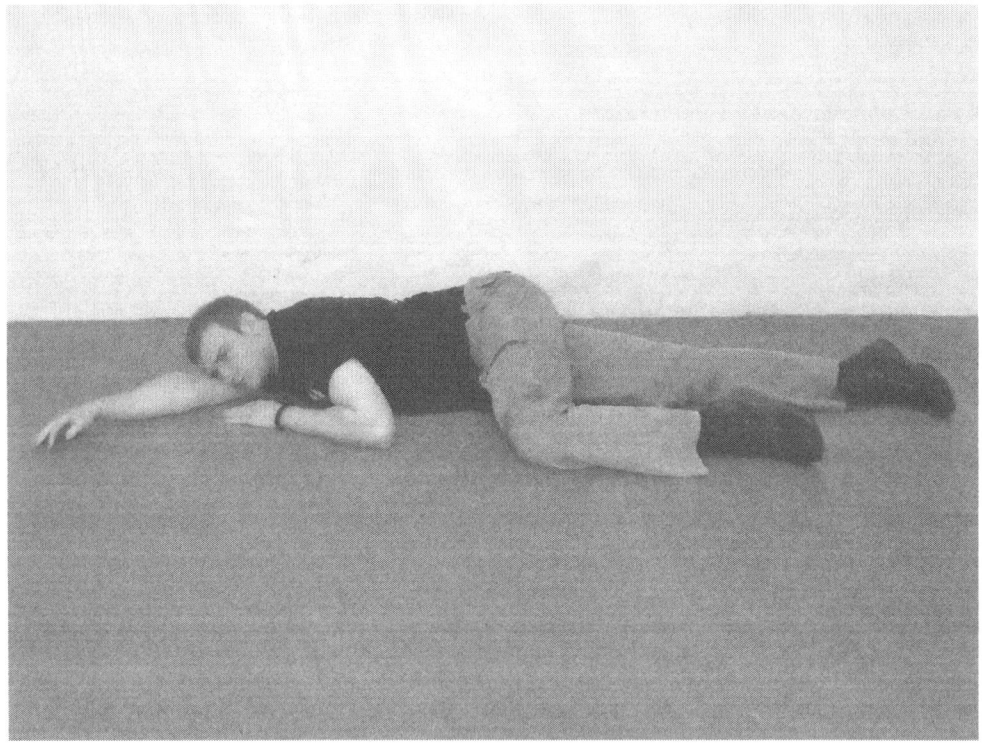

Lie on your side and try to maintain slow, shallow breathing. Obviously holding your breath if you suspect a subject is near. The reason for lying on one's side is to disguise breathing movements. If you are lying on your front or back, the inflation of the chest raises the upper body. However, if you are on your side, your body will not move up and down and as such will be less likely to be noticed.

If there are any others near you who are wounded, use their blood to smear on yourself to add to the ruse.

If the subject's do not move on, you may need to escape. However, remember the 2 second rule in a shooting and the 21 foot rule in a stabbing – if you are too far away from cover/escape and you try to run to either, the subject(s) will be able to target you. You could consider using the sniper crawl to get you to within a 2 second distance from cover/escape. This is essentially just using your finger tips and toes to slowly move you along the ground when the subject(s) are not looking. This may take several sets of movements.

If this allows you to get close enough to cover/escape, then wait for the right time and run for it.

Because the subjects may follow up with head shots or kick you to check you are really dead, you must be prepared to take action if that appears to be the case. This could be because you see this happening around you, or the subject is approaching you after having appeared to have finished their attack. Zigzag/lateral running or attacking the subject are your only viable options at this stage.

Essentials:
- Can be used in conjunction with 'Drop n roll' technique
- Relax your muscles
- Lie on your side
- Keep your eyes open for a shooting and nearly closed for a stabbing
- Breathe shallow and slow
- Use blood to smear on yourself
- Use the sniper crawl to get closer to cover/escape
- Be prepared to take action if the subjects appear to be checking if victims are really dead

Technique specific exercises:
Carry out scenario training with a BB gun. The usual safety advice should be heeded. PLEASE REFER TO SECTION ON BB GUN TRAINING BEFORE CARRYING OUT THIS DRILL.

One or two people take the role of the subject(s).

They should come into the training room and shoot at everyone.

All students should drop to the floor and play dead. The 'subject(s)' should walk around the 'bodies' and try to detect movement or signs of life. Should any be detected, the student gets shot with the BB gun as a reminder.

Defence against active killer – building tactics

What is it?
This is a guide to aide decision making when an active shooter is in the same building as you are.

Why do it?
Chaos is likely to be widespread in these circumstances, so a set of three easy to remember tactics will help you make quick and effective decisions to increase your chances of survival.

How to execute the technique:
Firstly, get into the habit of noting at least 2 exits in every room you go in your daily life. If there is ever an active shooter incident in the future, you know of at least one potential escape route even if the subject is blocking the other.

There are three options when faced with an active shooter in the same building as you. In order of preference, they are:

- Run
- Hide
- Fight

Run:

If you will not come into the path of the subject(s), then evacuation is the best option. It allows you to get to relative safety, gives you far more mobility and options and allows you to raise the alarm.

However, the initial attack may be an attempt to drive victims outside into one place where an explosive is detonated or more subjects are waiting to shoot you. As such, move to a non-obvious evacuation point as soon as possible.

If the subject(s) are close by, use 'Zigzag' or running at a 90 degree angle to them where possible (as learnt in Level 1 and Level 5).

Hide:

If you are in a corridor, you have nowhere to run but forwards or backwards – you are in the 'fatal funnel' meaning, you cannot escape the flying bullets.

If possible, get into a room that allows escape or at least 'onward movement'. Onward movement means that there is an adjoining room or hallway that you could move to should you need to, giving you more options.

Get out of the doorway as this too is a 'fatal funnel'.

If there is no escape, then barricade the door.

Then hide behind the best cover you can find that allows you movement – i.e. don't squeeze into a cupboard that will take you 10 seconds to get out of. Instead, squat behind a filing cabinet, so at least you can run or attack the subject instantly if you have to.

Case studies have shown that subject's on shooting sprees tend to only carry out cursory searches when mass casualties are the goal, so hiding gives a good chance of survival. That said, if they are looking for you specifically, then attacking the subject upon entering the room may be the best option.

Stay quiet. Turn your phone to silent. Make a call to the Police if possible. If you cannot speak, leave the line open to allow a 'passive' call.

Beware of deceptive 'cries for help'. This could be the subject trying to lure people out. It could even be the subject coercing one of the victims to lure people out.

Fight:

If you attack a subject that comes into the room, be mindful that there may be other subjects that could follow them in.

With the door closed, you should stand on the handle side if possible so you don't have to manoeuvre around a door to get to the subject. Stay behind an imaginary 45 degree line extending from the door jam and into the room as this reduces the chances of the subject seeing any part of you before you attack them.

The attack could utilise improvised weapons such as a fire extinguisher used as an impact weapon to the subject's head. However, you will need to control their weapon as soon as possible and carry out the appropriate technique. As such, carry out one strike, then control the weapon.

A group attack tactic, is having several victims stacked and hidden next to the door way with several others hidden elsewhere in the room. As the subject enters the room, these victims throw objects at the subject to act as a distraction whilst those that were stacked next to the door aggressively control the weapon and the subject.

Essentials:
- Always have 2 exits in mind
- 'Run'
- 'Hide'
- 'Fight'

Technique specific exercises:
With a little imagination an active killer scenario training drill with airsoft weapons or rubber knives could test all of these tactics. PLEASE REFER TO SECTION ON BB GUN TRAINING BEFORE CARRYING OUT THIS DRILL.

Defence against active killer – execution indicators

What is it?
Execution indicators are behaviours of subject's that suggest they are likely to execute you.

Why do it?
If you recognise any of the indicators, then you should try to fight or escape. Otherwise you will simply be letting the subject kill you. At least these indicators give you a chance to make a last ditch attempt at surviving.

How to execute the technique:
As discussed in Level 1, most humans are not natural born killers of other humans. As such, the subject is likely to want to de-humanise you to make it psychologically easier for them to kill you.

- They may tell you to turn around (this is so they cannot see your face)

- They may tell you to kneel (this is so you are not 'human' size)

- They may tell you to do both

- They may cover your face – perhaps with a bag or pillow case (again, this is so they cannot see your face)

- They may ask for you by name (indicating you are a specific target)
- Other more general indicators include binding you or moving you to another location.

If you look at the subject, this may cause them to feel you are a threat or that you could identify them. As such, just look towards the floor – it is non-confrontational and you can still see movement of the subject(s).

This is not an exhaustive list, nor is it a 100% guarantee that the subject WILL execute you under the circumstances described. However, if they are an armed criminal/terrorist and demonstrate one or more of the above, you should fight or escape as it is very likely to be your only chance at survival.

Essentials:
    Indicators:
- Tell you to turn around
- Tell you to kneel
- Cover your face
- Ask for you by name
- Bind you
- Move you to another location

    Response:
- Do not look at the subject(s) directly
- Fight and/or escape if an indicator is displayed

Technique specific exercises:
The scenario of a bank robbery could be used (not necessarily an active shooter incident, but works perfectly well) and the subject armed with an airsoft gun demonstrates one or more of the execution indicators. Those who comply, get shot.
PLEASE REFER TO SECTION ON BB GUN TRAINING BEFORE CARRYING OUT THIS DRILL

Defence against a liquid attack

What is it?
This is a defensive technique to be used when liquid is thrown at your face. This could be just a pint of beer or it could be bleach or acid for example. It could also include someone spitting in your face.

Why do it?
Criminals use throwing liquid in a victim's face to act as a distraction prior to a more serious attack, or as the attack itself using some form of noxious liquid. Spitting is also a common method of distraction and/or assault.

How to execute the technique:
If you are alert, then when a subject approaches with something in their hand, you should be at least stood in the 'Alert stance' described in Level 1.

However, you may not be as alert as you should be and/or taken by surprise.

Either way, as the liquid is thrown towards your face, you will naturally flinch, raising your arms. Use this natural response to shield your face.

As you do so, turn your head away and close your eyes.

Do not breathe at this point. That doesn't mean take a deep breath and hold it. If the liquid is noxious, then that deep breath may have caused you to inhale something dangerous. So do not breathe means close your mouth at whatever stage of the breathing cycle you are.

Step away from the subject and use your right bicep to wipe the right side of your face – up and outwards only once. Do the same with the left bicep for the left side of your face. Wiping any more times may cause the liquid to be reintroduced to your eye having soaked into your sleeve. As you wipe, use the forearm of each arm to wipe the scalp at the same time to help prevent any liquid on top of your head from dripping back down into your eyes.

Bear in mind, you may have only a few seconds of visibility, or possibly none at all, so at this point, you must either escape or acquire your target (know where the target is either visually, or by attaching to them with a grab) and attack until the subject is neutralised.

As soon as it is safe to do so, decontaminate your eyes and face and seek emergency medical treatment immediately.

Decontaminate flushing your eyes with plenty of clean water for at least 20 minutes. Whilst clean water is best, the liquid you are attacked with may be burning you chemically, so other cold beverages may be suitable as a temporary measure until you can obtain clean water.

Essentials:
- Get into alert stance if possible
- Shield your face with your arm's natural flinch response

- Turn your face
- Close your eyes
- Don't breathe
- Step away
- Wipe your face once with each of your biceps and your scalp with your forearms
- Escape or acquire your target and attack
- Decontaminate and seek emergency medical treatment

Technique specific exercises:
To make this more realistic, a plastic cup of water can be held by your training partner during a simulated argument. At a time of their choosing, they should throw the water in your face and you should of course carry out the technique.

Defence against a hand grenade attack

What is it?
This is a technique to improve your chances of survival when you realise a grenade or Improvised Explosive Device (IED) is about to be used.

Why do it?
80% of terrorist attacks include the use of small explosives and firearms. It has been known for criminals to use grenades, pipe bombs etc. as well.

How to execute the technique:
A hand grenade is designed to explode on the floor and shrapnel be sent up and out towards standing victims. As such, by getting on the floor before it explodes, you have already significantly increased your chances of survival. Other IED's such as pipe and nail bombs are likely to explode in a similar way.

A hand grenade has an internal fuse. This can be set for various different times. A method of using a grenade is to 'cook' it prior to throwing it, so it goes of instantaneously. 'Cooking' a grenade means pulling the pin and releasing the spoon to start the fuse count down. The subject will hold the grenade for a few seconds before throwing it, to give the victim's less time to react. So if the grenade has a 5 second fuse, they may hold it for 3 seconds prior to throwing it. Other IED's can be used in a similar way.

Hand grenades will generally roll on the floor before coming to a natural stop or exploding. This makes it difficult to decide which way to dive to the floor. If you dive too quickly, you may not be able to guess accurately where the grenade will end up and it could roll around right next to your head. Equally, if you wait until it comes to a natural stop, it could be too late and explode beforehand.

As such, you need to take a measured risk. That is to briefly observe the grenade in order to make a reasonable guess as to where it may land.

As you observe shout "GRENADE" so that others around you may take action. Most will not unless they have Military training, but there's only so much you can do for others in such a short period of time.

Dive in the opposite direction of where the grenade is likely to land.

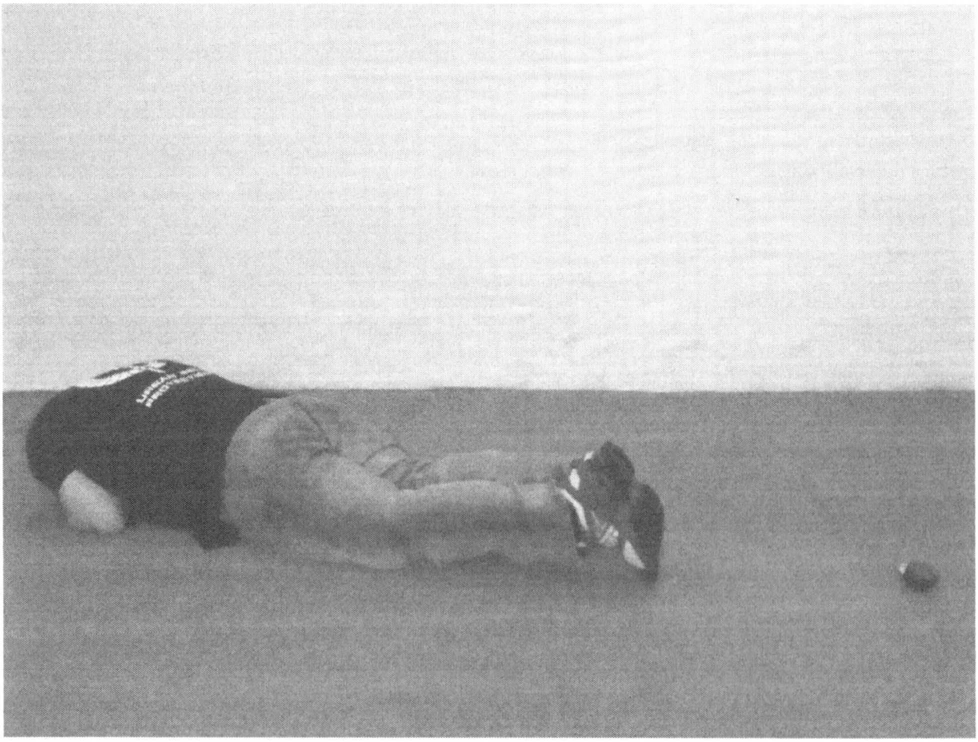

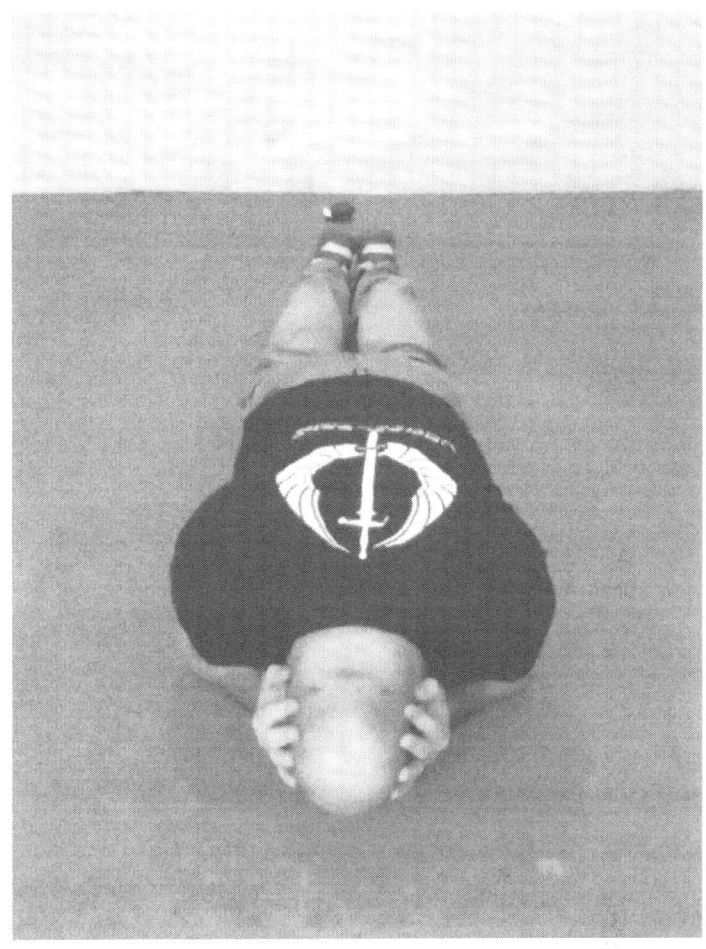

Put your feet together and tips of the toes on the ground. The bottom of your shoes in this position is the first place any shrapnel may hit. The shoes should offer some protection. Even if the shrapnel makes it through the soles of the shoes, it must continue all the way up your leg until it hits a vital area, again improving your chances of survival.

Place your forehead on the floor. This is so that when the blast wave of the explosion hits you, your head doesn't get thrown about and strike the floor causing injury.

Close your eyes – there will be huge amounts of debris and dust which could cause eye injury.

Open your mouth – this is to prevent air pressure build up and helps to protect the eardrums and lungs.

Put your hands over your ears – this is to prevent the shock wave causing damage to your ear drums.

Keep your elbows tucked into your ribs – if they are not tucked in, there is more potential for shrapnel to hit your arms and ribs. Your arms tucked in will help shield your ribs and the arteries in the arm pit should any shrapnel move towards that area.

Essentials:
- Shout "GRENADE"
- Briefly observe the grenade
- Dive away from it
- Feet together, on your toes
- Elbows tucked in
- Hands over ears
- Forehead on the floor
- Eyes closed
- Mouth open

Technique specific exercises:
Every so often, throw a simulated grenade when in training so you and those you are training with have to act immediately.

Defence against a suicide bomber – dead man's switch

What is it?
This is a last resort technique to disable a suicide bomber.

Why do it?
Terrorist attacks are sadly becoming very common. As stated above, 80% of terrorist attacks will include firearms and explosives. This includes explosives warn by the terrorist which inevitably kills them upon detonation, hence the name 'suicide bomber'.

Of course, the best thing you can do if you spot a suicide bomber is to evacuate the area and warn others. However, you may spot a bomber and feel they are about to detonate the bomb or you will be unable to evacuate those around you. As such, this is a dangerous, last resort tactic which should only be used when there is no other choice.

How to execute the technique:
There are many variations on suicide bombs. They could be hidden in a rucksack, in shoes, even in under wear. However, the most common is the suicide vest. The two common methods of detonation switch, is the dead man's switch and the plunger. As such, these are the two methods we will look at defending against.

A dead man's switch, is usually held like a plunger in the bomber's hand. The button is already depressed and will only detonate the explosive when the plunger button is released. As such, if the bomber is shot and killed, the explosive will detonate anyway as he will automatically release the button on the plunger.

Approach the bomber covertly from behind them.

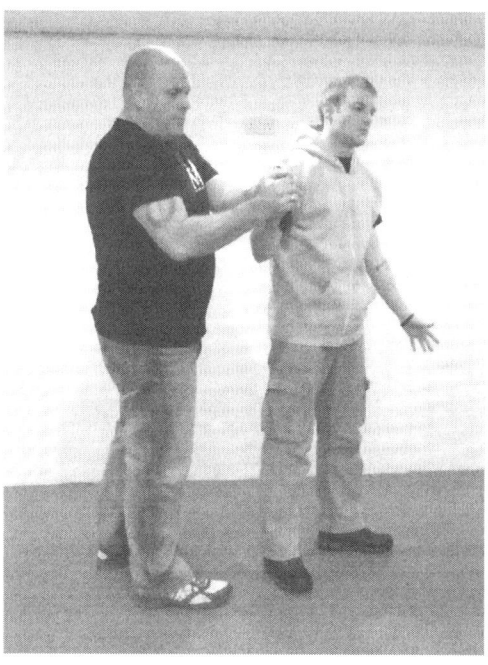

Place your inside hand over the thumb of the bomber's plunger hand to ensure they do not release the button. Use your outside hand to cup the bomber's plunger hand ready to carry out a cavalier take down.

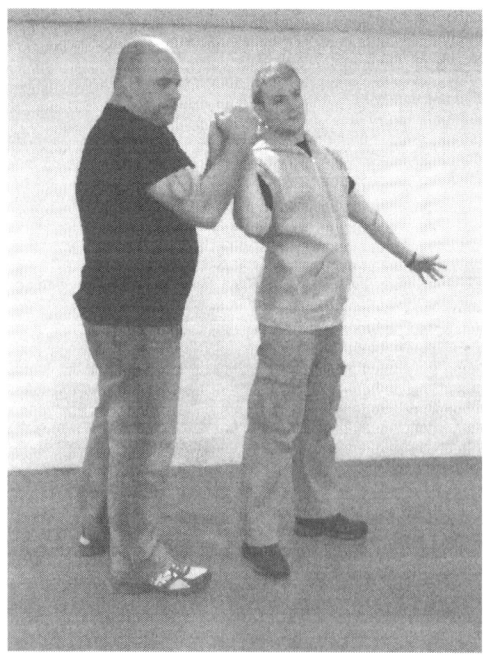

Act quickly and decisively carrying out a cavalier takedown.

Take care to land the bomber on their side by pulling their plunger arm upwards slightly. This is because there is often a secondary detonation switch on the front of the vest so throwing them onto their front may actually detonate the explosive.

Immediately stand on their other arm with one foot. This is to prevent them from triggering any secondary switches.

Remember, the device could be detonated remotely by an accomplice as well, so even if you are successful in your takedown, this is still an incredibly dangerous technique and as already stated should only be used as a last resort.

Incapacitate them however you can – obtain assistance and/or knee strike their head/throat until they are neutralised. Remember to keep the plunger button depressed. From here, you will require professional assistance. If you are concerned the device will detonate anyway and cannot wait for professional assistance, consider taping the plunger button down before you run to cover.

Essentials:
- Approach from the rear
- Cover the plunger with your inside hand
- Carry out a cavalier take down
- Keep the subject on their side and control their other hand with one of your feet
- Neutralise the subject

- Consider taping the plunger to aide an escape to cover

Technique specific exercises:
Use a small torch with a button on the cap. Depress the button which turns the light on. Then depress it again so that it is still on, but will turn off if you release the button. If your training partner can take you down without the light going out, this is a good indicator of a successful takedown.

Defence against a suicide bomber – plunger switch

What is it?
This is a last resort technique to disable a suicide bomber.

Why do it?
As stated before, the best thing you can do if you spot a suicide bomber is to evacuate the area and warn others. However, you may spot a bomber and feel they are about to detonate the bomb or you will be unable to evacuate those around you. As such, this is a dangerous, last resort tactic which should only be used when there is no other choice.

How to execute the technique:
There are many variations on suicide bombs. They could be hidden in a rucksack, in shoes, even in under wear. However, the most common is the suicide vest. The two common methods of detonation switch, is the dead man's switch and the plunger. As such, these are the two methods we will look at defending against.

A plunger switch, is usually held in the bomber's hand. The button has not yet been depressed and will only detonate the explosive when it is. You will be able to make an educated guess as to this being the case if their thumb is away from the button and the button is visible to you.

Approach the bomber covertly from behind them.

Place your inside hand around the thumb of the bomber's plunger hand to ensure they do not depress the button. Use your outside hand to cup the bomber's plunger hand ready to carry out a cavalier take down.
Act quickly and decisively carrying out a cavalier takedown.

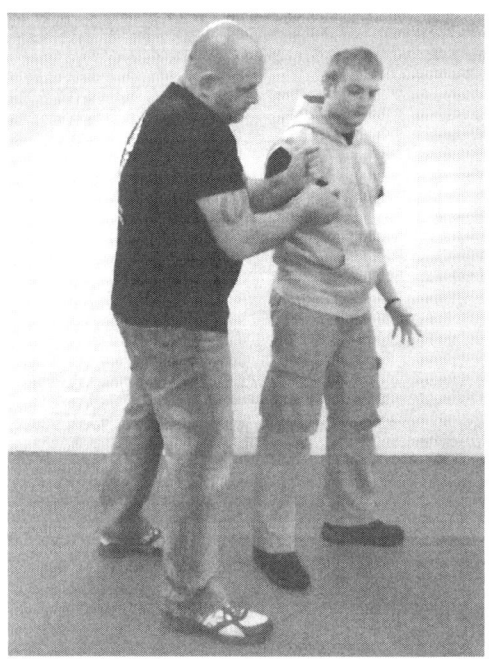
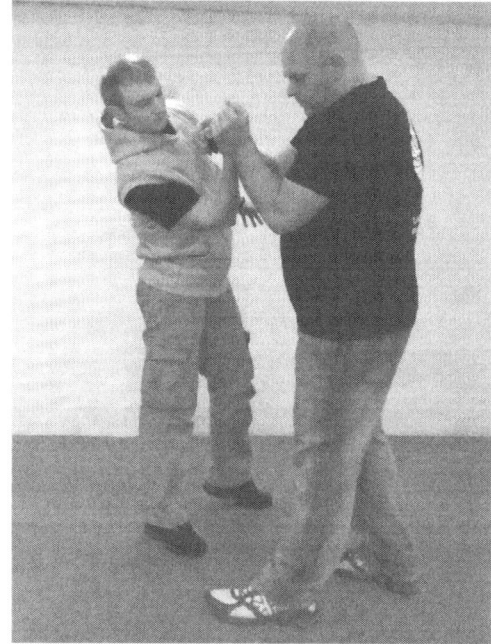

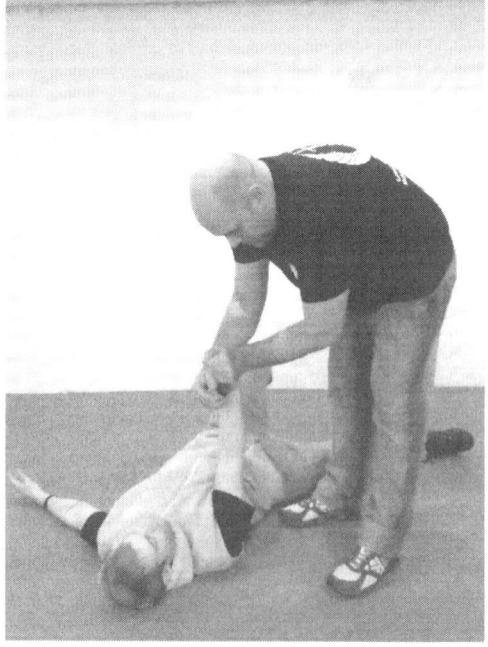

Take care to land the bomber on their side by pulling their plunger arm upwards slightly. As mentioned in the previous technique, this is because there is often a secondary detonation switch on the front of the vest so throwing them onto their front may actually detonate the explosive.

Immediately stand on their other arm with one foot. This is to prevent them from triggering any secondary switches.

Remember, the device could be detonated remotely by an accomplice as well, so even if you are successful in your takedown, this is still an incredibly dangerous technique and as already stated should only be used as a last resort.

Incapacitate them however you can – obtain assistance and/or knee strike their head/throat until they are neutralised. Remember to protect the button on the plunger from being depressed. From here, you will require professional assistance. If you are concerned the device will detonate anyway and cannot wait for professional assistance, consider taking the plunger out of the subject's hand (assuming they are dead/unconscious) and placing it on the ground before you run to cover.

Essentials:
- Approach from the rear
- Grab the subject's thumb with your inside hand
- Carry out a cavalier take down
- Keep the subject on their side and control their other hand with one of your feet
- Neutralise the subject
- Consider removing the plunger from the dead/unconscious subject's hand and placing it on the ground to aide an escape to cover

Technique specific exercises:
Use a small torch with a button on the cap in the off position. If your training partner can take you down without the light going on, this is a good indicator of a successful takedown.

Knife use – alert stance

What is it?
Knife use tactics are taught for times when it is necessary to use a knife or other edged weapon in a defensive situation. These will be improvised weapons in the UK as it is illegal to carry a pointed or sharply bladed instrument (which obviously includes knives) here in public, unless it is a folding pocket knife (no locking mechanism) with an edge no longer than 3 inches. The other exception is that you are carrying the instrument with good reason.

Self-defence is not considered a good reason in the eyes of UK law.

Examples of a good reason include taking knives that you use at work to and from your place of work and a fisherman taking a fishing knife to and from the place he is fishing. However, a court will decide what a good reason is and every situation is different.

Make sure you are aware of and adhere to the local laws regarding weapons wherever you are in the world.

The knife use alert stance is a covert ready stance prior to deployment of the weapon.

Why do it?
An improvised edged weapon can greatly improve your chances of surviving an attack as it gives you advantages of posturing, stabbing and slashing attacks. Improvised edged weapons of opportunity are plentiful and are generally very easy and simple to use to good effect.

Examples of improvised edged weapons are:

- A kitchen knife
- A screwdriver
- A piece of glass
- Keys
- Pens/pencils

(For training, we generally use a rubber knife or safe rigid plastic version).

You should make it a habit to spot these types of objects when you are out and about. For example, in your place of work is there a pen nearby that you could pick up.

Each object should be considered for it's individual characteristics. For example, a screw driver would not be able to slash very effectively, but it would be easy and effective to stab with. Glass would be good to slash with, but unlikely to cause deep puncture wounds.

That is not to say that you should look for the perfect object for the specific situation as time is of course, of the essence. But you should have some idea of the differences in characteristics and a good way to do this is to handle these various objects as part of your training. This will help weed out objects you think would be effective, but actually may be of little use to you in a conflict.

The reason for this specific technique – 'Knife use alert stance', is to allow you to covertly ready your improvised weapon so it is easy to deploy from a defensive stance.

Improvised weapons that are not to hand are very difficult to deploy under the pressure of a real confrontation due to the loss of fine motor skills.

For example, a sharp nail file at the bottom of a handbag is of no real value. You should be alert in 'Colour Code Yellow' and when in 'Colour Code Orange' (considering your options regarding a potential threat), consider putting an improvised weapon in your hand and hiding it from sight until it is needed so you don't fumble with it at the vital moment.

How to execute the technique:
The stance is the same as the 'Alert stance', described in Level1, with the exception that your rear hand is on, or holding, the improvised edged weapon. The edged weapon should be on your rear side, perhaps hidden in a pocket, waist band or behind your back.

You should try to make your rear hand look natural and not give away the fact that you have a weapon to hand.

Essentials:
- As per 'Alert stance'
- Hand on/holding weapon
- Hidden on rear side

Knife use – grip/stance

What is it?
A method of holding a knife or improvised edged weapon once deployed.

Why do it?
When utilising an improvised weapon in a confrontation, the most dangerous thing that could happen is your weapon falling into the hands of the subject or a third party and used against you. It is particularly difficult to retain a weapon once your hands get blood and/or sweat on them which they inevitably will in this situation. As such, the correct grip and stance will help you retain control of the knife.

How to execute the technique:
The ideal way to hold the knife is with the tip pointing up, with the edge towards knuckles. However, if you are grabbing a kitchen knife from a knife block in your kitchen for example, you may just grab it and hold it tip down or 'ice pick' grip. Whilst there is nothing wrong with this grip, the tip upwards method is more versatile so use it wherever possible.

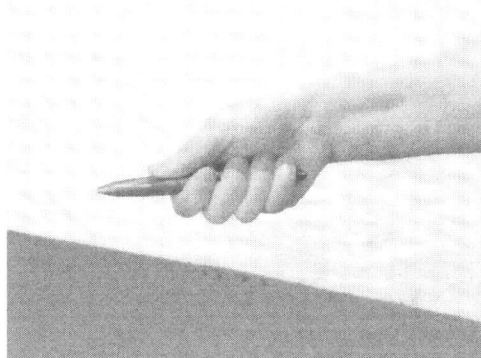 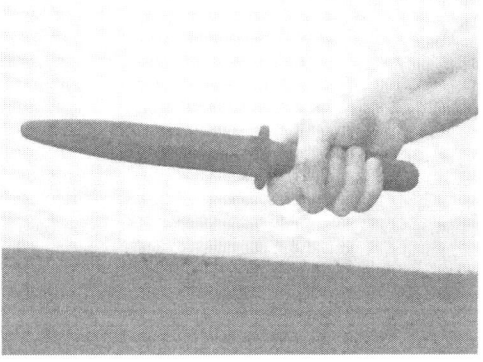

For the tip up grip, the weapon should be held tightly in the fist. The pad of the thumb tip should press firmly against the handle. A loose grip means a much higher chance of accidentally dropping the knife. An even tighter grip would be making a complete fist around the knife handle (full fist grip). The full fist grip works well for larger knives with thicker handles, whereas the grip using the pad of the thumb tip is better for thinner handles and smaller knives – or improvised weapons such as pencils or screwdrivers.

For the tip down or 'ice pick' grip, again grip the weapon tightly in your fist and this time place the pad of your thumb tip on the top of the butt of the knife handle, this is to prevent the weapon slipping through your hand if the tip strikes something hard like bone. As before, larger knives with thicker handles are best gripped using a full fist grip.

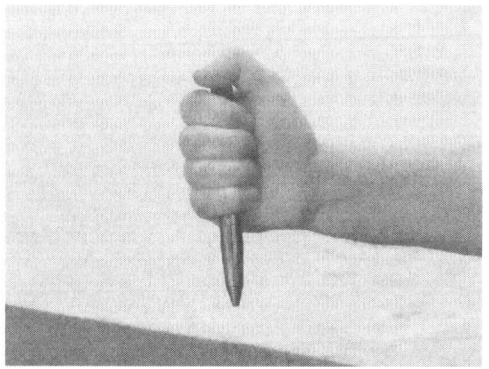
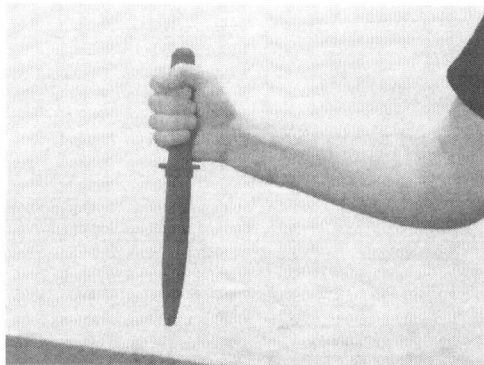

The stance for either grip is no different to a fighting stance, with the knife in the rear hand. This allows better weapon retention as the knife is further away from the subject.

However, it also means that your strikes with the weapon are slower than if they were in the lead hand. The only thing that is slightly different to a normal fighting stance is that the knife hand can be positioned in various ways depending on the characteristics of the knife (length, weight etc) your preference and the dynamics of the incident. As long as it is drawn back then you should be able to retain it.

Essentials:
- Tip up is best
- Grip the handle tightly with pad of thumb tip pressed against the handle or full fist grip for larger knives
- If using tip down, grip the handle tightly with pad of thumb tip on the butt of the handle or full fist grip for larger knives
- Knife should be in rear hand
- Stance is as per fighting stance

Technique specific exercises:
Hold a training knife for 30 minutes whilst training. If you drop it, your training partner dislodges it or you put it down, then give yourself a punishment as this reminds you that failing to retain your weapon can have consequences.

'Musical weapons' can also be used:

This is where safe versions of the weapons you are trained in are placed in the centre of a circle. Both you and your training partner walk around opposite sides of the circle with music playing. A third person turns the music off at which point, you and your training partner both rush in and grab the first weapon you can and begin sparring with it, improving your adaptation.

Knife use - 10 Angles

What is it?
Strikes using a knife or edged/pointed object.

Why do it?
The use of an improvised weapon is a force multiplier, meaning that smaller weaker defenders will have a greater chance of neutralising larger and stronger subjects. Knife like objects are readily available in everyday life, whether it's a pencil, screwdriver, dinner fork or a snapped credit card.

How to execute the technique:
Targets need to be considered when striking them, particularly with a weapon. Please refer back to the impact weapon trauma chart. Remembering that this is a very serious and high level use of force, it can be legally justifiable given the right circumstances.

Generally speaking, stab wounds are more effective at stopping the subject as they tend to penetrate deeper. That said, a slash wound may not cause as much physical damage, but it can help take the fight out of the subject if they see what looks to be a large horrific slash wound as opposed to a puncture wound produced by a stab.

In any event, any knife attack is usually highly effective. Don't forget though, people can carry on fighting even with multiple stab wounds, so don't rely on them dropping like a stone when you stab them.

As with all strikes, retract quickly. Although unlikely, there is a chance that there may be some suction caused by a stab wound making withdrawal of the blade from the subject harder. As such, carry out a short sharp twist before retracting to prevent this.

Bear in mind that clothing can prevent the knife from penetrating as effectively or even at all.

Body targets can be seen in a very similar way to that of impact weapon target acquisition, in that, stabbing or slashing the arms, legs, hands or feet are less likely to be lethal strikes than stabbing or slashing the face, head, throat, torso or groin. That said, bear in mind there are major arteries on the inside of the thigh and in the arm pits too.

Consider the characteristics of various knife like objects. Some will allow both stabbing and slashing (a kitchen knife for example), some will allow only a stabbing attack (a pencil for example) and some will only allow a slashing attack (a snapped credit card for example).

The following photographs only depict a tip up grip. Train with an ice pick grip and find out which angles are appropriate and which ones are awkward.

Forwards angle – hold the weapon in your rear hand and drive it forwards as you would for a cross punch, bending your wrist to point the tip of the weapon at the target. Turn it so the blade is horizontal as this will penetrate ribs more easily. This is also to increase the stopping power and effectiveness of the strike; veins in the body run vertically, so you are likely to damage more this way.

A tip down (ice pick) grip makes it awkward to carry out a forward angle strike, although it is possible. This is a stab only angle and as such a slash only weapon such as a snapped credit card will not be effective.

Backwards angle - Hold the weapon in one hand and look over your shoulder on the side you're holding it (remember that by looking over your shoulder, you will lose depth perception as you will effectively have only one eye on the target). If you are in a passive stance, take a step backwards and swing the weapon backwards along the horizontal plane and strike the target as you would with a rear hammer fist strike. If you are using a tip up grip, then the strike will be a slash. If you are using a tip down (ice pick) grip, then the strike will be a stab.

Horizontal plane, right to left (from right fighting stance, mirror if in left fighting stance) – you can both stab and slash in either grips at this angle. However, slashing with the tip up grip is usually the most natural.

Horizontal plane, left to right (from right fighting stance, mirror if in left fighting stance) – you can both stab and slash in either grips at this angle. However, slashing with the tip up grip is usually the most natural.

Vertical upward angle – you can stab or slash with the tip up grip on this angle. With the tip down grip you can only attack using a slash. Pivot your feet accordingly.

Vertical downward angle – you can only slash using a tip up grip on this angle. You can only stab with a tip down grip on this angle. Raise the knife like object up and back. Strike down the centre line on the vertical plane as you would for a downward hammer fist strike. This may be to target the head in a serious attack or perhaps a limb in a less dangerous incident. Drop your weight as you make contact with the target and pivot on your rear foot.

Diagonal angles: The weapon moves along an imaginary 'X' on the subject's body.

Diagonal down, right to left (from right fighting stance, mirror if in left fighting stance) – you can both stab and slash in either grips at this angle, although slashing in a tip down grip is awkward.

Diagonal down, left to right (from right fighting stance, mirror if in left fighting stance) – you can slash in a tip up grip on this angle and stab in a tip down grip.

Diagonal up, right to left (from right fighting stance, mirror if in left fighting stance) – you can slash or stab in a tip up grip on this angle, but only slash with a tip down grip.

Diagonal up, left to right (from right fighting stance, mirror if in left fighting stance) – you can both stab and slash in either grips at this angle, although both slashing and stabbing in a tip down grip is awkward on this angle.

Technique specific exercises:
To gain power and skill, a rubber knife used against a punch bag is very useful.

Use of a realistic training mannequin is good too as it assists with target acquisition.

Rubber knives can be used as a safe training tool and could be laying on the ground when you spar with your training partner or practice a technique and if it's appropriate to pick it up, then it can be used to strike.

You could also spar with rubber knives, wearing eye protection of course.

Consider using safe versions of improvised knife like weapons for training too – for example, marker pens with their lids on are a fairly safe way to represent a pen, or perhaps a soft plastic toy screwdriver from a toy shop to obviously replicate a screwdriver.

Knife use – flow combinations

What is it?
Combinations of strikes using an edged weapon.

Why do it?
Remembering that this is a very serious and high level use of force, it can be legally justifiable given the right circumstances. As mentioned above, stab wounds are generally more effective at stopping the subject as they tend to penetrate deeper. That said, a slash wound may not cause as much physical damage, but it can help take the fight out of the subject if they see what looks to be a large horrific slash wound as opposed to a puncture wound produced by a stab. In any event, any knife attack is usually highly effective. Don't forget though, people can carry on fighting even with multiple wounds, so don't rely on them dropping like a stone when you stab or slash them.

Flow combinations allow you to strike multiple times and multiple targets in a short space of time, increasing the stopping power and effectiveness of your defence. They also teach you how to add power and what types of strike combine well with others.

How to execute the technique:
As this is not a set combination, you can of course carry out any strikes you like in whatever order you like. However, you will soon find that stabbing and slashing flow together better when utilising a few principles:

If you are carrying out repeated slashes, then slash from one side to the other and then back. I.e. inward slash, then outward slash (horizontally, diagonally – up or down - or vertically downwards) or outward slash then inward slash. To just slash inwards repeatedly is awkward and unnatural as is just repeatedly slashing outwards. However, side to side allows continuous motion.

The opposite is true for stabbing. If you repeatedly stab on one side (be it upward, diagonal upward or horizontal) then you are achieving the most economy of motion. To stab inwards and then outwards straight afterwards is also unnatural and awkward.

To slash and follow with a stab would mean that if you were slashing outwards, then you could transition to stabbing inwards and if you were slashing inwards, then you could transition to stabbing outwards.

To stab and follow with a slash would mean that if you were stabbing outwards, then you could transition to slashing outwards and if you were stabbing inwards, then you could transition to slashing inwards.

This may all sound complex, but when you get a rubber or plastic training knife and try to carry out a 6-10 strike combination on a punch bag or realistic training dummy, it will all become much clearer.

Now the angles and motions have been explained, it is time to consider how to achieve a powerful strike. You will be using the principle of 'torque'. This is essentially making sure your strikes are quick, but that you are putting your body weight into each one and powerfully dragging the slashes across the body.

Lastly, you must incorporate one of the overall guiding principles from DAMSB and this is: Move. As you carry out your combination, you should, wherever possible, be moving around to the side of the subject, out of their fighting arc, but so they remain within yours.

Essentials:
- Slashes = side to side
- Stabs = same side
- Use torque – speed and body weight
- 6-10 strikes continuous motion
- Move out of their fighting arc and keep them inside yours

Technique specific exercises:
Both rigid and rubber training knives can be good for training this technique. Ideally, practice on a realistic training dummy that you have dressed with an old hoody or similar.

If you are practicing on a training partner, use only a rubber training knife and ensure that they are wearing eye protection.

Flow combinations can be mixed into sparring and blocking/countering drills (described shortly in a more appropriate section)

Knife use – blocking

What is it?
Blocking strikes using an edged weapon.

Why do it?
A knife is solid and as such possible to block the path of incoming strikes. A knife blocking a subject will likely cause them more injury than blocking with your hand and as such makes your defence more effective. This can be used against a subject with a knife.

How to execute the technique:
In a tip up grip, block against the wrist of the subject's attacking arm by blocking it's path at 90 degrees.

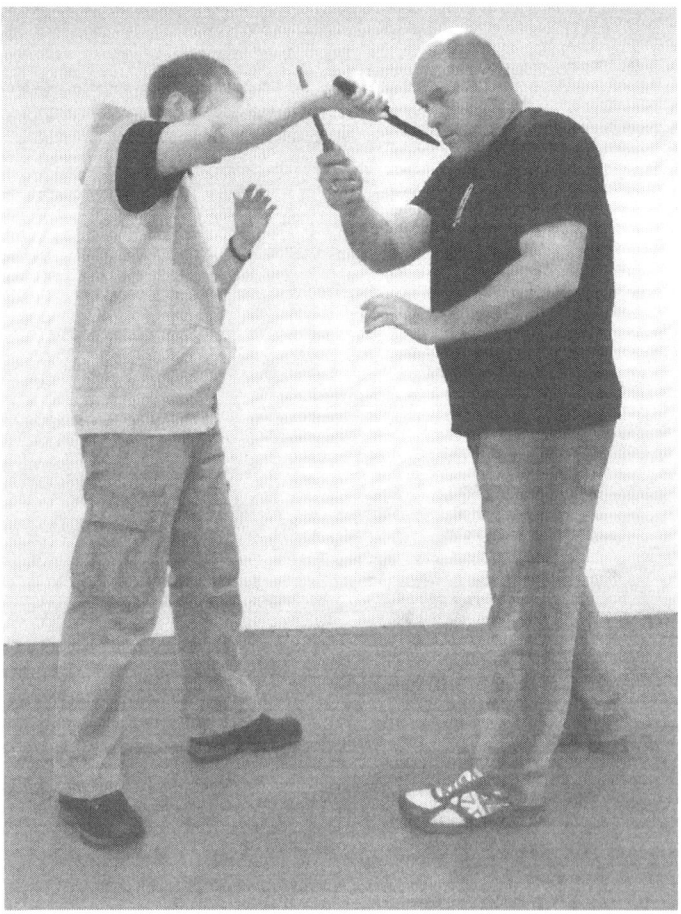

The blocks can be outward as per 360 blocking, or inward as per inside palm blocks, depending on the angle of attack.

Use your empty hand to 'check' the subject's attacking arm in case your knife is too small and misses it's target.

As the attacking arm comes in, try to move in the same direction as it is moving to effectively reduce it's impact speed. If the angle of attack is straight forwards or downwards, then of course move to one side.

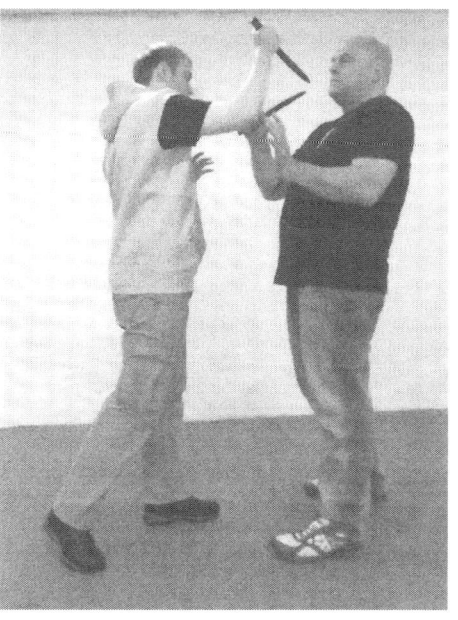 

Counter attack as soon as possible using a flow combination, moving out of the subject's fighting arc and keeping them within your own.

Essentials:
- Block knife to wrist
- Use your empty hand to 'check' the attacking arm
- Try to move in the direction of the attack, or to the side for straight forwards or downwards
- Counter with a flow combination

Technique specific exercises:
If you are practicing on a training partner, ensure that you are both wearing eye protection.

This technique can be mixed into sparring and blocking/countering drills.

The blocking/countering drills can be carried out as follows:

You and your training partner both have training knives and eye protection.

Your training partner carries out a random knife attack angle, but holds it in position to allow you to carry out your block and counter attack. Once you have finished, your training partner carries out a different angle of attack.

The next level of training comes when you carry out the same drill, but your training partner carries out their next angle of attack after only three seconds, (your training partner must stick to three seconds, perhaps by saying slowly in their head "One Mississippi, two Mississippi, three Mississippi") whether you've finished your counter attack or not. This applies pressure on you but is still not completely realistic.

The next level is the same drill, but with only two seconds before your training partner carries out their next angle of attack for even more pressure.

The next level is knife sparring.

A rolled up magazine as an improvised weapon can be used in almost exactly the same way as a knife. Try the drills above but knife vs. rolled up magazine and adapt as necessary.

Use of improvised edged weapons

What is it?
Considerations given to different types of improvised edged weapons.

Why do it?
Considering where you may quickly obtain an improvised edged weapon and how it may perform can help prevent hesitation/delay during a confrontation.

How to execute the technique:
As with any improvised weapon, you need to look out for examples of them in your everyday life as stated before. Examples include keys, a pen, a screw driver or a piece of broken glass. Do you have these items to hand in your everyday environment? Remember, in some countries it is illegal to carry any item if your intention is to use it to injure, therefore, we are only talking weapons of opportunity.

You also need to consider it's characteristics – a screw driver will deliver stabs well, but is less effective as a slashing tool and the opposite is true for a broken piece of glass. Some specific examples and their use are set out below to give you some guidance on how to think about improvised edged weapon use:

A bottle – despite what is shown in the movies, a smashed bottle will only be good for around two stabs/slashes. Of course this depends on the quality of the bottle, but this is a good guide. Stabbing or slashing a subject through their clothing is normally fairly ineffectual. As such, provided it's reasonable, only attack exposed areas such as the face and arms. The best use of a bottle is as an impact weapon and IF it breaks, then use it as an edged weapon.

A snapped credit card will slash skin very effectively (although not at all well through clothing), but not very deeply. As such, aim for the forehead as the head bleeds profusely. This has a psychological effect on the subject making them think the wound is worse than it really is and the blood may well drip into their eyes causing them difficulty in seeing and giving you a tactical advantage.

Essentials:
- Consider what edged weapons are likely to be available to you in your daily life
- Consider the types of attack they can be used for
- Consider what targets are most effective for the specific object

Technique specific exercises:
Take a mental note of any potential improvised edged weapons you see in your daily life.

Where there is a safe substitute, train with improvised edged weapons. An example would be using a thick marker pen with it's lid on to simulate a sharp pen or pencil. You could cut a plastic bottle in half and tape over the cut edge to simulate a broken bottle.

Defence against a knife threat inside a vehicle

What is it?
A defensive tactic to deal with a subject who is in your car (either sat next to you or behind you) and they are threatening you with a knife. This is most likely to be to your throat but the principles are the same with any type of knife threat.

Why do it?
Car jacking is far more likely these days as newer cars tend to have immobilisers in their keys. As such, a thief needs the keys to be able to drive the car. Gone are the days of hot wiring a car or shoving a screw driver in the ignition to start it.

Therefore, the use of a weapon to threaten a driver in these circumstances is common.

These principles parallel the 'Frenzied knife attack defence' and as such will be easy to learn and retain.

How to execute the technique:
Grab the subject's weapon arm at the wrist/forearm with both of your hands to control it.

Pin the arm to prevent the knife from flailing around as per defence against a frenzied knife attack – if the subject is behind you with the knife to your throat, pin their arm against your chest, the seat or the door pillar. If they are to your side or in front of you, pin it against the steering wheel, the dashboard or the door pillar.

Bite the subject's thumb joint until they release the knife. This is because we are unable to strike with the legs whilst confined in a vehicle and if we try to escape at this point, we'd lose control of the knife.

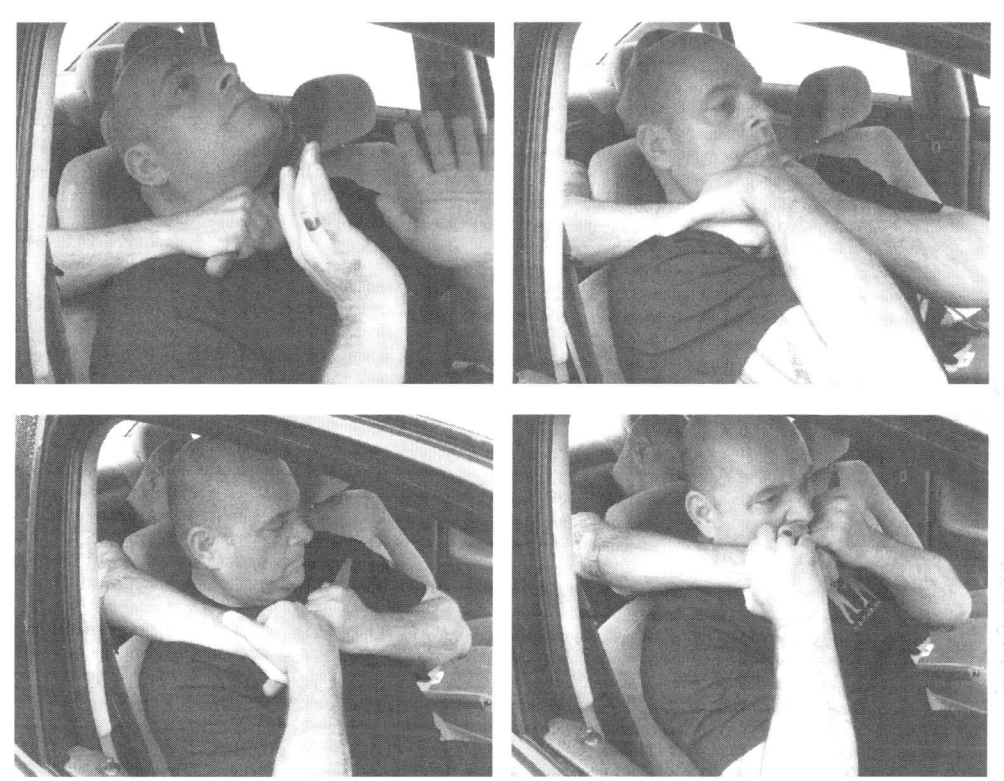

Once they have released the knife, escape if you can or continue to attack until the subject is neutralised. If you continue to attack, make sure you keep the subject from regaining the knife.

Essentials:
- Grab
- Pin
- Bite
- Escape/attack

CONFLICT KNOWLEDGE

Active killer knowledge

The following information describes what an active killer is, how they prepare, the tactics they employ and indicators for different types of attackers.

This knowledge is useful to be able to spot someone in the stages prior to an attack giving you more time to be able to deal with the situation. Knowing the types of tactics used may aide your decision making process during such an incident and increase your chances of survival. Indicators are useful to be able to predict how the attacker(s) may behave and to be able to provide first responders with useful information.

The definition of an active killer is:

"Someone who is ARMED, has used DEADLY FORCE and CONTINUES to do so."

ARMED can mean with a firearm, a knife or other type of weapon. This can include the use of a vehicle as a weapon.

'DEADLY FORCE' does not mean they have necessarily killed someone, but they have carried out a type of attack that could kill someone.

'CONTINUES' means that they are still on the rampage. If they have stopped and given up or been neutralised, they are no longer 'active'.

Stages prior to the event:

The subject will almost always go through the following stages to one degree or other:

- Imagining the incident.
  This may mean they discuss their thoughts with others. If they do so, this must be reported.
- Planning the incident.
  This includes the who, (i.e. consideration of targets and possibly accomplices) what (i.e. what they are going to do – perhaps carry out a mass shooting) where (i.e. location(s) to carry out the incident) and when (i.e. date and time). Planning will also likely include logistics. This could include how they will get to the location, how much ammunition they may need, how to communicate with accomplices etc. These plans may be committed to paper, discussed in emails, in telephone conversations etc. Again, if you suspect someone is in the planning stage you must report this.
- Preparing for the incident.

This includes obtaining the equipment they might need and hiding/stashing it somewhere. They may make a video or write a note or social media piece ready to be published on completion of / during the incident. They may also give warnings to certain people they do not want getting hurt to avoid the targeted area. So you may become aware of one or more of these preparations. If so, report it.
- Approach to the incident.
  The subject(s) will be armed and on route to the incident. Again, if you see anyone armed you obviously must report it.

Subjects in mass killings will almost never stop until they run out of ammunition, there are no more victims (all dead or escaped), they kill themselves or they are killed.

There are generally 2 categories of active killer's and their indicators/tactics are as follows:

Terrorist
- Can be a group or individual
- Multiple venues hit with a co-ordinated simultaneous attack
- They will continue until they are stopped
- What they say may indicate if they are a terrorist
- They are likely to target those in a uniform

Non Terrorist
- Alone or with one other
- One venue or consecutive venues rather than a co-ordinated attack
- They will usually commit suicide before being stopped
- What they say may indicate if they are a non-terrorist
- They are also likely to target those in a uniform

Bear in mind though, that tactics are constantly changing in terms of terrorist attacks. As this book is being written, Spontaneous Violent Extremists also known as Lone Wolves or Lone Actors are becoming more prevalent – these attackers tend to work alone and use low tech methods of attack such as bladed weapons, home made explosives or vehicles. As such, know your enemy by keeping up with the news.

Essentials:
- ARMED, DEALY FORCE, CONTINUES
- There are stages leading up to the incident that can sometimes be inadvertently revealed by the subject
- Terrorist and non-terrorists have some differences in tactics and indicators

Technique specific exercises:
Know your enemy by keeping up with the news.

Hostile vehicle attacks

Whilst this is not a new tactic used by terrorists, it is becoming more frequently used. Quite simply, the terrorist drives a vehicle into as many unsuspecting members of the public as possible, often followed by exiting the vehicle and carrying out armed attacks.

Treat the threat of a mobile vehicle attack in the same way you would with many other terrorist tactics - avoid concentrations of people, in this case it's at the roadside, particularly on bridges as these are 'bottle necks', providing less avenues to escape and as such are target rich environments for the terrorist.

You also need to get into a habit of good positioning - have a solid fixed object between you and vehicles. Whilst a lamp post won't necessarily stop a vehicle, it is likely to give you time to get to safety.

Listen for screeching tyres and vehicle acceleration - look to see what's causing the noise and be ready to get to safety.

Lastly, if you cannot escape in time, leap aside as quickly as you can - a sideswipe from a vehicle is more survivable than frontal impact and the dive may at least move your head and vital organs out of the most dangerous area.

Essentials:
- Avoid concentrations of people at the roadside – particularly bridges.
- Get into the habit of having a large fixed object between you and vehicles.
- Listen for excessive vehicle noise and look towards it.
- If you are caught in the path of a hostile vehicle, dive as far to the side as you can.

Suicide bomber traits

Identifying suicide bombers in time is one of the toughest challenge facing Security, Military and Law Enforcement Officers everywhere. If you know the common signs, you may be able to act before a detonation.

The traits change from country to country, but there are some universal characteristics to watch out for:

- Unreasonably bulky clothing – if the subject is sweating, he may be overdressed to hide a bomb belt/vest.

- Mismatched clothing – Military or civilian uniforms that are missing logos or standard issue kit – for example, a Police Officer with no radio.

- Components of a bomb – suicide bombs are usually crudely made and as such are not packaged well. The subject will need to handle the switch and as such, component parts will need to be close to hand. Perhaps there are wires protruding from the subject's sleeve for example.

- Unusual behaviour – the subject may be walking around alone, looking indecisive. They may be scratching at their clothes or repeatedly adjusting their rucksack.

- Locked on gaze – bombers have often been reported as fixing a stare into Security Officer's eyes prior to detonation. There are several theories as to why this might be, but suffice to say it is a common trait.

These characteristics on their own may mean nothing, but as part of a bigger picture, they may give you time to act.

Essentials:
- Unreasonably bulky clothing
- Mismatched clothing
- Component parts
- Unusual behaviour
- Locked on gaze

Technique specific exercises:
Know your enemy by keeping up with the news.

Escape methods

The following is a list of tips to help you escape should you be held captive, be that during a siege, kidnapping or other similar incident.

Whilst rare, people do get kidnapped, held hostage and caught in sieges. Being able to escape restraints, locked doors, fencing or even a car could all be very useful and be the difference between life and death.

Firstly, make sure that during the capture phase you try to hide any equipment that may be useful. Most obviously a mobile phone. If possible put it on silent and hide in the front of your underwear – even if you're searched, the subject is unlikely to feel comfortable checking your genital region.

Other items could be a pocket knife or multi tool, water, food, torch, compass in case of overland escape, improvised weapon and so on.

Escaping restraints:
Whilst the restraints are being put on, flex your wrists and forearms as much as possible without making it obvious to the subject. This will make it easier to slip out of the restraints later.

When you are alone, bring your hands to the front if not already in this position, by passing them under your legs and feet. With your hands at the front, even if you are unable to escape the restraint, you will still have better mobility when running or fighting.

If the restraints on your wrists are mechanical (i.e. handcuffs or similar) then you can attempt to pick the lock. This however, is incredibly difficult, so don't waste time on this option if you don't have the know-how. Alternatively, you can try to break or file down the bracelet/chain using friction against something hard like brick or metal. This of course will take a long time.

You could also try to break the handcuffs at the hinge point. This involves sliding something solid between the 'double bar' section of the handcuff bracelet (i.e. the part with two metal pieces) and twisting it violently. A seat belt buckle or a door handle could be used for example. This may part the double bar section and allow you to separate the 'single bar' and the double bar at the hinge section.

If the restraints on your wrists are tape, rope, cable or similar, then try to use anything you can to snag the bindings in order to wear through them or loosen any knots. For example a door handle or corner of a desk can be used.

If the restraints are rope, chain or similar and are being used around your body, then inhale and flex your muscles whilst it is being applied. Again, do not make it obvious to the subject that you are doing so. This will make it easier for you to slip out of the restraints later.

Plastic zip ties used around the wrists can be removed by using friction from a shoe lace. Undo your shoe lace and place the end of one of the laces in your teeth and pull it tight. Then rub the zip ties quickly up and down the lace whilst trying to prise your wrists apart. Be warned, the friction can cause a lot of heat. This should take only a few seconds to work. However, be warned that some shoe laces will break before the zip tie and others won't, so you may have to adapt the method.

Padlocks on doors:
Use something heavy and strong to smash a padlock, by directing the force so that the base separates from the shackle. Alternatively, in the unlikely event that a saw or file is available, then of course you can try to cut through the shackle. Again, picking the lock is another alternative, but requires skill and luck.

Escaping from a room:
Consider lifting / breaking through floor boards, ceiling boards or wall boards to find an escape route.

Brick walls – chisel at the mortar around one brick with a small solid object like a screw driver. Once you have removed one brick, the rest will be considerably easier to remove with blunt force such as a kick or a strike with a heavy object.

Doors – execute a 'Forward kick' at the locking point if the door opens outwards.

If it opens inwards, try removing the hinge pin.

Many doors can have holes kicked in them with persistence and a strong kick.

Glass – scratch an 'x' into the glass to weaken it before striking it with something hard and sharp.

Strike the corner of a window as the middle is the most flexible area and therefore least likely to break.

If this doesn't work and the glass is full height – i.e. a door – then run at it full force with something hard leading the strike e.g. a chair or rock. Cover your neck and face whilst doing so.

Escaping over dangerous fences:
If you suspect a fence is electrified, touch the fence with a blade of grass – if you feel a tingle in your hand, then it is.

Throw something like a coat over barbed wire before climbing over it to protect you from the barbs.

Digging a shallow dip under a fence can also be considered.

Escaping from a car boot:
Obviously jumping from a car that is moving is inherently dangerous. If you must do so, try to wait until the driver has to slow down and/or a soft landing area such as grass is available.

Depending on the circumstances, you can try to force the rear seats to fold down and escape from the rear seats.

You can try and find a cable release in the boot which will allow the boot lid to be opened.

If there are tools in the boot, try to use these to pry open the lock.

Smash the car's rear lights through and try to attract attention through the whole either with your hand or by forcing objects/debris through it.

Essentials:
- Expand your body when restraints are being placed on you
- Get your hands to your front
- Snag restraints or try to ware through them
- Zip ties can be broken using the friction of a shoe lace
- Smash or cut through padlocks
- Consider escaping a room through the floor/wall or ceiling boards
- Remove one brick and the rest will be easier to move
- Kick at door locks or remove hinge pins
- Strike the corner of a panel of glass with something hard to break it and cover your face/neck
- Test electric fences with a blade of grass
- Cover barbed wire before climbing
- Dig under fences
- In a car, force down seats, find the boot cable release, pry the lock or smash the rear lights through to attract attention

Technique specific exercises:
Training in escaping restraints holds its own specific dangers including positional asphyxiation, detailed earlier in this book as well as wrist damage and secondary injuries from falling over.

As such, your training partner must be watching you the whole time and be ready to release you from the restraints instantly. If this means having safety medical scissors on hand to cut through rope, tape or zip ties, then they should be available.

It is not safe/sensible to practice many of these techniques and simply having the knowledge of what to do should be enough to improve your chances in a real life situation. Stick to trying to escape restraints in your training and leave other techniques for use in an emergency only.

Surviving as a hostage

The following is a list of tips to help improve your chances of survival if you are held hostage in a siege type situation.

Whilst rare, people do get caught in sieges. There are several things you can do to improve your chances of survival and spot indicators of imminent violence.

Escape attempts:
The best time to make an escape attempt is during the takeover. After this only make an escape attempt if success is guaranteed, or if you will be killed imminently anyway.

Blending in:
It is dangerous to appear to be any form of threat to the hostage taker(s) as such, you need to 'go grey'. This means behaving in a way that attracts the least amount of attention to you.

If you are an athletic male, keep your sleeves rolled down and maintain a slumped posture to make you look less of a physical threat.

Avoid any behaviour or speech that could be classed as flirtatious – particularly if you are female and the hostage takers are Islamic extremists as this will likely be seen as offensive and make you a target.

Keep your gaze on the floor. If you are spoken to, look at the hostage taker's chest, not their eyes. Eye contact with the hostage taker(s) can be seen as threatening.

Accessories:
The majority of terrorist incidents are motivated by religious extremism. As such, remove and dispose of any religious icons and any identification that ties you to an enemy state/group/organisation.

Consider travelling with a separate wallet to offer that does not identify you as a target.

As per escape methods, if you have a mobile phone with you, set it to silent and hide it in your underwear.

Well-being:
Eat, drink and rest whenever possible as the siege may last a considerable amount of time.

Be careful not to fall into the Stockholme Syndrome – essentially sympathising with your captors as a result of a bond building during the incident. However, do not agitate the hostage takers either.

Helping the authorities:
Telephoning the Police and whispering details or even just leaving the line open is helpful, but do not get caught doing so as you will likely be a target for violence from the hostage takers.

Important details the Police will require include; the number of hostage takers and weapons (including explosives) at their disposal.

Stay alert and listen for inconsistencies between the truth and what the hostage takers are telling negotiators. For example, are the hostage takers exaggerating or down playing their numbers? This information needs to be passed to the Police if possible.

Indicators of immediate deadly attack from the hostage takers:
The attack could include detonation of explosives or a mass shooting etc.

Lying to negotiators may be an indicator of a likely deadly attack.

If the hostage takers are Islamic Extremists, then their playing recordings of Arabic worship may be an indicator, as may ritualistic behaviours. The phrase "Allahu Akbar" is an Arabic phrase used frequently in the Islamic faith and means "God is Greater" or "God is the Greatest". This phrase is often shouted prior to a deadly attack.

Last minute bullying and provocation of hostages may be an indicator that the hostage taker(s) are looking for an excuse to begin executing people.

Execution indicators described earlier are of course indicators of a deadly attack too.

Action to take:
If you feel there is an imminent deadly attack, then you must take action. If you don't, then you will likely die anyway.

If you feel you have time, spread the word amongst fellow captors you deem trustworthy, trying not to cause panic but to recruit as many able people as possible, ready for your assault on the hostage taker(s).

Charge the hostage taker(s) going first for those who are able to detonate bombs and then anyone you consider to be a leader of the group. Use improvised weapons if there are any to hand, but do not hesitate – if you do not have one immediately to hand, then carry out the attack unarmed – speed, aggression and surprise are the most important factors.

Rescue attempts by authorities:
When a rescue attempt is made by authorities, drop to the floor and display your hands as being empty.

Do not run.

Expect to be roughed around by the authorities and handcuffed, as they will treat everyone as a potential threat until their identity can be clarified. Offer no resistance.

Essentials:
- During the takeover is the best opportunity to escape
- Go 'grey'
- Remove items that could suggest you are an enemy to the hostage taker(s)
- Hide your phone
- Look after yourself physically and mentally
- Covert calls to the Police should include numbers of hostage taker(s) and their arsenal
- Listen for inconsistencies
- Watch and listen for indicators of an attack
- If an attack is suspected, form a group and attack
- If a rescue is attempted, drop, display your hands and expect to be treated roughly by the authorities

Technique specific exercises:
Scenario training is a good way to practice use of these tips, as is mental rehearsal.

Survival rule of 3's

The rule of 3's describes the priorities in an emergency survival situation, essentially by giving you a guide as to how long a human can survive without various things.

The emergency survival situation could be a natural disaster, a terrorist attack, a hiking accident, escaping overland from captivity, your car breaking down in the middle of nowhere and a host of other incidents.

These rules are very easy to remember therefore easy to recall in the panic of an emergency survival situation.

The rules help you prepare for and deal with emergencies that could occur when you're at home, in your car, at work or when you are travelling.

The rule of 3's:

OXYGEN:
A human can survive for 3 minutes without oxygen.

How can you prepare for a lack of oxygen? Well, perhaps you could carry a dust mask in your bag in case the atmosphere becomes polluted suddenly with dust from an explosion or a chemical attack.

Preparing for a lack of oxygen also includes having smoke detectors in your house and knowing to get low in a smoke filled environment when trying to escape.

Oxygen is obviously the TOP priority and is more important than anything else.

SHELTER:
A human can survive for 3 hours when exposed to the elements.

The elements being rain, wind, water, cold and heat. We can be protected against these elements with appropriate clothing, a tent, a cave, a car or even just by having a fire in the case of the cold. However, without them, 3 hours exposure is likely to be as long as we'll last before we become close to death.

As such, shelter needs to be your second priority after being able to breathe. This is normally as simple as making sure you have a jacket if it's going to rain. However, if you were stuck in your broken down car in the middle of a cold night, a blanket may be an essential survival item. If you are hiking, then a survival bivvy bag or tent would be one of the first things to pack for an emergency. Methods to create fire would also be important so carry a disposable lighter and have knowledge of how to make a fire.

Whatever happens, if you are in an emergency survival situation, find shelter and warmth as soon as you can.

WATER:
A human can survive for 3 days without water.

Water is vital to keep our body and all it's organs working. If we are without it for too long, our body gives up and we die. So, once you have found shelter, a water source is your next priority.

Have a bottle of water in your car. Carry a bottle of water with you when hiking.

Water purification is essential as drinking polluted water can induce vomiting and dehydrate you quicker.

One method is to use water purification tablets. They are tiny, cheap and available at camping shops. These may be useful if you find yourself in the middle of nowhere and have only river water to drink. Another consideration is a method to carry water. The smallest and easiest way is to carry a condom with you – this can be filled with water and placed into your sock to add strength to the improvised drinking vessel.

FOOD:
Humans can survive for three weeks without food, so once you can breathe, have shelter and water, you should begin searching for a food source.

Again, preparation can be very simple: some high calorie cereal bars kept in the boot of your car may get you through an emergency or the same in your rucksack when hiking.

Without this preparation, you will have to resort to scavenging or hunting food and without specialist knowledge, both are difficult.

Essentials:
- 3 Minutes without oxygen
- 3 Hours without shelter
- 3 Days without water
- 3 Weeks without food

Technique specific exercises:
Reading survival books, going on courses and practicing survival skills are all useful ways to improve your chances of survival in an emergency.

Driving skills

Defensive / Evasive / Offensive driving

Defensive driving is all about looking ahead, recognising and dealing with hazards before they become a danger to you. You can learn this by training with the IAM (Institute of Advanced Motorists).

Becoming an advanced driver enhances your safety by improving your driving skill, thus preventing road rage and of course avoiding accidents. This information is not designed to be a driving manual, however, it is highly recommended that you become an advanced driver to enjoy the benefits outlined above (and cheaper car insurance!)

Evasive driving is the term given to escape techniques often only taught to Close Protection Operators (Bodyguards), Military and Police personnel. However, these techniques can be of use to you if you find yourself ambushed perhaps by a road block, a group of hostile people or some armed criminals.

Therefore, it is prudent to describe these methods. Unfortunately, being professionally trained in these techniques is very costly and the alternative of practising in your local car park or on the roads is dangerous and illegal so do not do so under any circumstances. To physically learn these methods, the only way to do so is via professional tuition.

However, the information within may be enough for you to be able to avoid an ambush.

The overall goal of evasive driving is essentially to change direction quickly.

Handbrake Turn:

- Change to a low gear but keep the revs high
- At around 20-25 MPH in the wet, 30-40 MPH in the dry, pull up hard on the handbrake whilst depressing the clutch
- At the same time spin the wheel to the right or left just over half a turn, depending on which side of the road you're driving on
- This will cause the rear wheels to lock and the back end will spin round
- When 100 degrees or so has been reached, release the hand brake and clutch and straighten the wheel
- Start to accelerate
- At 180 degrees you should be straightened up and accelerating forward in the opposite direction

This technique is sometimes hard to predict, depending on the road surface, speed, vehicle type etc. so should only be used as a last resort.

If you can safely carry out a 'U' turn quickly, this is obviously the best choice.

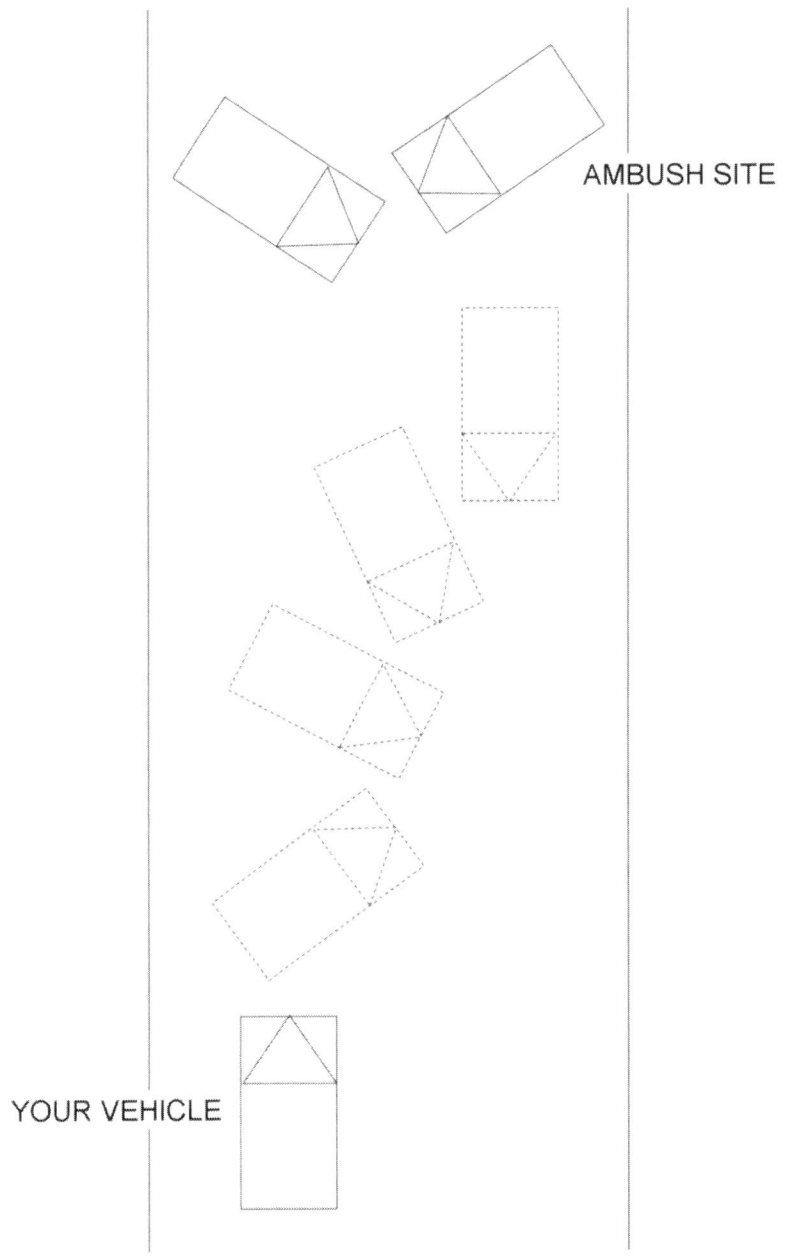

J' Turn:

- Check your mirrors to make sure the road behind you is clear
- Stop driving forwards as soon as possible
- Engage reverse gear
- Accelerate back down the road keeping straight
- Go back until the car has reached around 25 MPH
- Engage the clutch DO NOT USE THE FOOT BRAKE AT ALL DURING THIS MANOUVER
- Release the accelerator simultaneously
- 'Flick' the steering wheel around half a turn
- The weight of the engine will swing the front of the car around
- Once you have turned 90 degrees, engage first gear, straighten the wheel and accelerate
- At 180 degrees you should be straightened up and accelerating forward in the opposite direction

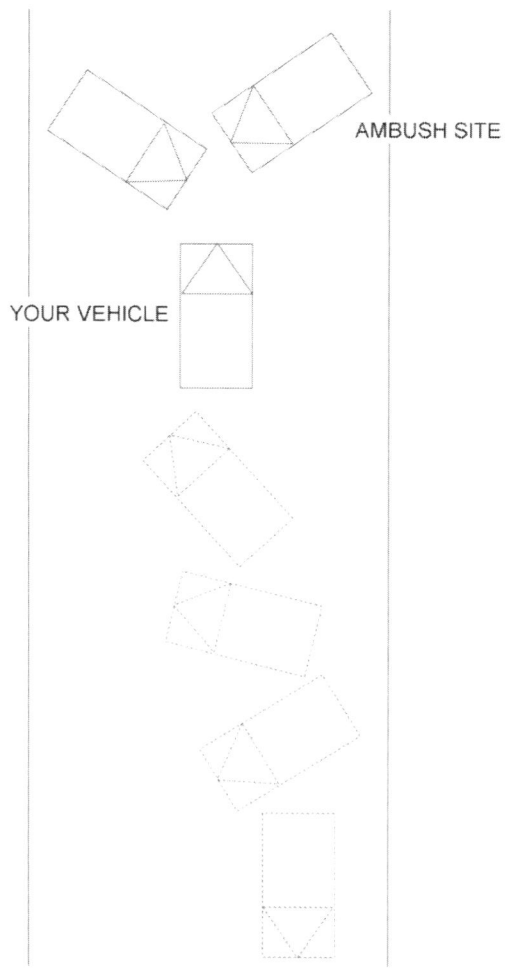

Offensive driving is the term used for ramming through vehicle road blocks, using your car as a weapon or to shove a subject's car off the road or into a spin. Hopefully, using 'Defensive driving' and maybe even 'Evasive driving', you will never need these techniques, however, just in case, here are a few that could save your skin. As with 'Evasive driving' methods, do not practice these anywhere unless you are being professionally tutored.

Knocking a car in front, off of the road

- Go 10-20 MPH faster than the car in front
- Hit the right corner of their rear bumper with the left corner of your front bumper
- Hit, don't push
- Remember that your airbag may be deployed now – this does not disable the car so about a second later it will deflate in your lap (it will be quite hot) and you can continue on
- The subject's vehicle will go sideways until the tyres gain traction again, then it will continue in the direction it's pointing – hopefully off the road

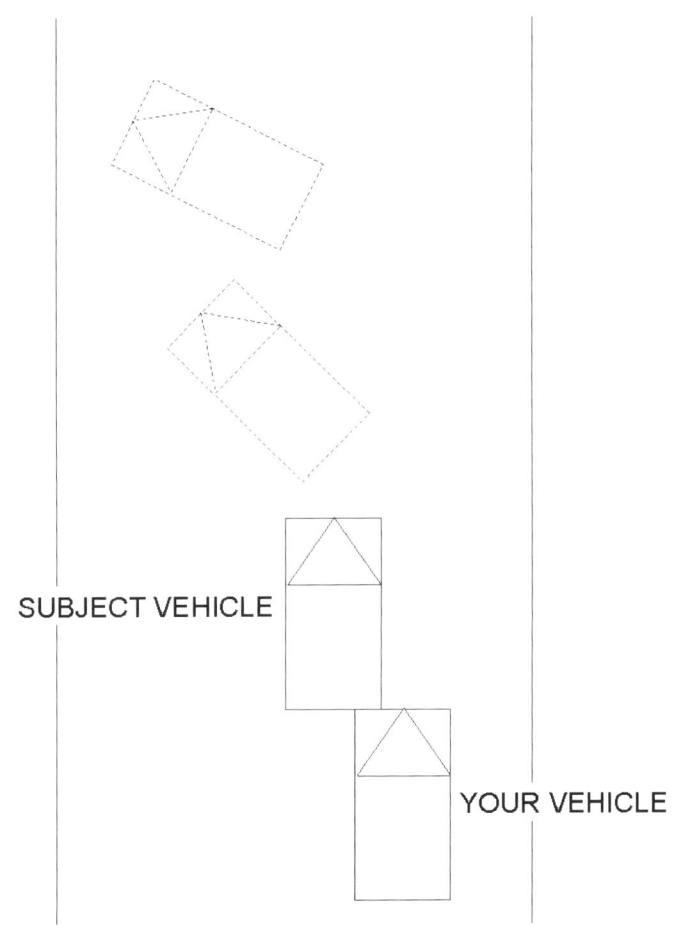

The second method of knocking a car off the road is as follows:

- The subject's vehicle needs to be beside yours, with your front bumper between their rear wheel and rear bumper
- Jerk the steering wheel in the direction of the subject's vehicle and hit their car smartly with your own
- They will spin in front of you so be prepared to brake and manoeuvre around

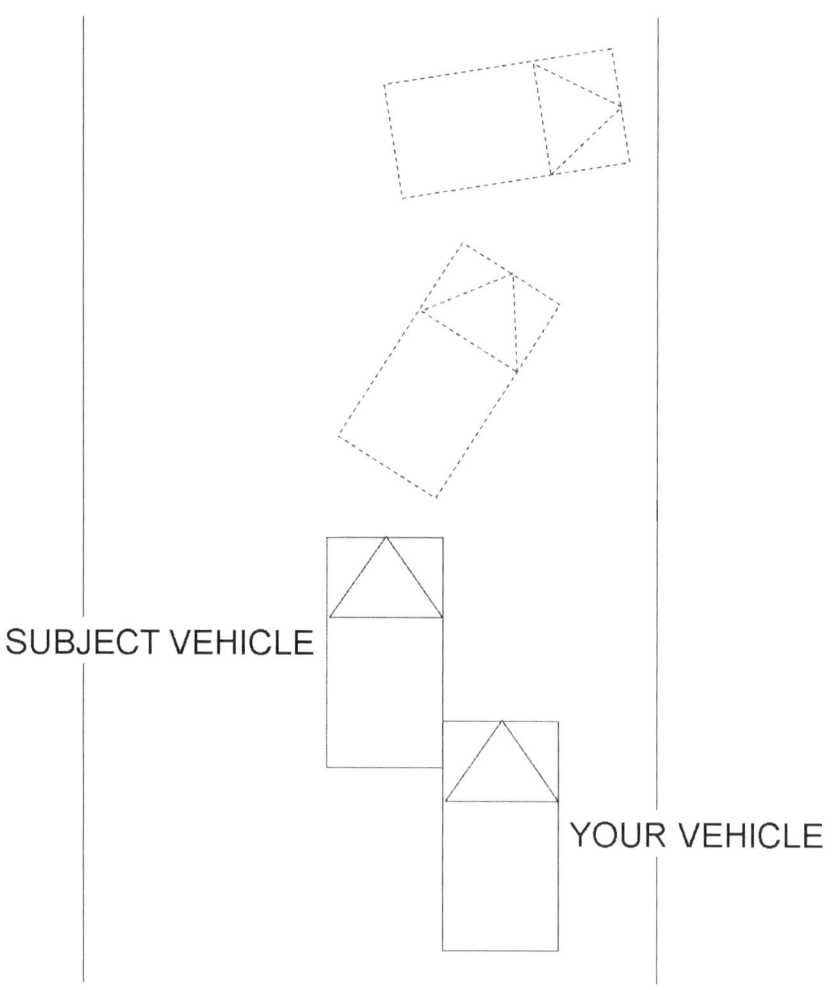

Offensive driving is the term used for ramming through vehicle road blocks, using your car as a weapon or to shove a subject's car off the road or into a spin. Hopefully, using 'Defensive driving' and maybe even 'Evasive driving', you will never need these techniques, however, just in case, here are a few that could save your skin. As with 'Evasive driving' methods, do not practice these anywhere unless you are being professionally tutored.

Knocking a car in front, off of the road

- Go 10-20 MPH faster than the car in front
- Hit the right corner of their rear bumper with the left corner of your front bumper
- Hit, don't push
- Remember that your airbag may be deployed now – this does not disable the car so about a second later it will deflate in your lap (it will be quite hot) and you can continue on
- The subject's vehicle will go sideways until the tyres gain traction again, then it will continue in the direction it's pointing – hopefully off the road

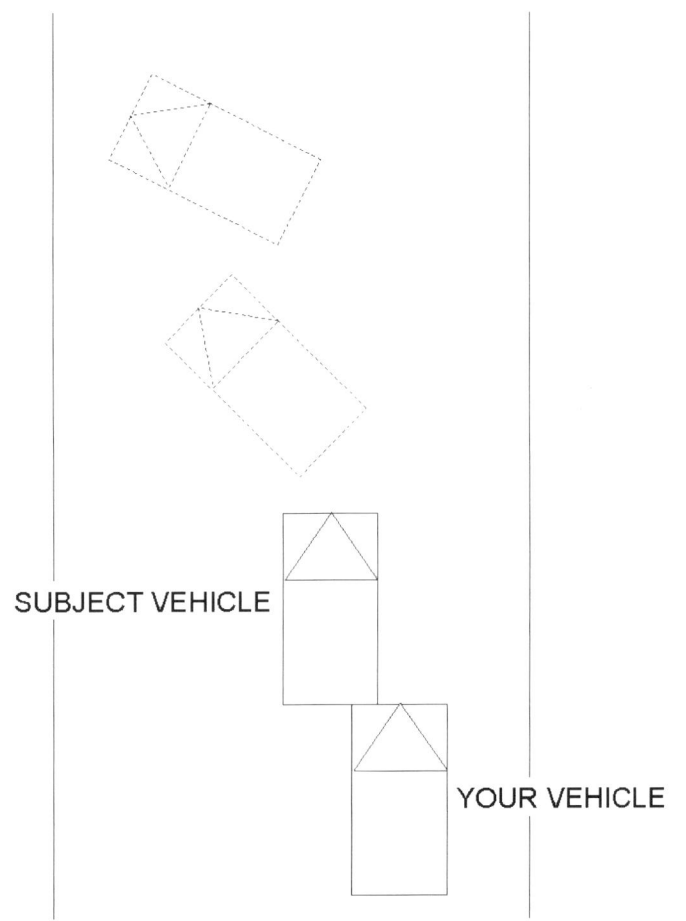

The second method of knocking a car off the road is as follows:

- The subject's vehicle needs to be beside yours, with your front bumper between their rear wheel and rear bumper
- Jerk the steering wheel in the direction of the subject's vehicle and hit their car smartly with your own
- They will spin in front of you so be prepared to brake and manoeuvre around

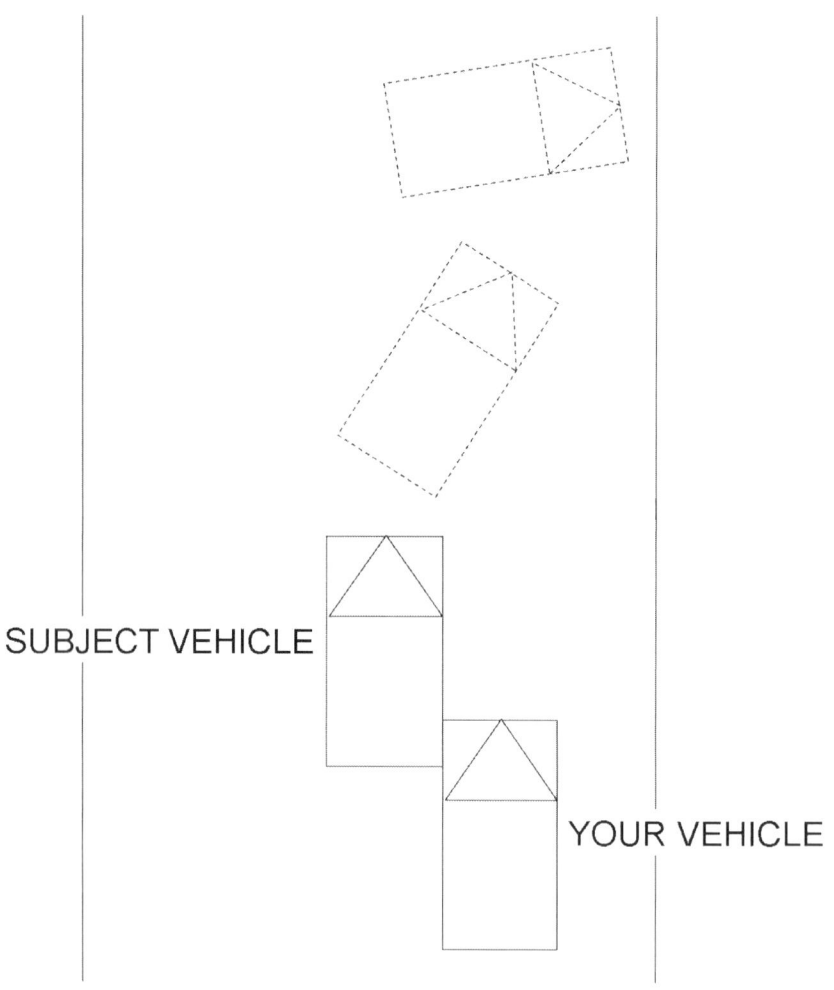

Road block

Of course using an evasive manoeuvre would be best here, but if that is not possible, you will need to ram the blocking vehicle.

- Slow to almost a stop and engage first gear
- Accelerate hard and hit between their rear wheel and rear bumper if possible
- Second choice is between the front wheel and front bumper
- Keep the accelerator floored until you push past the blocking vehicle
- This is a push, not a smart hit

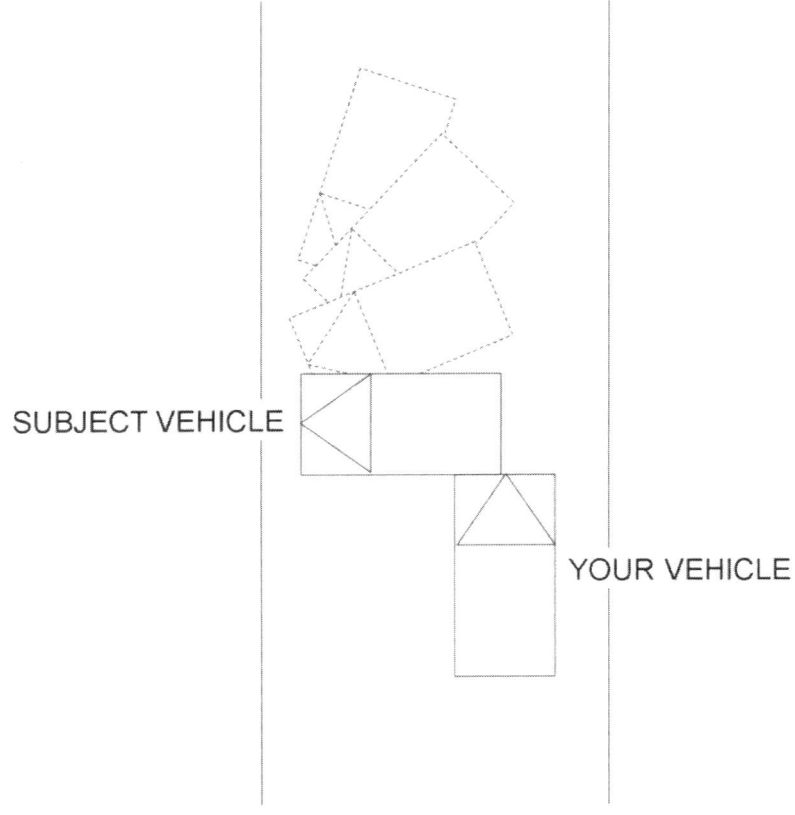

Thank you for reading 'The Complete Guide to Urban Self Protection Volume 2'

If you ever have to apply anything you've learned from this book in a real life situation, we'd love to hear from you. Your feedback will be invaluable to us as we continue to develop and improve the system.

Web: **www.u-s-p.co.uk**

Email: **u-s-p@hotmail.co.uk**

Find us on Facebook: **'Urban Self Protection'**

Printed in Great Britain
by Amazon